GW01376762

THE AMERICAN EXPRESS POCKET GUIDE TO
BERLIN

Derek Blyth

Mitchell Beazley

The Author
Derek Blyth is a European writer, journalist and translator. He has spent more than a decade exploring the art and culture of Northern Europe, and has published several travel books including *Flemish Cities Explored* and *The American Express Guide to Amsterdam*. He is currently based in Brussels, where he writes travel articles for *The Bulletin* magazine.

Acknowledgments
The author would like to thank the German National Tourist Office in Berlin, Gutenberg Buchhandlung in Brussels, Henriette Heimgärtner and Doug and Cathy Hutchinson for their invaluable help.

The publishers also wish to thank the American Express Publishing Corporation Inc., New York, and Gary Walther, Editor-in-Chief of *Departures*, for their co-operation during the production of this book, and Coleman Lollar for his careful reading of the typescript.

The editor would also like to thank the German National Tourist Office staff in London and Berlin, Staatliche Museen zu Berlin, Staatliche Museen Preussicher Kulturbesitz and Verwaltung der Staatlichen Schlösser und Gärten for their help with picture reference, and Mike de Mello of Triptych Systems Limited for his technical assistance.

The *American Express Travel Guide Series* was conceived under the direction of Susannah Read, Douglas Wilson, Hal Robinson and Eric Drewery.

For the series
General Editor   David Townsend Jones
Map Editor   David Haslam
Indexer   Hilary Bird

For this edition
Edited on desktop by   Eileen Townsend Jones
Art editors   Castle House Press
Illustrator   Sylvia Hughes-Williams
Jacket illustration   Fred Gambino
Gazetteer   Anne Evans

For Mitchell Beazley
Senior Executive Art Editor   Tim Foster
Managing Editor   Alison Starling
Production   Sarah Schuman

Edited and designed by Mitchell Beazley Publishers, part of Reed International Books, Michelin House, 81 Fulham Road, London SW3 6RB for the American Express (R) Travel Guide Series

© American Express Publishing Corporation Inc. 1992
All rights reserved
No part of this work may be reproduced or utilized in any form by any means, electronic or mechanical, including photocopying, recording or by any information storage and retrieval system, without the prior written permission of the publisher.
A cataloguing-in-publication record for this book is available from the British Library.
ISBN 0 85533 952 7

Maps in 2-color and 4-color by Lovell Johns, Oxford, England.
Desktop layout in Ventura Publisher by Castle House Press, Llantrisant, Wales.
Typeset in Garamond and Univers.
Linotronic output through Tradespools Limited, Frome, England.
Produced by Mandarin Offset. Printed and bound in Malaysia.

Contents

How to use this book	4
Key to symbols	5

Berlin: past, present, future 6

Basic information
Before you go	8
Getting around	10
On-the-spot information	12
Useful addresses	15
Emergency information	17

Culture, history and background
Landmarks in Berlin's history	18
Architecture in Berlin	22
Art in Berlin	26
Guide to Berlin's galleries	27
Film in Berlin	28
Berlin porcelain	30
Selected reading	31

Planning, walks and trips
When and where to go	31
Calendar of events	33
Walks and trips	34

Berlin
Sights and places of interest	43
Major sights classified by type	44
Sights A to Z	45
Where to stay	101
Hotels classified by location	101
Hotels A to Z	101
Eating in Berlin	103
Restaurants classified by cuisine	105
Restaurants A to Z	105
Cafés	108
Beer halls and beer gardens	109
Nightlife and the performing arts	110
Shopping in Berlin	115

Potsdam
Introduction, history, walks	119
Sights and places of interest: A to Z	125
Hotels, restaurants, cafés, shopping, boat trips	131

Special information
Other excursions	132
Berlin and Potsdam for children	132
Sports and activities	133
German in a nutshell	135
List of street names	137
Index	139

Maps
Key	
Berlin City	Maps 1-4
Berlin environs	Maps 5-7

How to use this book

How to find it   (**1**) For the organization of the book, see CONTENTS on the previous page. (**2**) Wherever possible, sections are arranged alphabetically, with headings appearing in **BLUE CAPITALS**. The headings are followed by addresses, telephone numbers and other practical details printed in *blue italics*. (**3**) Subject headers, similar to those used in telephone directories, appear in **bold black type** in the top corner of each page. (**4**) If you still cannot find it, look in the INDEX (on pages 139-144).

Cross-references   These are printed in SMALL CAPITALS, referring the reader to other sections or entries in the book.

Using the maps   The full-color maps at the end of the book have a standard grid system, to which the map co-ordinates given throughout the book refer. For example, the Brandenburger Tor is on map **3**C7 and Schloss Charlottenburg on map **1**B2. A complete list of Berlin street names with their map co-ordinates, which includes all streets that fall within the area of our maps, appears on pages 137-138.

Bold and italic type   **Bold type** emphasizes points or topics of interest. As well as being used conventionally for titles, foreign words etc., *italic type* is also used within brackets for addresses, telephone numbers and other practical details.

Abbreviations   These include days of the week and months; N, S, E and W (points of the compass); Str. (Strasse); St (Saint); rms (rooms); C (century); and measurements.

Floors   The European convention is used: "first floor" means the floor above the ground floor, and so on.

Price categories   Price categories for hotels and restaurants are represented by the symbols ☐ ▯ ▯▯ ▯▯▯ and ▯▯▯▯, which signify cheap, inexpensive, moderately priced, expensive and very expensive, respectively.

These correspond approximately with the following actual prices, valid as of spring 1991, which provide a guideline at the time of printing. Although actual prices will inevitably increase, price categories relative to each other should remain stable.

Price categories	Corresponding to approximate prices for **hotels** *double room with bath; single slightly cheaper*	for **restaurants** *meal for one with house wine, incl. service and taxes*
☐ cheap	under DM 150	under DM 40
▯ inexpensive	DM 150-200	DM 40-60
▯▯ moderate	DM 200-300	DM 60-80
▯▯▯ expensive	DM 300-400	DM 80-100
▯▯▯▯ very expensive	over DM 400	over DM 100

Key to symbols

- ☎ Telephone
- ⓕ Facsimile (fax)
- ★ Recommended sight
- 🏛 Building of architectural interest
- ⋖ Good view
- ⋎ Guided tour
- ✵ Special interest for children
- ♿ Facilities for disabled people
- 🕭 Hotel
- 🍴 Restaurant
- ☕ Cafeteria
- ▢ Cheap
- ▯▯ Inexpensive
- ▯▯▯ Moderately priced
- ▯▯▯▯ Expensive
- ▯▯▯▯▯ Very expensive
- AE American Express
- ⬥ Diners Club
- ⬤ MasterCard/Eurocard/Access
- VISA Visa

A word from the General Editor

Our authors and editors go to great lengths to ensure that all the information is accurate at the time the *American Express Travel Guides* go to press. However, no travel book can be completely free of error or totally up to date. Politicians the world over are prone to announce sweeping new initiatives, and in Germany in particular, new developments are an almost daily occurrence. Moreover, telephone numbers and opening hours change without warning, and hotels and restaurants come under new management, which may affect their standards.

We are always delighted to receive corrections or suggestions for improvements from our readers, which where appropriate can be incorporated in the next edition.

I am particularly indebted to readers who wrote during the preparation of this book. Please continue to stay in touch — your feedback is very important to our efforts to tailor the series to the very distinctive tastes and requirements of our sophisticated international readership.

Send your comments to me at Mitchell Beazley Publishers, Michelin House, 81 Fulham Road, London SW3 6RB; or, in the US, c/o American Express Travel Guides, Prentice Hall Travel, 15 Columbus Circle, New York, NY 10023.

The publishers regret that they cannot accept any consequences arising from the use of this book or from the information it contains.

David Townsend Jones

INTRODUCTION

Berlin: past, present, future

That November night in 1989 when the guards at the Berlin Wall unexpectedly began to allow people to cross the border *without* formalities was a rare moment of joy in 20th century German history. The world was briefly caught off guard by dramatic images of young Berliners scrambling onto the wall that had divided their city for 28 grim years. Scenes of East Berliners flooding through the breached Wall into the glare of television floodlights were strangely reminiscent of that moment in Beethoven's opera *Fidelio* when prisoners emerge from captivity into the blinding daylight.

For a few months, travelers savored the exhilaration of poking around abandoned checkpoints, or strolling unchallenged past a solitary Soviet guard on the reopened Glienicker Brücke. The euphoria may have worn off by now, as romanticism merges into pragmatism, but *die Wende* (the change) has totally transformed Berlin from a melancholy, divided city into the capital of a confident new Germany. The combined metropolis now spreads across an area of 1,000 square kilometers (386 square miles), with a population of three-and-a-half-million.

The merger of two almost independent cities has created an embarrassment of riches. No other European city can boast three opera houses, two national art galleries or two large zoos. For the first time since the Wall was built, visitors are free to explore the astonishing wealth and diversity of culture in Berlin: the reconstructed Greek and Roman temples, pastel-tinted Baroque palaces, melancholy Romantic paintings and Neoclassical urban spaces. They can also feast on a remarkable diversity of cultural attractions, from classical opera in grandiose settings to moonlit jazz serenades on lakeside stages.

Berlin is a city with two centres — the cluster of expensive hotels, bars, cinemas, shops round the Memorial Church, a sparkling nucleus of light, like a sham diamond, in the shabby twilight of the town; and the self-conscious civic centre of buildings round the Unter den Linden, carefully arranged. In grand international styles, copies of copies, they assert our dignity as a capital city — a parliament, a couple of museums, a State bank, a cathedral, an opera, a dozen embassies, a triumphal arch; nothing has been forgotten. And they are all so pompous, so very correct — all except the cathedral, which betrays in its architecture, a flash of that hysteria which flickers always behind every grave, grey Prussian facade.

Christopher Isherwood, *Goodbye to Berlin* (1939)

Founded in the 13th century in an inhospitable region of sandy pine woods and dark lakes, Berlin became the principal residence of the Hohenzollern family and, later, the center of political power in Prussia, developing into a handsome Neoclassical city molded by crisp Prussian ideals of order and elegance. The character of Berlin changed dramatically when it became capital of the German Reich in 1871. Its rulers transformed it into the most progressive European city, dazzling visitors with its technological prowess. The world's first electric tram ran through the Berlin streets, while the U-Bahn (underground) and S-Bahn (overground) railroads were models of Prussian efficiency.

Berlin's cultural vitality reached a thrilling climax under the Weimar Republic of the 1920s, but the city sank to unspeakable depths of evil a decade later under the Nazi regime. Berlin

Introduction

seemed to symbolize everything that was bad about Germany, and, in retribution, the heart of the city was devastated by Allied bombers during World War II.

The postwar division of the city into East Berlin (the Soviet sector) and West Berlin (the Allied sector) created a sinister tension that hovered on the brink of war. But now that Berlin is once again capital of Germany, it has assumed a role at the leading edge of European history. It is perhaps here, more than anywhere else in Europe, that you feel most keenly the effects of the revolution that swept through the Communist states in 1989.

Haunted by memories of the Nazi years, many visitors think of Berlin as a restless, nervy city: the cafés filled with the seedy characters from 1920s Otto Dix paintings, or sinister spies lurking in the shadow of the S-Bahn viaducts. Yet compared with many large cities, contemporary Berlin has a surprisingly peaceful spirit. Its peculiar postwar status made it a refuge for many German pacifists, ecologists and alternative thinkers, who give districts such as Kreuzberg a creative vitality tinged with occasional anarchic outbursts. The city has relatively few high-rise buildings, and about one-third of the metropolitan area is taken up by forests, fields and lakes.

Yet there is a certain raw edge to the city. The broken spire of the Kaiser-Wilhelm-Gedächtniskirche and the wasteland at the Anhalter Bahnhof perhaps reflect Berliners' occasional need for a sense of *Sturm und Drang* (storm and stress) in their lives. Berlin seems to have been in a state of constant flux since the 1870s, and virtually every statue in Berlin has been moved at some time in its life. Changing names of streets and bridges seem symptomatic of the restless spirit of Berlin; Adolf-Hitler-Platz was renamed Theodor-Heuss-Platz after World War II, and Stalinallee was renamed Karl-Marx-Allee when the Soviet leader fell from grace. *Die Wende* has added to the confusion, as old maps are redrawn, disused U-Bahn stations reopen, and museum collections are shuffled around.

Who can tell what will happen in Berlin in the coming years? No one in 1871 could have predicted that the second Kaiser of Germany would end his days in exile in the Netherlands, nor that women would toil throughout the 1950s to construct hills out of the rubble of Berlin's buildings. Karl Marx, who studied law at Berlin University, predicted that capitalism would wither away, but the reality was exactly the opposite. East German socialism collapsed almost overnight, and the once-terrifying Berlin Wall was broken into pieces to be sold as souvenirs.

One of the saddest sights in former East Berlin was a solitary bear imprisoned in a concrete pit behind the Märkisches Museum. The bear is Berlin's motto — an allusion to Albrecht the Bear of the House of Askanier, who drove the Slavs from Brandenburg — but the captive bear in a concrete pit seemed a particularly appropriate symbol of postwar Berlin, hemmed in on all sides by a wall of concrete. But Berlin and its people have been liberated, and the city is rapidly recovering its centuries-old role as a European haven of freedom, tolerance and culture.

You sense the change in Berlin most acutely along the scar of wasteland that was once a death strip between East and West, but there are signs of transformation throughout the city. Berliners debate incessantly the various plans to develop the rubble-strewn wasteland that was once Potsdamer Platz, the busiest square in Europe. They face agonizing choices, such as the dilemma about what to do with the remains of the concrete bunker where Hitler shot himself in 1945. The past still haunts many Berliners, who are

BASIC INFORMATION

painfully aware of their city's part in the horrors of World War II. The city is dotted with memorials to victims of the Holocaust and ruins that have been left as a warning to future generations.

The political change is a perhaps an occasion for rejoicing mingled with restraint. Sighing with world-weariness, Maria in the German television series *Heimat* epitomized the developments with the complaint: "Six times in my life there's been a *new age* — they never stop coming." Visitors to Berlin in the coming years must judge for themselves how this latest new age in German history is taking shape.

Before you go

Documents required
US citizens need a valid **passport**, while for citizens of EC countries, a passport or **national identity card** is the only document required if your visit to Berlin does not exceed 3mths.

If you intend to drive in Germany, you must have a valid national **driver's license**, and if taking a vehicle into the country, you will need a **national identity plate** and the **vehicle registration certificate**.

Travel and medical insurance
It is advisable to travel with an insurance policy that covers loss of deposits paid to airlines, hotels, tour operators, etc., and the cost of dealing with emergency requirements, such as special tickets home and extra nights in a hotel, as well as a medical insurance policy. To obtain on-the-spot cover, contact your local travel agent before departure.

For US citizens, the **IAMAT** (International Association for Medical Assistance to Travelers) has a list of English-speaking doctors who will call, for a fee. IAMAT has member hospitals and clinics throughout Europe, including a number in Germany. Membership of IAMAT is free. For further information on worldwide traveling, and a directory of doctors and hospitals, write to **IAMAT** (*417, Center Street, Lewiston, NY 14092*).

Money
The unit of currency is the Deutschmark (DM), divided into 100 Pfennig. There are coins for 1, 2, 5, 10, 20 and 50 Pfennig and DM 2 and DM 5. Banknotes are issued in denominations of DM 10, DM 20, DM 50, DM 100, DM 500 and DM 1,000.

Travelers checks issued by all major companies and, for Europeans, Eurocheques, are widely accepted. It is important to note separately the serial numbers of your checks and the telephone number to call in case of loss. Specialist travelers check companies such as American Express provide extensive local refund facilities through their own offices or agents.

Currency may be changed and travelers checks and Eurocheques cashed at all banks, and at *Wechselstube* in major railroad stations and airports, which have the advantage of longer opening hours. Some department stores, such as **KaDeWe** (*Tauentzienstrasse 21*), will also handle foreign exchange.

American Express also has a **MoneyGram** (R) money transfer service that makes it possible to wire money worldwide in just minutes, from any American Express Travel Service Office. This service is available to all customers and is not limited to American

Before you go

Express Card members.

Major charge and credit cards such as American Express, Diners Club, and Visa are widely accepted in stores and hotels in Berlin, though restaurants often do not accept payment by charge or credit card.

Customs
The completion of the European Single Market takes place at the end of 1992. Duty- and tax-free shopping will still be available to travelers departing directly for countries outside the European Community, such as the US, and for non-EC citizens a list of duty-free allowances can be obtained at German tourist offices and airports. Within the EC, it is probable that as of January 1, 1993, the sale of goods at duty-free prices will no longer apply, and that no duty will be payable on goods brought into Germany by EC citizens. British residents can obtain information from the **Single Market Unit, HM Customs and Excise** (☎ *071-865 5426*).

Visitors are exempt from paying Value Added Tax (*MWS* or *Mehrwertsteuer*) on purchases above a certain amount, on completion of a simple form and presentation of a passport at the time of purchase. However, to validate the refund, which will be made to you at your home address, or through a charge or credit card refund, you must present the paperwork and goods at a checkpoint before the passport control on leaving the country. Leave enough time to do this.

German National Tourist Offices
UK 65, Curzon St., London W1Y 7PE ☎ (071) 495 3990.
USA 747 3rd Avenue, 33rd floor, New York NY 10017 ☎ (212) 308 3300.

There is also an office in **Toronto** ☎ (416) 968 1570.

Getting there
By air Berlin's Tegel airport (☎ *(030) 41011*) and Schönefeld airport (☎ *(0372) 67870*) are major international airports with direct flights from all over the world.
By rail The rail network throughout Germany is run by *Deutsche Bundesbahn* (*DB*). Rail links to Berlin have improved greatly since German unification, and fast, comfortable international trains run directly to Berlin from many capital cities including Paris (13-14hrs), Brussels (11-12hrs), Copenhagen (8hrs), Warsaw (10hrs), Moscow (31hrs), Prague ($6\frac{1}{2}$hrs), Vienna (12hrs), Budapest ($16\frac{1}{2}$hrs), Sofia (23hrs) and Belgrade ($22\frac{1}{2}$hrs). The opening of the Channel Tunnel in 1993 should cut the journey time from Britain to Berlin by several hours.

Most trains to Berlin stop at Potsdam, Bahnhof Zoologischer Garten (usually known as Bahnhof Zoo), Bahnhof Friedrichstrasse and Hauptbahnhof. Leave at Zoo for destinations in the Tiergarten, Charlottenburg and Kreuzberg districts, and at Friedrichstrasse for addresses in Mitte and Prenzlauer Berg.

In Berlin ☎(030) 19419 for information on train services. Information can also be obtained from the **German National Tourist Offices** in London or New York. See above for addresses.
By sea From Britain, regular train-and-ferry services operate from London's major railroad stations. There are two main ferry routes: from Harwich to Hoek van Holland (6hrs) and from Dover to Ostende (3hrs 45mins).

The fastest sea crossing is by Jetfoil from Dover to Ostende (1hr

Getting around

45mins). The total journey time to Berlin from London is 17-19hrs via Ostende and about 30hrs via Hoek van Holland.

Climate
Berlin has a continental climate, with cold winters, hot summers, and rain throughout the year. The best times for visiting are spring and early summer. *Berliner Luft* (Berlin air) has been praised in song for its invigorating qualities, but it now suffers the pollution typical of most large cities.

Clothes
Pack warm clothes if you are visiting Berlin in winter, and take strong shoes if you intend to go walking in the woods. Germans tend to wear casual clothes, and there are no rigid rules about dress in Berlin.

General delivery (Poste restante)
Letters to be collected should be marked *poste restante* and addressed to Bahnhofpostlagernd, Postamt 120, Bahnhof Zoo, 1000 Berlin 12 (☎ *(030) 3139799*). They can be collected at the desk marked *Postlagernde Sendungen*: take a passport for identification. **American Express** offers the same service to its customers. Write to: Client Mail, American Express Travel Service, Kurfürstendamm 11, 1000 Berlin 15 (☎ *(030) 8827575*).

Getting around

From the airports to the city
Bus 109 runs from Tegel airport to Budapester Strasse, stopping at Adenauerplatz, Uhlandstrasse, Kurfürstendamm and Bahnhof Zoo. The **S-Bahn** provides a frequent service to Schönefeld airport. The **Airport-Transfer bus** runs between Tegel and Schönefeld airports, stopping at Bahnhof Zoo and other central locations.

Public transportation
Berlin has an excellent public transportation network, run since 1929 as an integrated system by **BVG** (*Berliner Verkehrs-Betriebe, Potsdamer Strasse 188* ☎ *(030) 2165088*). The **U-Bahn** (subway/underground), founded in 1896, is the fastest means of getting around the city. Trains run from 4.30am-1am, while lines U1 and U9 continue through the night. Stations (marked at street level with a white **U** on a blue background) are clean and well designed. Wittenbergplatz, opened in 1913, is the station of most architectural interest, with polished wooden ticket booths, ornate clocks, and iron columns topped with Ionic capitals. Some of the suburban stations on line U2 bear a resemblance to rural farmhouses.

The **S-Bahn** (*Stadtbahn*) elevated railroad network was begun in 1875. The main routes are the *Ost-West* and *Nord-Süd* lines, which intersect at Friedrichstrasse station. Administered by East Germany after 1945, the S-Bahn became rather dilapidated, and many stations were closed after the Wall was built, resulting in a boycott by West Berliners. Now run by BVG, the system has greatly improved. The S-Bahn is useful for getting to outlying districts such as Wannsee, Potsdam and Köpenick. Trains normally run at 10min intervals from 4.30am-1am, and line S3 from Charlottenburg to Friedrichstrasse continues through the

Getting around

night. Stations (many of them impressive 19thC iron and glass structures) are marked by a white **S** on a green background.

Buses are slower, but useful for reaching remote corners of the city. You enter the bus at the front, using the door marked *Kasse* if you need to buy a ticket, or *Sichtkarten* if you have a pass (which must be shown to the driver). You leave by the rear door, using the stairs at the back on double-decker buses. Buses are well designed for wheelchairs and prams, which use the rear door to get on and off. Safety belts are provided to help secure wheelchairs. Bus stops are marked with a green **H** on a yellow background. Night buses, indicated by a yellow number on a green background, continue on several routes throughout the night.

BVG also operates a regular **ferry** service across the Havel from Wannsee to Kladow. Some antiquated **trams** (*Strassenbahn*) still rumble through the streets of East Berlin, offering a slow and rather bumpy ride.

The dilapidated trams are far removed from Berlin's most advanced transportation system: the prototype **M-Bahn** (*Magnetbahn*), which glides along an elevated track from Gleisdreieck to the well-designed stations at Bernburger Strasse and Kemperplatz. The fully-automated train currently offers a rather limited service (*Mon-Fri 3-10pm; Sat, Sun 8am-10.30pm*), but it is fun to use.

Tickets

These are issued for one-way trips (*Normaltarif*) and multiple journeys (*Sammelkarte*). A *Normaltarif* ticket allows you unlimited travel on the BVG network for 2hrs from the time stamped. Children aged 6-14yrs pay a reduced rate (*Ermässigungstarife*). A *Sammelkarte* covers five separate journeys. The *Ku'damm-Ticket* is a reduced fare for travel along Kurfürstendamm on buses (except number 109) between Rathenauplatz and Wittenbergplatz. The *Kurzstrekenfahrausweise* is a reduced rate for short journeys by bus, not valid for transfers. Timetables posted at bus stops indicate the zone in which the ticket is valid.

If you are planning to make four or more journeys in a single day, it is cheaper to buy a *Berlin-Ticket* (*24-Stunden-Karte*) valid for 24hrs on all U-Bahn, S-Bahn, bus and tram services. It is also valid on the Wannsee to Kladow ferry run by BVG, and on S-Bahn and bus services from Berlin to Potsdam, but not on special excursion buses from Wannsee (marked with a triangle) or local buses and trams in Potsdam. The *Familien-Tageskarte* is a one-day ticket valid on weekends, entitling a family of two parents and all children under 16 to unlimited travel. All tickets, including 24hr passes, must be stamped in the red *Entwerter* on station platforms and in buses.

The combined day ticket (*Kombi-Tageskarte*) is valid for 24hrs on all BVG services, and on scheduled boat services (known as *Linienverkehr*) run by Stern und Kreisschiffahrt from Apr-Oct. It can also be used on certain excursions on the paddle steamer *Havel Queen*. Boats sail from Tegel, Spandau, Wannsee, Pfaueninsel, Glienicker Brücke and other major landing stages on the Havel. For sailing times ☎(030) 8100040.

Tickets can be bought from counters marked *Fahrausweise* at U-Bahn and S-Bahn stations, and from automatic machines. Tickets, maps and timetables are sold at the **BVG-Pavillon** (*Hardenbergplatz, opposite Bahnhof Zoo* ☎ *(030) 2562462, open Mon-Fri 8am-6pm, Sat 7am-2pm, Sun 9am-4pm*).

On-the-spot information

Taxis
Taxis can be ordered by telephone (*in West Berlin* ☎ *6902, 240024, 240202 or 261026; in East Berlin* ☎ *3644*), or picked up at one of the taxi stands at Bahnhof Zoo, Savignyplatz and other central locations.

Getting around by car
There is no need ever to use a car in Berlin or Potsdam, but, if you have to drive, remember that it is strictly prohibited to pass a stationary tram. The legal minimum age for driving is 18, throughout Germany.

Renting a car
Most major international car rental firms have branches at Tegel airport. Payment by charge or credit card avoids the need for a large cash deposit. A current driver's license is required, and the minimum age is normally 18.

Renting a bicycle
West Berlin has an extensive network of bicycle lanes (they often run along the sidewalk), and there are numerous attractive routes in the Grunewald to follow. Bicycles may be taken on the S-Bahn (use the doors marked with a bicycle symbol), and on the U-Bahn (*Mon-Fri 9am-2pm and 5.30pm-closing time*). You use the reduced rate ticket (*Ermässigungstarif*) for a bicycle.

Bicycles can be rented for one or more days at the **Fahrradbüro** (*Hauptstrasse 146* ☎ *(030) 7845562, closed Tues, Sat afternoon, Sun*). In the summer months, bicycles are rented at Grunewald S-Bahn station and in the Freizeitpark at Tegel.

New destinations can be reached now that the W part of the city is no longer encircled by the Wall. The best map for serious cycling around Berlin is the 1:100,000 ADFC-Radtourenkarte, which covers *Berlin und Umgebung* (Berlin and environs).

Getting around on foot
Distances in Berlin are often too great to cover on foot, but some districts are pleasant for wandering, such as Tiergarten, Kreuzberg and Prenzlauer Berg. The Grunewald is the main forest where Berliners stretch their legs on weekends. For sugested walks and rambles see also PLANNING AND WALKS on pages 31-40. The Falkplan patent folded map of Berlin is indispensable for rambles in the city and forests.

On-the-spot information

Public holidays
Jan 1; *Karfreitag* (Good Fri), *Ostersonntag* (Easter Sun) and *Ostermontag* (Easter Mon); May 1; *Himmelfahrt* (Ascension); *Pfingstsonntag* (Whit Sun) and *Pfingstmontag* (Whit Mon); *Fronleichnam* (Corpus Christi); *Gesetzlicher Feiertag*, Jun 17; Day of German Unity, Oct 3; *Allerheiligen* (All Saints), Nov 1; *Busstag* (Day of National Repentance), 3rd Wed in Nov; *Weihnachten* (Christmas Day) and *2 Weihnachten* (Dec 26).

Time zones
Germany, like most Western European countries, is 1hr ahead of **Greenwich Mean Time** in the winter and 2hrs ahead in the summer, i.e., 1hr ahead of Great Britain most of the year. It is

On-the-spot information

6hrs ahead of (US) **Eastern Standard Time** and 7-9hrs ahead of the other US time zones.

Banks and currency exchange

Currency transactions are dealt with at the desk marked *Devisen*, and the money is handed over at the *Kasse* (cash desk). Banks in Berlin are normally open Mon-Fri 9am-3.30pm, and two afternoons a week until 6pm. The **Berliner Commerzbank** (*Maison de France, Kurfürstendamm 211*) remains open Mon-Fri until 6pm, Sat 10am-1pm; branches of the **Sparkasse der Stadt Berlin** (*Kurfürstendamm 11* (☎ *(030) 8827671), Savignyplatz 9, the ICC, and other locations where a spätservice (extended service) operates*) are open similar hours. The bank at the **KaDeWe** department store (☎ *(030) 2114182*) is open Mon-Fri 10am-6.30pm, Sat 10am-2pm, extended to 6pm on *langer Samstag* ("long Saturday" — the first Sat of every month). The *Wechselstube* (currency exchange) at **Bahnhof Zoo** (☎ *(030) 8817117*) is open Mon-Sat 8am-9pm, Sun 10am-6pm, and at **Tegel airport** (☎ *(030) 4135049*) daily 8am-10pm.

Shopping hours

Shop opening hours in Germany are strictly regulated by law. Normally, shops are open Mon-Fri 9am-6pm, Sat 9am-1pm and, possibly, Thurs until 8.30pm, although department stores may stay open Mon-Fri until 6.30pm and Sat until 2pm. Shops remain open until 4pm on *langer Samstag*, the first Sat of the month, and the four Sats before Christmas. Only florists and bakers are allowed to open on Sun, perhaps because many Germans could not face the prospect of a day without *Kuchen* (cake). Turkish stores in Kreuzberg and Neukölln are sometimes open on Sat and Sun, while shops in a few U-Bahn stations such as Kurfürstendamm open late and on weekends.

Postal, telephone and fax services

Post offices (marked *Post* or *Postamt*) are normally open Mon-Fri 8am-6pm, Sat 8am-noon. The **Main Post Office** (*at Bahnhof Zoo*) has one counter that never closes.

Public telephones (marked *Fernsprecher*) are normally located at main squares, railroad and U-Bahn stations, cafés and department stores. Phones take 10 Pfennig, DM 1 and DM 5 coins. Phones marked *Kartentelefon* or *Telefonieren ohne Münzen* are operated by a phonecard (*Telefonkarte*) sold at post offices.

Berlin **telephone numbers** are preceded by three different area codes: **West Berlin** is **030**, while **East Berlin** is **9** when dialing from West Berlin and **0372** when dialing from elsewhere.

West Berlin from the UK	☎**010-4930** + number;
West Berlin from the US	☎**011-4930** + number;
West Berlin from elsewhere in Germany	☎**30** + number;
West Berlin from East Berlin	☎**849** + number;
East Berlin from the UK	☎**010-49-372** + number;
East Berlin from the US	☎**011-49-372** + number;
East Berlin from West Berlin	☎**9** + number;
Potsdam from West Berlin	☎**03733** + number;
Potsdam from East Berlin	☎**003733** + number.

International calls from Berlin should be preceded by **00** and the country code (**1** for US, **44** for UK, **353** for Ireland), then the telephone number minus any initial 0 digit of the area code.

The notoriously inefficient East German telephone network is being improved. Until completion (and no date is yet fixed) you

On-the-spot information

may have difficulty dialing an international call from East Berlin.

Urgent documents can be sent from the public **fax** at **Bahnhof Zoo post office**, or from **Trigger** (*Pohlstrasse 69* ☎ *(030) 2616037* ⊕ *(030) 2617038, U-Bahn to Kurfürstenstrasse*). Most major hotels will send faxes for nonresidents.

Telegrams can be sent from any post office or by telephone (☎ *1131*).

Museums
Museums in Berlin are normally open Tues-Sun 9am-5pm. All museums are closed Mon, except the Ägyptisches Museum, Antikenmuseum, Bauhaus-Archiv, Brücke-Museum, Museum für Deutsche Geschichte and Zille-Museum. A few museums stay open in the evening, including the Martin-Gropius-Bau, the Berlin Museum and the Haus am Checkpoint Charlie. Large museums normally stop admitting visitors about 30mins before closing time. Be sure to deposit coats, large bags and umbrellas in the cloakroom, and keep back from paintings to avoid triggering invisible alarms.

Public rest rooms (toilets)
Public rest rooms are located on main squares, in department stores and in U-Bahn, S-Bahn and railroad stations. A charge of 50 Pfennig is normally made.

Electric current
The electric current in Germany is 220V. Plugs are standard European, with two round pins. Take an adaptor with you.

Laws and regulations
The written and unwritten laws of Germany are rather zealously enforced by the public, and you may be scolded for jaywalking, loitering at a shop entrance or even taking a baby out without a hat. This somewhat nagging tone is reflected in the signs that appear at almost every flight of steps in Germany, warning users, *Betreten bei Schnee und Glätte auf eigene Gefahr* (use in snow and ice at own risk). German intolerance is at its worst on autobahns, where it is customary for cars to flash their headlights angrily at slower vehicles blocking their lane.

So many activities in Germany are *streng verboten* (strictly forbidden) that it comes as a shock to many visitors to discover that nudist sunbathing is widely tolerated on beaches and in parks and forests. Although officially permitted only in areas designated *FKK* (*Freikörperkultur*), nudity crops up in unofficial places without apparently causing offense.

Etiquette
It is normal to shake hands when you meet someone in Germany. Say *Guten Tag* when you enter a store and *Auf Wiedersehen* as you leave. Be sure to apologize with *Entschuldigen Sie* or *Pardon* (sorry) if you accidentally tread on someone's foot. Men and women should always cover their heads when entering a Jewish cemetery or synagogue, out of respect for religious custom.

Tipping
In restaurants and cafés in Germany, service charges are almost invariably included in the check, although it is customary to round up the sum to the nearest DM. Taxi drivers will expect about 10 percent of the fare.

Disabled visitors

The provision for disabled people in Germany is generally excellent. Berlin buses have specially designed rear doors for wheelchair access, and safety straps to attach a wheelchair firmly. A booklet, *Berlin-Stadtführer für Behinderte*, available free from **Landesamt für Zentrale Soziale Aufgaben** (*Sächsische Strasse, 1000 Berlin 31* ☎ *(030) 8676114*) contains detailed information on facilities for handicapped people in Berlin.

Local and foreign-language publications

The monthly *Berlin Programm*, available from tourist offices, provides a comprehensive listing of theater, opera, dance, music, cabaret, museums, exhibitions and other events in Berlin and Potsdam, plus international train and airline timetables. German tourist offices abroad also often stock a few copies.

The thick fortnightly magazine *Zitty* is crammed with listings of movies, plays, children's events, workshops and television in Berlin. *Tip*, a more glossy magazine published every 2wks, is easier to use but less comprehensive.

Several German newspapers are published in Berlin. The weighty leftish weekly *Die Zeit* is written in ponderous prose that even Germans sometimes find daunting. *Tageszeitung*, known as *TAZ*, is a serious alternative daily, but the best paper for local news is the *Berliner Morgenpost*.

Useful addresses

Tourist information

Europa-Center (*Budapester Strasse entrance* ☎ *(030) 262603 1*) is open daily 8am-10.30pm.

Other information offices, open daily from 8am-11pm, are located at **Tegel airport** (☎ *(030) 41013145*)and **Bahnhof Zoo** (☎ *(030) 3139063*). In Mitte, there are offices at the Fernsehturm and at the s wing of the Brandenburger Tor (☎ *(0372) 2124675 for both offices*). Good general information can be had from the **Informationszentrum** (*Hardenbergstrasse 20, 2nd floor* ☎ *(030)310040, open Mon-Fri 8am-7pm, Sat 8am-4pm*). The **Fraueninfothek** (*Leibnitzstrasse 57* ☎ *(030) 3245078, open Tues-Sat 9am-9pm, Sun 9am-3pm*) provides information to women visiting Berlin.

American Express Travel Service (*Kurfürstendamm 11, 2nd floor* ☎ *(030) 8827575, open Mon-Fri 9am-5pm, Sat 9am-noon*, or, in East Berlin, at Berlin Tourist, *Alexanderplatz 5* ☎ *(0372)2150*) is a valuable source of information for any traveler in need of help, advice or emergency services.

Telephone services

Directory inquiries   Germany ☎1188, abroad ☎00118
Telegrams   ☎1131

Boat tours

The following companies organize boat excursions in Berlin:
Reederei Bruno Winkler   ☎(030) 3917010. River trips from Schloss Charlottenburg.
Reederei Horst Schlenther   ☎(030) 4162732. Daily 6hr Havel cruise from Tegeler Weg in Charlottenburg to Potsdam.
Reederei Triebler   ☎(030) 3315414. Trips from S-Bahnhof Wannsee to Potsdam.
Spreefahrt Horst Duggen   ☎(030) 3944954. Trips on the

Useful addresses

Spree and Landwehrkanal, departing from the Kongresshalle.
Stern und Kreisschiffahrt ☎(030) 8100040. Regular services on the Havel between Tegel, Spandau, Wannsee and Pfaueninsel, and trips to Potsdam and Tempelhof.
Weisse Flotte Berlin ☎(0372) 2712327. Cruises in East Berlin from Treptow pier.

Bus tours
Departure times and dates of bus tours appear in *Berlin Programm*. The following companies run bus excursions:
BBS Buses leave from Gedächtniskirche (☎ *(030) 2134077*) and Alexanderplatz (☎ *(0372) 2124362*). Tours of Berlin and day trips to Dresden and the Spreewald.
BVB ☎(030) 8859880. Buses leave from Kurfürstendamm 225. Tours of Berlin and day trips to Dresden and the Spreewald.
BVG ☎(030) 2567039. Tours of Berlin in a replica 1920s bus with an open roof. Bus departs from Gedächtniskirche.
Berolina Sightseeing ☎(030) 8822091. Buses leave from Kurfürstendamm 220 and Karl-Liebknecht-Strasse. Tours of Berlin and day trips to Dresden and the Spreewald.
Kultur Kontor ☎(030) 310888. Informed cultural tours on topics such as 1920s Berlin, architecture and literature. Buses leave from Savignyplatz 9.
Severin & Kuhn ☎(030) 8831015. Buses leave from Kurfürstendamm 216. Tours of Berlin and Spreewald day trips.

Walking tours
Stattreisen Berlin Stephanstrasse 24 ☎(030) 3953078. Well-researched guided tours in German, taking you to Potsdam, Wedding district, the abandoned Jewish cemeteries of East Berlin or the eerie wasteland near Potsdamer Platz.

Airlines
Air France Europa-Center ☎(030) 261051
British Airways Europa-Center ☎(030) 691021
Lufthansa Kurfürstendamm 220 ☎(030) 88751
Pan Am Europa-Center ☎(030) 01305566

Major libraries
Amerika-Gedenkbibliothek Blücherplatz, Kreuzberg ☎(030) 69050
Staatsbibliothek Preussischer Kulturbesitz Potsdamer Strasse 33, Tiergarten ☎(030) 2661

Places of worship
Französisch-reformierte Friedrichstadt-Kirche Platz der Akademie, Mitte ☎(0372) 2291760
Kaiser-Wilhelm-Gedächtniskirche Breitscheidplatz ☎(030) 245023. Service in English every Sun at 9am.
St David and St George Preussenallee 16-17 ☎(030) 3091. Anglican service.
St. Hedwigs-Kathedrale Bebelplatz, off Unter den Linden, Mitte. Catholic service.

Consulates in Berlin
Canada Europa-Center ☎(030) 2611161
Ireland Ernst-Reuter-Platz 10 ☎(030) 34800822
Japan Wachtelstrasse 8 ☎(030) 8327026
United Kingdom Uhlandstrasse 7 ☎(030) 3095292
United States Clayallee 170 ☎(030) 8324087

Emergency information

Emergency services
Coins are not needed for emergency calls from public telephones.

For **Police** ☎110; for **Fire** ☎112; for **Ambulance** ☎112, or in East Berlin ☎115.

Emergency telephone numbers are likely to be standardized throughout the EC from Jan 1993.

Medical and dental emergencies
Doctors' emergency service (24hrs)   ☎310031
Dentists' emergency service (24hrs)   ☎1141

There is no English or American hospital in Berlin, except those that cater solely to the military.

First aid
For first-aid assistance ☎310031.

24-hour pharmacy
Pharmacies are open during normal shop hours. A list of those open at night and on Sun is placed in the window of every pharmacy. The **Europa-Apotheke** (*Tauentzienstrasse 9* ☎ *2614142*) is open daily 9am-9pm. For information on all-night pharmacies ☎(030) 1141.

Automobile accidents
- Do not admit liability or incriminate yourself.
- Ask any witness(es) to stay and give a statement.
- Contact the police.
- Exchange names, addresses, car details and insurance company details with any other drivers involved.
- Give a statement to the police, who will compile a report acceptable to insurance companies.

Car breakdowns
- Put on flashing hazard warning lights, and place a warning triangle 50m (55yds) behind the car.
- ☎ police, or the **ADAC** (road patrol) (☎ *(030) 19211*).

Lost passport
Contact the local police and your consulate immediately.

Lost travelers checks/charge/credit cards
Notify the local police immediately, then follow the instructions provided with your travelers checks, or contact the issuing company. Contact your consulate or **American Express** (☎ *(030) 8827575*) if stranded with no money.

Lost property
Contact the police lost property office (**Fundbüro im Polizei-Präsidium**) (*Platz der Luftbrücke 6* ☎ *(030) 6990*). If you have lost something on public transportation, go to the **Fundbüro der BVG** (*Potsdamer Strasse 188* ☎ *(030) 2161413*). Report all losses to the police immediately, as insurance claims may not be accepted without a police report.

Emergency phrases
Help!   *Hilfe!*
There has been an accident.   *Ein Unfall!*
Where is the nearest telephone/hospital?   *Wo ist das nächste Telefon/Krankenhaus?*
Call an ambulance!   *Bitte, einen Krankenwagen, schnell.*
Call the police!   *Die Polizei, bitte.*

CULTURE, HISTORY AND BACKGROUND

Landmarks in Berlin's history

Electors of Brandenburg
c.1230: Two small settlements established on the Spree River: Berlin, a trading outpost on the right bank, and Cölln, a fishing village on the island opposite. **1369**: Berlin became a leading member of the Hanseatic League, a powerful group of German trading towns. **1380**: Robber barons terrorized Berlin, and trade declined. **1414**: Robber barons crushed by Burggraf Friedrich of Nuremberg, of the House of Hohenzollern.

1415: Friedrich elected *Kurfürst* (Imperial Elector) of the N German region of Brandenburg. **1440**: Elector Friedrich II built the Stadtschloss on the island town of Cölln. Berlin became royal residence and administrative center. Medieval privileges were eroded, but prosperity increased.

1517: Martin Luther led the Reformation in Germany, nailing 95 anti-Catholic theses to the door of the Schlosskirche at Wittenberg, SW of Berlin. **1539**: Elector Joachim II introduced Reformation to Berlin.

1618-48: The Thirty Years' War, a struggle between Protestant and Catholic states, fought mainly on German soil. Berlin repeatedly plundered by Swedish troops.

1640: Succession of the Great Elector, Friedrich Wilhelm I of Brandenburg. He trebled the strength of the army from 8,000 to 23,000, and increased the state's power by eroding civil liberties and granting privileges to the nobility. **1675**: Swedish army defeated at Battle of Fehrbellin. Brandenburg became the strongest German state after Austria.

1685: The Great Elector enacted the Potsdam Edict, opening Berlin to Huguenots driven from France by the Revocation of the Edict of Nantes. Some 20,000 Protestant exiles settled in Brandenburg, including 5,000 in Berlin (mainly in the suburbs of Friedrichswerder and Dorotheenstadt), where they worked as merchants, artists, inventors and linen manufacturers. The Great Elector modeled Berlin on the mercantile cities of the Dutch Republic, where he had spent his youth. Quays were constructed along the Spree waterfront, and a canal was built between the Spree and the Oder.

1688: Friedrich III succeeded his father, and engaged Baroque architects to embellish the city, while Queen Sophie Charlotte, a friend of Descartes and Leibnitz, encouraged art, philosophy and the sciences. Berlin became known as the Athens on the Spree. **1695**: Zeughaus (arsenal) was built by Andreas Schlüter. **1696**: Academy of Art founded in Berlin.

The Kingdom of Prussia
1701: The Kingdom of Prussia was founded, combining Brandenburg and the duchy of Prussia. Friedrich Wilhelm III crowned King Friedrich I at Königsberg, East Prussia (now Kaliningrad in the USSR). Academy of Science founded in Berlin, based on proposal by the philosopher Leibnitz, who became its first director.

1709: Berlin expanded to include Cölln, Friedrichswerder, Dorotheenstadt and Friedrichstadt. **1713**: King Friedrich Wilhelm I, the "Soldier King," succeeded his father, and devoted his energies to building up the army to 83,000 soldiers. Austere and devout, he was the first European king to wear uniform constantly, and elevated the Prussian officer corps to the highest rung of the aristocracy. Friedrich Wilhelm laid out large parade grounds such as Pariser Platz, Leipziger Platz, Mehringplatz and the Tempelhofer Feld (later Tempelhof airfield). They were

Historical landmarks

linked by broad streets named after the king: Friedrichstrasse and Wilhelmstrasse (the latter renamed Otto-Grotewohl-Strasse in honor of the postwar East German prime minister).

1730: The future Frederick the Great rebelled against his father's strict regime. He attempted to flee Prussia, but was captured. **1735**: The city was encircled by a wall to facilitate collection of tolls.

1740: King Frederick II, later named "the Great," succeeded his unloved father. Pursuing a more enlightened policy, he embellished Berlin, building the Forum Fridericianum, Unter den Linden, the Alte Königliche Bibliothek and the Staatsoper.

1740-48: The War of the Austrian Succession was sparked off by Prussia's invasion of Silesia. Austrian troops occupied Berlin briefly in 1742.

1756-63: The Seven Years' War, during which Austria, France, Russia and Saxony combined forces against Prussia. Frederick the Great occupied Saxony. **1759**: Prussia narrowly avoided defeat at battle of Kunersdorf. **1760**: Russian troops occupied Berlin. Russia dropped out of the alliance in 1762 and the war ended through exhaustion, leaving Prussia intact as one of the five major European powers.

1786: Friedrich Wilhelm II succeeded his father. **1791**: The Brandenburg Gate was built. **1792**: Prussian army defeated by French at Battle of Valmy. **1797**: Friedrich Wilhelm III succeeded his father.

1806: Napoleon defeated Prussian army at Battles of Jena and Auerstadt, and entered Berlin in triumph through the Brandenburg Gate. He abolished the Holy Roman Empire, a loose German confederation founded in the 10thC. **1813**: Wars of Liberation. Napoleon defeated at Battle of Leipzig. French occupation ended, and Prussia recovered the Ruhr. **1815**: The timely arrival of General Von Blücher's Prussian army played a decisive role in the defeat of Napoleon at Waterloo. A German Confederation under Hapsburg rule was established at the Congress of Vienna. **1838**: Berlin's first railroad line built to Potsdam.

1840: Friedrich Wilhelm IV succeeded his father. **1848**: The German Revolution, sparked off by overthrow of French King Louis Philippe. Demonstrations in Berlin and elsewhere led to drafting of German constitution in Frankfurt. Assembly asked Friedrich Wilhelm IV of Prussia to become king of a united Germany, but he refused.

1862: Bismarck appointed Minister-President of Prussia. **1866**: Prussian army led by Count Helmuth von Moltke defeated Austrians at Battle of Königgrätz.

1870-71: The Franco-Prussian War, begun by Napoleon III. Germany encircled entire French army at Sedan, and occupied Alsace and Lorraine.

Imperial Germany

1871: Bismarck forged a united German Empire (the Second Reich) out of 39 independent kingdoms and principalities that once belonged to the Holy Roman Empire. The Second Reich was proclaimed at Versailles. Wilhelm I, King of Prussia, crowned Emperor. Berlin became the imperial capital of an increasingly authoritarian society. Bismarck's policies ensured peace in Europe for 20yrs, but German military build-up continued. **1878**: Attempted assassination of Kaiser Wilhelm I in Berlin provided Bismarck with an excuse to persecute socialists.

1888: Kaiser Wilhelm II succeeded his father. He dismissed Bismarck and assumed control of the army.

Historical landmarks

1914: Austria attacked Serbia, in response to the assassination of Crown Prince Ferdinand at Sarajevo. Germany entered World War I to protect Austria against threatened attack from Russia. Germany attacked France, Russia's ally, through neutral Belgium, drawing Britain into the 4yr conflict.

1918: German spring offensive on Western Front failed. Realizing inevitability of defeat, German generals persuaded the Reichstag to negotiate peace. Under the Treaty of Versailles, Germany forced to pay massive war reparations. Naval mutiny at Kiel garrison sparked off November Revolution. Anarchy in Berlin as Social Democratic Party (SPD) followers fought with Communists. Kaiser Wilhelm II fled to the Netherlands.

The Weimar Republic

1919: In elections, SPD gained majority of seats, and Friedrich Ebert elected President of new republic. Reichstag moved from Berlin to Weimar, where model federal constitution drawn up. **1920**: National Assembly returned to Berlin. Law of April 27 created the metropolis of *Gross-Berlin* (Greater Berlin), population 4 million, through the fusion of seven towns, 59 villages and 27 estates. The Kapp Putsch, led by a Prussian civil servant, failed to topple the government. **1922**: Walter Rathenau, the Jewish foreign minister, assassinated by right-wing extremists angered by a treaty signed with Russia.

1923: France and Belgium occupied the Ruhr after German default on reparations payments. General strike in Germany led to massive inflation. Failure of right-wing military putsch in Munich led by Göring, Ludendorff and Hitler (who was imprisoned for 8mths for high treason).

1924: US loans to Germany led to economic boom. Occupation of the Ruhr ended. Painting, theater and cabaret flourished in Berlin in conditions of relative political stability. **1925**: General Field Marshall von Hindenburg succeeded Ebert as president. **1926**: Joseph Goebbels, appointed by Hitler as Nazi party chief in Berlin, orchestrated clashes between Nazi stormtroopers and local Communists.

1929: Wall Street Crash in Oct halted US loans to Germany, and unemployment soared to 3 million. **1930**: Nazi party gained 107 seats in Reichstag. **1932**: Nazis gained 230 seats, to become largest party in Reichstag. Street violence in Berlin escalated. Jewish businesses, theaters and cabarets attacked. Nazis lost 34 seats in Nov elections.

Nazi Germany

1933: Hitler appointed Chancellor of Germany by Hindenburg. Weimar Republic suspended in Mar. Jewish shops boycotted in Apr, and Nazis burned books on the Opernplatz in May. Trade unions and opposition political parties outlawed. Brecht, Kandinsky and others fled from Berlin. **1934**: Night of the Long Knives (June 30), during which SA officers were murdered by Nazis.

1936: Berlin Olympics exploited for Nazi propaganda. **1938**: The Generals' Plot, an attempt on Hitler's life led by General Ludwig Beck, ended in failure. Hitler invaded Sudetenland region of Czechoslovakia. Jewish properties in Berlin destroyed in widespread riots in Nov.

1939: Britain and France declared war on Germany after invasion of Poland in Sept. **1943-44**: The Battle of Berlin, during which the RAF dropped more than 30,000 tons of bombs on Berlin in an attempt to crush morale.

1944: The Von Stauffenberg Plot. Colonel Von Stauffenberg planted a bomb under Hitler's conference table at Rastenberg in

Historical landmarks

East Prussia. Hitler survived the assassination attempt and the conspirators were executed.

1945: Soviet troops led by Marshall Zhukhov entered Berlin on Apr 21. Hitler shot himself in his underground bunker nine days later. The German army surrendered on Apr 30, after fierce street fighting. The term *Stunde Nul* (Zero Hour) coined, to describe Germany's ruin in 1945. Potsdam Agreement signed by US, Russia and Britain. Germany divided into four sectors under US, British, French and Soviet control. Berlin ceased to be capital of Germany. The Nuremberg Trials, Nov 1945-Oct 1946, led to execution of prominent Nazis for crimes against humanity; Rudolf Hess and Albert Speer imprisoned in Spandau prison.

Divided Germany

1948: The Berlin Blockade imposed in June by Soviet Union in attempt to force West Berlin into submission. Road and rail links through East Germany closed, preventing essential supplies from reaching US, British and French sectors of the city. Berlin Airlift immediately organized by General Lucius D. Clay, to land essential supplies at Tempelhof airfield. Some 2.2 million tons were landed in 274,418 flights. East and West Berlin polarized.

1949: Blockade lifted in May. The division of Germany formalized by the enactment of the Basic Law in May, creating the German Federal Republic (West Germany), with Konrad Adenauer as the first Chancellor. The German Democratic Republic (East Germany) was established in Oct, with Otto Grotewohl as its first prime minister. Ernst Reuter elected first Mayor of West Berlin.

1950: A constitution was drawn up for Berlin as a special West German *Land* (state) under the control of the four powers. It became the *de jure* capital of West Germany, with Bonn as the *de facto* capital. **1952**: East Germany cut telephone links between East and West Berlin.

1953: East German government insisted on 10 percent increase in productivity for no increase in pay, prompting strikes. Rebellion crushed by Soviet troops — a foretaste of things to come in Prague and Budapest.

1961: Fearing war between US and Soviet Union, East Germans flooded into West Berlin. Walter Ulbricht ordered construction of the 47km (29-mile) Berlin Wall as an "antifascist defense barrier" along boundary of Soviet sector.

1963: US President John F. Kennedy expressed solidarity with West Berliners in speech at Rathaus Schöneberg, West Berlin's town hall. **1969**: Chancellor Willy Brandt, former West Berlin mayor, launched *Ostpolitik*, a policy of reconciliation with East Germany.

1971: The Four Powers Agreement on Berlin reduced Cold War tension by improving access to West Berlin through East Germany, and easing restrictions for West Berliners visiting relatives in East Berlin.

German Unification

Late 1989: *Die Wende* (the turning point). After massive demonstrations in Leipzig and other East German cities, resignation of East German government. Berlin Wall was opened to East Germans on Nov 9.

1990: Border checks between East and West Berlin abolished. West German Deutschmark became sole legal tender in both countries. Fears of mass unemployment in East Germany led to acceleration of unification process. East and West Germany formally united on Oct 4. **1991**: *Bundestag* (parliament) restores Berlin as capital of Germany.

Architecture

Architecture in Berlin

The bombing of Berlin in World War II destroyed a massive stock of palaces, churches, cinemas and apartments, leaving little of the old city. The Nikolaikirche and the Marienkirche are the only medieval buildings still standing in central Berlin, and virtually all the Renaissance architecture commissioned by Joachim II — Berlin's first Protestant Elector — has disappeared, except for the Jagdschloss in the Grunewald.

Baroque

Nor have many buildings survived from the long reign of Friedrich Wilhelm, the Great Elector (from 1640-88), who rebuilt Berlin at the end of the Thirty Years' War in a Baroque style, modeled on the Dutch towns where he had spent his youth. The principal mementos of the Great Elector are the monumental 17thC urban spaces, such as Unter den Linden and the Lustgarten.

The formal Baroque new towns of Friedrichswerder (w of Cölln) and Dorotheenstadt (N of Unter den Linden) were laid out at this time to accommodate Berlin's rapidly growing population of Huguenot craftsmen, although most of the buildings now standing were built in the 19th or 20thC.

Berlin continued its westward push in the era of Friedrich III (reigned 1688-1713), the first king of Prussia, who created the suburbs of Friedrichstadt (s of Unter den Linden) and Charlottenburg (w of the Tiergarten). The reconstruction of Schloss Charlottenburg for Sophie Charlotte, the king's second wife, turned the former village at Charlottenburg into one of Berlin's most elegant suburbs. Johann Arnold Nering's compact palace, built 1695-99, came to mirror the growth of Prussian power in the extensions that were soon added. Courtyards, wings, a cupola and an orangery were completed within 30yrs, while Georg Wenzeslaus von Knobelsdorff's new wing was added in 1740-46 for Frederick the Great, and additions were still being made 100yrs later.

Schloss Charlottenburg

Many new buildings were designed for Friedrich III by Andreas Schlüter (1664-1714), a Polish architect and sculptor invited to Berlin in 1694. After a 2yr study tour of France and Italy, he returned to Berlin to complete the royal arsenal, or Zeughaus,

Architecture

(now the Museum für Deutsche Geschichte) on Unter den Linden, a monumental Baroque building begun by Johann Nering. Schlüter subsequently reconstructed the Stadtschloss (city palace) on the Spree, which was bombed in 1945, and finally demolished in 1950. A scale model in Schloss Charlottenburg shows the grandeur of Schlüter's Baroque design, of which all that now remains are a few charred Baroque statues in the Bode-Museum.

Schlüter's most famous sculptural work — an equestrian statue of the Great Elector, made in 1700 — stood until World War II on the bridge beside the palace. It now graces the courtyard of Schloss Charlottenburg. Schlüter was dismissed from his post following the collapse of a tower of the Stadtschloss, and his last completed work in Berlin was the Villa Kamecke in Dorotheenstadt. It, too, was destroyed in 1945, and all that remains are some sculptures from the balustrade, which are to be seen in the Bode-Museum.

Friedrich Wilhelm I, the Soldier King (reigned 1713-40), had little time for architecture. Interested only in expanding the Prussian army, he laid out the Pariser Platz and the Tempelhofer Feld (now an airport) as military parade grounds. His son, Frederick the Great, was a keen soldier too, but nurtured grand architectural schemes for the capital. He turned Unter den Linden into one of Europe's finest streets, lined with monumental Baroque edifices such as the Staatsoper, designed by Georg Wenzeslaus von Knobelsdorff (1699-1753), the Palais des Prinzen Heinrich by Johann Boumann (1706-76), and the Alte Königliche Bibliothek by Christian Unger (1743-1812). Karl von Gontard (1731-91) built the Deutscher Dom and the complementary Französischer Dom (the cathedral of the Huguenot community) on the Gendarmenmarkt (now the Platz der Akademie), and Georg Wenzeslaus von Knobelsdorff designed St Hedwigskirche (later the Catholic cathedral) in the style of the Pantheon in Rome. Schloss Bellevue was built on the edge of the Tiergarten in 1785, prompting the development of an elegant residential quarter around the woods.

Frederick the Great flirted briefly with the Rococo style at his summer palace, Schloss Sanssouci, at Potsdam. The palace and its terraced grounds were designed by Knobelsdorff, while Johann Gottfried Büring created the Chinesisches Teehaus (1745), a delightful Rococo whimsy.

Neoclassical

Neoclassical architecture proved more suited to the stern Prussian temperament than flighty French Rococo. The Brandenburger Tor, erected in 1793 by Carl Gotthard Langhans (1732-1808), was Berlin's first Neoclassical building, in Classical Athenian style. The Greek revival was developed by Friedrich Gilly (1772-1800), who abandoned Neo-Gothic in favor of Neoclassical in his 1796 design for a national monument to Frederick the Great. After completing a study tour of France and England, Gilly was appointed Professor of Optics and Perspective at the newly-founded Academy of Architecture.

Schinkel

Karl Friedrich Schinkel (1781-1841), a pupil of Gilly's, designed much of Neoclassical Berlin. A German Romantic at heart, Schinkel was fond of painting melancholy scenes of Gothic churches. But he later converted to a disciplined Neoclassical style that exactly suited the quiet mood of confidence in Berlin following the defeat of Napoleon in 1815.

Appointed to the public works department in 1815, Schinkel

Architecture

Schinkel's **Altes Museum**

designed the Neoclassical Neue Wache on Unter den Linden in 1816. Two years later, he resorted to his beloved Neo-Gothic style in a War Memorial on the Kreuzberg. But he returned to sober Neoclassicism for the Schauspielhaus on the Gendarmenmarkt (now Platz der Akademie) in 1818-21, the exquisite Schinkel-Pavillon at Schloss Charlottenburg (1824), and Schloss Tegel (1822-24), built for his scholarly friend Wilhelm von Humboldt. Schinkel also completed several buildings at Potsdam, including Schloss Charlottenhof (1826) and the Nikolaikirche (1830), and he designed a Neoclassical palace and other smaller buildings in the nearby Volkspark Klein-Glienicke.

Schinkel's masterpiece was the Altes Museum on the Spree (1823-30), a handsome museum incorporating a domed hall modeled on the Pantheon in Rome. But medieval architecture never entirely lost its hold on Schinkel, and the designs for the Friedrichswerdersche Kirche (1824-30) and Schloss Babelsberg near Potsdam (1833) are pure Neo-Gothic.

Wilhelmine

The Wilhelmine period at the end of the 19thC led to the development of a heavy, bourgeois style of architecture for hotels, government offices and apartment blocks in Mitte, Charlottenburg and other prosperous districts.

Meanwhile, speculators were erecting massive tenement blocks (*Mietskaserne*) in the poorer districts of Kreuzberg, Neukölln, Wedding and Prenzlauer Berg. Many of these grim apartments were lit only from deep courtyards — the notorious *Hinterhöfe*, as they were known.

A new simplicity of design was introduced by Peter Behrens (1868-1940), a disciple of William Morris. After producing Art Nouveau posters, he was appointed chief architect for the giant Berlin electricity company AEG in 1907. Behrens developed a unified modern corporate design for AEG's factory buildings, electrical products (such as kettles and fans), canteen cutlery and stationery.

Bauhaus

Walter Gropius (1883-1969), who worked in Peter Behrens' firm until 1910, built factories in a severe functional style that heralded the Modern Movement. In 1919, he moved to Weimar, sw of Berlin, to replace the Belgian architect Henry van de Velde as director of the School of Arts and Crafts. Renaming it the *Bauhaus* (House of Building), Gropius transformed it into a revolutionary school based on medieval ideals of craftsmanship. Although it lasted only 14yrs, the Bauhaus had an enormous influence on 20thC architecture and design, employing Paul Klee, Wassily Kandinsky and Theo van Doesburg as teachers.

Harassed in Weimar by the Nazis, the Bauhaus moved in 1925 to the left-wing town of Dessau, mid-way between Weimar and Berlin. But even here Gropius was harangued, and he was finally forced to resign in 1928.

Architecture

After the Dessau Bauhaus was closed down in 1933, the school moved to Berlin, but lasted there only a few months. Although finally crushed in Germany, Bauhaus architects such as Walter Gropius and the last director, Mies van der Rohe, went on to play a major role in the development of postwar American architecture. Several American skyscrapers were the realization of Bauhaus projects for Berlin frustrated by the Depression and the Nazi regime.

The closure of the Bauhaus marked the beginning of a dark age in German architecture. Adolf Hitler outlawed modern design in Germany, and conspired with the architect Albert Speer to create a terrifying Neoclassical Nazi capital to be called Germania. Few of his megalomaniacal plans were ever realized, and almost all traces of Germania have vanished.

Postwar reconstruction

The first task after World War II was to shift the millions of tons of rubble. Reconstruction of the devastated city began in the Soviet sector, where a heroic attempt was made at Stalinallee (later Karl-Marx-Allee) to create a modern Berlin in harmony with Schinkel's Neoclassicism. Driven by the tense rivalry of the Cold War, West Berlin responded by commissioning a team of international architects to design new apartments in the devastated Hansaviertel.

Mies van der Rohe's **Neue Nationalgalerie**

Gropius returned to Berlin in 1957 to submit a design for the competition. He also designed the Bauhaus-Archiv on the edge of the Tiergarten. Mies van der Rohe was invited back to the city he had fled, to design the Neue Nationalgalerie, a strikingly simple square structure with glass walls overhung by a black steel roof, which was completed in 1968, only a year before his death.

IBA architecture

But the Bauhaus style largely failed to create a livable city out of the rubble. A major turning point came in 1979, when the International Building Exhibition (IBA) was set up by the West Berlin *Land* (state) to transform the inner city into an attractive environment for living. The IBA has sponsored imaginative schemes in Kreuzberg, employing international architects who have created colorful and quirky apartment blocks alongside the gloomy buildings of the Wilhelmine age. Sometimes the new buildings incorporate fragments of old houses or Neoclassical touches, generating the rudiments of a recognizable Berlin style once again.

Now that Berlin is capital of Germany once more, grand architectural projects have been mooted, to adapt the city to its new role. The planned developments range from the rural idyll of creating a park along the strip of wasteland left by the Wall, to Daimler-Benz's massive office complex on Potsdamer Platz. The plans to transform Berlin have sparked off fierce controversy among architects and politicians, which adds immensely to the current mood of excitement in the changing metropolis.

Art

Art in Berlin

The great movements of German Gothic and Renaissance art did not touch Berlin, and the city only became an important center of European painting in the early 20thC, when a succession of radical art movements created a climate of bold experimentation. Artistic groups in Berlin tended to be short-lived and explosive, and artists often participated in several different movements.

The revolt against the established art of the 19thC began with the **Berliner Secession**, a group inspired by radical artists in Munich and Vienna who had seceded from the official art exhibitions. Max Liebermann (1847-1935), the foremost of the German Impressionists, founded the Berliner Secession in 1899 and served as its first president.

An idealistic group called **Die Brücke** (The Bridge) was founded at Dresden in 1905 by a group of art students that included Ernst Ludwig Kirchner (1880-1938), Emil Nolde (1867-1956) and Max Pechstein (1881-1955). Inspired by German woodcuts and the ethnography collection in the Zwinger Palace at Dresden, Die Brücke sought to express human emotions through violent colors and jarring compositions. The group dissolved in 1913, just 3yrs after its move to Berlin.

Meanwhile, the Secession had become rather too staid for the most radical of Berlin's artists, and in 1910 a new splinter group, the **Neue Secession**, was founded. Led by Max Pechstein, it drew recruits from Die Brücke, including Kirchner and Nolde.

The artists of the various German art movements that challenged 19thC Impressionism became collectively known as the **Expressionists**. Inspired by Munch and Van Gogh, they evolved a highly emotional, anxious style, employing vivid colors and distorted forms. Expressionism had a profound influence on early German cinema and (to a lesser degree) architecture.

The Utopian ideals of Expressionism were dashed by World War I. The **Novembergruppe**, founded in Berlin in 1918 by disillusioned Expressionist artists and architects such as Max Pechstein and César Klein, sought to heal a world broken by war through a socialist unification of arts, architecture and town planning. Some of the group's members later joined the Berlin **Dada** movement, founded in 1918 after the German poet Richard Huelsenbeck proclaimed an irrational Dada speech in Berlin. Reacting against German Expressionism, Berlin Dada was a provocative and revolutionary art movement born out of the savagery of war. But it lasted only a few years; after a brief explosion of creativity, Berlin Dada was officially pronounced dead in a meeting at Weimar in 1922.

John Heartfield (1891-1968), a communist and founding member of the Berlin Dada movement, continued to create biting photomontages ridiculing Hitler and the Nazis in the 1920s. He fled to England in 1938 and returned to East Berlin in 1950.

German **Impressionism** resurfaced in the 1920s, when Lesser Ury painted attractive Berlin street scenes, but the most powerful art movement in the Weimar Republic was **Neue Sachlichkeit** (New Objectivity), led by Georg Grosz (1893-1959) and Otto Dix (1891-1969). Scarred by their experiences in World War I, Grosz and Dix painted savage caricatures of the corrupt businessmen and generals of the Weimar Republic.

Neue Sachlichkeit and German Expressionism became prime targets for Hitler's notorious vilification of decadent art in the 1930s. Expressionist artists and galleries were hounded, modern paintings were ridiculed in exhibitions of "decadent art" staged by the Nazis, and the bulk of the works were sold abroad. What little remained was mostly burned in Berlin in 1939, in a sequel to the notorious book-burning. All that survives in Berlin of those astonishing years of creativity from 1899-1933 are the depleted collections in the Nationalgalerie, the Neue Nationalgalerie and the Brücke Museum in Dahlem.

German art took a long time to recover from the Nazi years. In the late 1970s, the Expressionism of the 1910s resurfaced in West Germany under the group known as **Die Neue Wilden** (the New Wild Ones). The permanent collection of 20thC Berlin paintings in the Martin-Gropius-Bau illustrates modern Berlin artists' understandable obsession with themes of violence and terror. But the most famous works of postwar Berlin art were the spontaneous murals sprayed onto the Wall by numerous artists. Now that the Wall has come down, little remains in Berlin of this playful and irreverent art — apart from fragments in the Berlin-Museum and the Museum für Deutsche Geschichte — but several books of photographs record these extraordinary works of graffiti art.

Guide to Berlin's galleries

There are more than 130 commercial art galleries in Berlin, exhibiting a broad range of painting, sculpture, ceramics and photography by Berlin and international artists. Galleries in Charlottenburg tend to deal in well-established artists, whereas those in Kreuzberg are more likely to show young, emerging talents. Most galleries are open Mon-Fri afternoon and Sat morning, but times are rather erratic; it is always wise to call ahead to check that a gallery is open. The *Berlin Programm* (available from tourist offices) provides a selective monthly listing of exhibitions. More detailed information is given in the quarterly *Kunstblatt*. The following list of galleries highlights some of the most interesting or unusual.

Aedes S-Bahn Bogen, Savignyplatz, Charlottenburg ☎(030) 3122598. Map **2**D4. Gallery located in the arches below S-Bahnhof Savignyplatz, exhibiting architectural plans and scale models ranging from the Acropolis to the Museumsinsel.

Brusberg Kurfürstendamm 213, Charlottenburg ☎(030) 8827682. Map **2**D4. Major modern Surrealist and Dada artists including Ernst, Dalí, Dubuffet, Miró and Picasso.

DAAD Kurfürstenstrasse 58, Tiergarten ☎(030) 31000336. Map **3**D6. U-Bahn to Nollendorfplatz. Exhibitions of work by foreign artists, sponsored by the *Deutschen Akademischen Austauschdienstes* (German academic exchange program). Situated on the first floor of a handsome Old Berlin mansion, above the fashionable Café Einstein.

Elefanten Press Galerie Oranienstrasse 25, Kreuzberg ☎(030) 6149036. Map **4**D9. Bookstore run by alternative Berlin publishing house, with an airy gallery exhibiting radical paintings and photographs.

Galerie am Chamissoplatz Chamissoplatz 6, Kreuzberg ☎(030) 6925381. Map **4**E8. Gallery situated in a former bakery, mounting shows of critical art including biting cartoons on German unification politics by Gerhard Seyfried. Also occasional readings and concerts.

Gelbe Musik Schaperstrasse 11, Wilmersdorf ☎(030) 2113962. Map **2**D4. Unique gallery and shop specializing in artists' records, tapes and videos.

Film

Nierendorf Hardenbergstrasse 19, Charlottenburg ☎(030) 7856060. Map **2**C4. Founded during the Weimar Republic, Nierendorf continues to exhibit 1920s German Expressionist art.

Pels-Leusden-Galerie Fasanenstrasse 25, Charlottenburg ☎(030) 8826811. Map **2**D4. Elegant art gallery situated in the restored Villa Grisebach, with major exhibitions of work by well-established contemporary artists.

Raab Potsdamerstrasse 58, Tiergarten ☎(030) 2619217. Map **3**D6. Ingrid Raab's discerning selection of contemporary Berlin artists.

Staatliche Kunsthalle Berlin Budapester Strasse 42, Charlottenburg ☎(030) 2617067. Map **2**D5. Major exhibitions featuring contemporary Berlin artists.

Weisser Elefant Almstadtstrasse 11, Mitte ☎(0372) 2823908. Map **4**B9. Situated in a decayed 19thC mustard factory near Alexanderplatz, the Weisser Elefant was formerly a forum for young East Berlin artists such as Wolf Leo — the artist who painted murals on the East side of the Wall.

Film in Berlin

The early German film industry developed at the Filmstadt Babelsberg, a film studio built near Potsdam in 1911. This became the UFA (Universum-Film-Aktiengesellschaft), Germany's largest film studios, which turned out numerous propaganda films during World War I.

German Expressionist Cinema developed in Berlin in the 1920s, heightening suspense by the use of unusual camera angles, moving cameras and light and shade. With its pioneering Expressionist techniques, Fritz Lang's *Cabinet of Dr. Caligari* (1919) profoundly influenced Hollywood style. *Metropolis* (1926), another Fritz Lang epic, provided a bleak prophecy of urban life in the year 2000. Constructed in UFA's Babelsberg studios at enormous cost, Lang's visionary city of skyscrapers looks more like Manhattan than Weimar Berlin, although the intersecting railroad tracks in the sky were perhaps inspired by the intricate engineering of the Berlin railroad network. Among the many experimental works shot in the 1920s, *Berlin, Symphony of a Great City* (1927) can still be admired for its fragmentary portrayal of a single day in the life of the metropolis.

One of the last great films of the Weimar years was *Der Blaue Engel* (1930), by Josef von Sternberg, a film both produced and set in Berlin. Based on the Heinrich Mann novel *Professor Unrat*, the film tells of the moral decline of a respectable German professor captivated by the Berlin cabaret singer Lola-Lola, played by Marlene Dietrich. Serious film fans should try to catch the German version with English subtitles rather than the inferior English remake.

Some of the most talented figures in the Berlin film world were lured to Hollywood in the 1920s, including Ernst Lubitsch, Emil Jannings (who played the professor in *The Blue Angel*) and Pola Negri. The rise of the Nazis led to further departures from Berlin, including Fritz Lang and Billy Wilder. But Pola Negri and Emil Jannings, hampered in Hollywood by their strong German accents, returned to Berlin to star in Nazi propaganda films. The talented Berlin director Leni Riefenstahl also worked under the Nazis to film documentaries of the Nuremberg rallies and the 1936 Berlin Olympics.

The bleak, bombed ruins of postwar Berlin provided the

background for melancholy films such as Roberto Rossellini's *Germany, Year Zero* (1947), in which a 13-year-old boy is haunted by the Nazi past, and Robert Stemmle's *Ballad of Berlin* (1948), telling of a defeated soldier returning home to be preyed upon by criminals and bureaucrats. Several movies shot in Berlin in the 1950s focused on international tensions in the postwar city. Carol Reed's *The Man Between* (1953) is a Berlin spy thriller modeled on his famous *The Third Man*. Sam Fuller's *Verboten!* (1958) is an unusual story of a US soldier's relationship with a German woman who saved him from a sniper in occupied Berlin.

The division of Berlin by the Wall offered an edgy setting for a spate of 1960s Hollywood spy thrillers such as Hitchcock's *Torn Curtain* (1966). Berlin is the setting, too, for several movies based on British author Len Deighton's complex thrillers, which include *Funeral in Berlin* (1966), starring Michael Caine, and *The Quiller Memorandum* (1966).

Bob Fosse's *Cabaret* (1972) is the screen version of a musical based on Christopher Isherwood's *Goodbye to Berlin*. Set in the tormented late years of the Weimar Republic, the Hollywood movie stars Liza Minnelli as a sexy singer in a louche Berlin cabaret. The smoky, sinful setting is similar to that in *The Blue Angel*, but Michael York, unlike Professor Unrat, remains almost untainted by the corruption all around. Swedish director Ingmar Bergman's *The Serpent's Egg* (1977) was a later attempt to re-create the atmosphere of Berlin in the early 1920s.

The realistic school of the 1970s, labeled New German Cinema, was developed by West German directors such as Rainer Werner Fassbinder and Werner Herzog. Their studios were based in Munich, dubbed "Hollywood on the Iser," but West Berlin sometimes provided an exotic setting. *Berlin Alexanderplatz*, the classic novel of 1920s Berlin, was made into a 15hr television movie by Fassbinder in 1980. Set in the late years of the Weimar Republic, the film deliberately evoked the smoky, seedy atmosphere of *The Blue Angel*. Contemporary Berlin was portrayed as a drab and menacing metropolis in *Christiane F* (1981) by German director Ulrich Edel. Filmed in the squalor of the Bahnhof Zoo (now far less sinister) and the modern tower blocks of the Märkisches Viertel, it recounts the true story of a 13yr-old heroin-addict-turned-prostitute. The Berlin gay world has been affectionately filmed by Rosa von Praunheim, a male American, in movies such as *City of Lost Souls* (1983). *Rosa Luxemburg* (1986) by the feminist director Margarethe von Trotta tells the moving tale of the Polish-born co-leader of the Spartacist revolt, who was brutally murdered in Berlin in 1919. Chris Petit's *Flight to Berlin* (1983) and *Chinese Boxes* (1984) are thoughtful films shot in Berlin by a British director deeply influenced by New German Cinema.

Cult German director Wim Wenders' *Die Himmel über Berlin* (1987) is an affectionate film about an angel who looks down on the city from the Siegessäule, then longs to become human when he falls in love with a melancholy trapeze artist at the Tempodrom circus. Set mainly on the desolate wasteland around Potsdamer Platz, the film has lingering shots of the Wall, the Staatsbibliothek, and the ruins of a World War II concrete bunker.

East Germany's state-run film industry (DEFA) was based at the old UFA studios at Babelsberg, where some 5,000 people were employed in the production of television shows, documentaries and feature films. Like much industry in the eastern part of Germany, DEFA was threatened with closure following reunification. But even if the Babelsberg studios close, Berlin is likely to remain a favorite location for German and foreign directors. The city's cinemas offer an impressive variety of movies, and the annual festival in February proves that Berliners are still enraptured by the art form pioneered in their city.

Berlin porcelain

Berlin has been a major center of ceramics manufacture since 1678, when an enterprising Dutchman, Pieter van der Lee, founded a factory producing blue-and-white Delftware. Other firms were established by Cornelius Funcke in 1699 and Karl Friedrich Lüdicke in 1756, and a factory opened nearby in Potsdam in 1740.

The coarse Dutch faience became unfashionable in the 18thC, with the introduction of finer quality porcelain. The hitherto secret Chinese formula for manufacturing porcelain was discovered in 1709 at Meissen, in Saxony, by Johannes Böttger and Ehrenfried Walter, Graf (Count) von Tschirnhausen. Despite strict security, the secret, or *arcanum*, was leaked by Böttger's assistant, and rival factories were soon founded in 1719 at Vienna and Venice.

Berlin's porcelain industry began in 1751 with the foundation of a factory by Wilhelm Caspar Wegeley, a local merchant. Johann Benckengraff, an arcanist trained at the Höchst porcelain works, was put in charge of the factory, which produced ware (marked with the letter W) imitating the elegant Rococo style of Meissen porcelain.

The Wegeley factory was patronized by Frederick the Great, who created a "Porcelain Room" at Schloss Charlottenburg. Inspired by Augustus the Strong's Porzellan-Zimmer at Dresden, it was crammed from floor to ceiling with precious vases. The Prussian ruler lost interest in the Berlin factory after gaining control of the Meissen factory and, deprived of essential royal patronage, the business collapsed in 1757.

A second factory was founded in 1761 by a Berlin banker, Johann Ernst Gotzkowsky. Frederick the Great bought the business in 1763, renaming it the **Königlichen Porzellan-Manufaktur**, or **KPM**. The Royal Porcelain Factory moved from its original site in Leipziger Strasse to its present location near S-Bahnhof Tiergarten in 1870.

The enthusiasm for Classical Antiquity in early 19thC Berlin led KPM to produce large Grecian urns modeled on Classical amphora. Known as *Ansichtsporzellan*, the vases were hand-painted with miniature scenes of Neoclassical Berlin or Potsdam. The factory also produced copies of Neoclassical works, such as Schadow's famous statue of the Princesses Luise and Friederike (now on view in the Nationalgalerie). After the Battle of Waterloo, KPM made a dinner-service (now in Apsley House, London) to present to the Duke of Wellington as a token of Anglo-Prussian friendship.

Art Nouveau (*Jugendstil*) ceramics were introduced at KPM by Theodor Hermann Schmuz-Baudiss, while in the 1920s prominent Bauhaus artists designed simple modern Berlin porcelain.

With the foundation of the Weimar Republic in 1918, the factory was renamed the **Staatliche Porzellan-Manufaktur** (State Porcelain Factory). Destroyed during an air raid in 1943, the factory was rebuilt in 1953, and the name KPM restored in 1988.

PLANNING, WALKS AND TRIPS

The largest collection of Berlin porcelain is at the Kunstgewerbemuseum. The Berlin-Museum, the Märkisches Museum and the Schinkel-Pavillon at Schloss Charlottenburg have a number of 18thC and 19thC KPM works, while the Bröhan-Museum has some striking Art Nouveau and Art Deco porcelain.

Selected reading

For fiction and historiography with a Berlin setting, dig into the following.

Alfred Döblin's *Berlin-Alexanderplatz*, inspired by James Joyce's *Ulysses*, is a classic 20thC German novel of working-class life, set in the 1920s amid squalor and corruption. Franz Biberkopf, a worker imprisoned for battering his wife to death, tries to make a new beginning, but is dragged down into crime and madness. The plot infuriated the Nazis, and they added the book to the pyre of decadent literature burned on the Opernplatz.

Christopher Isherwood based two novels on his experiences as a teacher in Berlin in 1929-33. *Mr Norris Changes Trains* (1935) is a sinister tale of a seedy Communist activist in late Weimar Berlin. *Goodbye to Berlin* (1939), a collection of sketches, includes the tale of Sally Bowles, a flighty cabaret singer, which inspired a play, a musical and the film *Cabaret*.

Len Deighton has written several spy thrillers set in postwar Berlin, including *Funeral in Berlin* and *Berlin Game*. Deighton's *Winter: A Berlin Family 1899-1945* is a powerful chronicle of the fortunes of a prosperous industrialist's family, from the turn of the century to *Stunde Null*.

Peter Gay's *Weimar Culture* (1969) is a fascinating account of the politics and art of the 1920s, written by a Berliner who fled from the Nazis. The story of the bombardment of Berlin is recounted in detail in **Martin Middlebrook's** *The Berlin Raids* (1988), which includes eye-witness accounts by both bomber crews and Berliners. *The Berlin Diaries* by **Marie Vassiltchikov** is an account of wartime Berlin by a woman who knew several of the conspirators in the failed Von Stauffenberg Plot. The American historian **Robert Darnton's** *Berlin Diary 1989-1990* describes the city immediately after the "Turning Point."

When and where to go

Berlin is a bustling, cosmopolitan city throughout the year, and there are plenty of excellent museums to visit in bad weather. Spring in Berlin tends to be mild, while summers are hot. Early summer is the time to catch the lime trees in blossom on Unter den Linden. From about May-Sept, you can sit in the leafy Tiergarten or enjoy open-air concerts in the parks and zoos. The beech and oak woods W of the city look their best in fall, while Berlin's winters, although often severe, offer an opportunity to explore uncrowded museums.

Orientation
The following list gives an idea of the character of Berlin's districts. Parts of East Berlin (Mitte, Prenzlauer Berg, Köpenick) tend to be rather shabby, with few shops or restaurants. For an overview of the city, see maps **5-7**.

When and where to go

Mitte (*Map 4; Central Berlin*). The former heart of the old city, with lingering traces of Imperial Berlin in the 19thC museums, churches and theaters. Now released from the grip of drab socialism, Mitte is fast becoming one of Berlin's most elegant quarters.

Charlottenburg (*Map 1; w of the old city*). An elegant 19thC district that developed around SCHLOSS CHARLOTTENBURG and KURFÜRSTENDAMM. It was the heart of West Berlin, and still has the city's most fashionable stores, cafés, hotels, galleries and movie theaters.

Tiergarten (*Map 3; between Mitte and Charlottenburg*). An elegant quarter bordering Berlin's principal park. Badly bombed in World War II, it is now a mixture of 19thC villas and modern apartment blocks. With the demolition of the Wall, the area around the NEUE NATIONALGALERIE seems poised to develop into a lively cultural quarter.

Kreuzberg (*Map 4; s of the old city*). A 19thC district of large apartments and factories. Partially destroyed by wartime bombardment, it has become an animated quarter settled by migrants, political activists, punks and artists. Dotted with radical galleries and chic restaurants.

Wedding (*Map 6; N of Tiergarten*). A working-class 19thC district of grim apartment blocks and factories. Interesting historically as the scene of many clashes between Communists and Nazis.

Dahlem (*Map 6; sw corner of the city*). A leafy suburb on the edge of the Grunewald, with imposing villas, university buildings and museums.

Grunewald (*Map 5; sw of Charlottenburg*). A vast expanse of woods and lakes, where energetic Berliners walk, jog, swim or cycle, while everyone else drinks beer.

Spandau (*Map 5; w edge of the city*). A historic town on the Havel, with an attractive old center.

Tegel (*Maps 5-6; N of Charlottenburg*). A pleasant old town surrounded by forests and lakes.

Prenzlauer Berg (*Map 7; N of the old center*). A fascinating 19thC working-class district of apartment blocks and factories, with a typical East Berlin mix of dilapidated grandeur and prim restoration. Alternative cafés, art galleries and 1950s milk bars generate an atmosphere akin to that in Kreuzberg.

Köpenick (*Map 7; SE corner of the city*). A run-down old town set among forests and lakes.

Organizing your time

On a trip to Berlin, you may get caught up in the frenetic, exhilarating pace of the city: crossing the city by U-Bahn, snatching a sausage at a stand-up *Imbiss* kiosk, returning to the hotel long after midnight. But it is just as important to capture the full flavor of the city by devoting some time to its more serious cultural attractions: the museums, Neoclassical architecture, classical concerts, quiet cafés and elegant restaurants are all very rewarding.

Four-day visit

Day 1 Spend the morning at the MUSEUMSINSEL, visiting the PERGAMON-MUSEUM, the BODE-MUSEUM and, if time permits, the NATIONALGALERIE. Lunch in the NIKOLAIVIERTEL, then wander along UNTER DEN LINDEN. Climb the tower of the FRANZÖSISCHER DOM for a captivating view of MITTE.

Day 2 Spend the day at SCHLOSS CHARLOTTENBURG, visiting the ÄGYPTISCHES MUSEUM, the Nationalgalerie and the Goldene Galerie. Lunch at Luisen-Bräu (see BEER GARDENS on page 109).

Day 3 Take in the collection of Old Masters at the GEMÄLDEGALERIE in the morning. Walk down Königin-Luise-Strasse and through the Grunewald to visit the JAGDSCHLOSS GRUNEWALD.
Day 4 Visit Potsdam (see pages 119-135).

Three-day architecture tour
Day 1 Visit Schinkel's ALTES MUSEUM, then walk down to UNTER DEN LINDEN to look at Schinkel's Schloss Brücke (now renamed the Marx-Engels-Brücke) and the Neue Wache. Go to the Schinkel Museum in the FRIEDRICHSWERDERSCHE KIRCHE, then walk to PLATZ DER AKADEMIE to climb the tower of the FRANZÖSISCHER DOM.
Day 2 Visit SCHLOSS CHARLOTTENBURG in the morning, looking especially at the Goldene Galerie and the Schinkel-Pavillon. Stroll through Kreuzberg (see WALK 2) in the afternoon. Visit the Aedes gallery (see GUIDE TO GALLERIES on page 27).
Day 3 Visit Potsdam, particularly the Baroque old town, the Rococo Chinesisches Teehaus, and Schinkel's Schloss Charlottenhof (see pages 119-135).

Three-day German art tour
Day 1 Study the German Renaissance art in the GEMÄLDEGALERIE (Wing B) and the SKULPTURENGALERIE at Dahlem.
Day 2 Look at the 19thC Romantics in the GALERIE DER ROMANTIK in the morning, then take bus 110 to Clayallee and walk through the woods to the JAGDSCHLOSS GRUNEWALD. Visit the BRÜCKE-MUSEUM for a glimpse of early 20thC Berlin art.
Day 3 Look at the postwar art in the NEUE NATIONALGALERIE in the morning, then go to the NATIONALGALERIE on MUSEUMSINSEL.

Two-day Berlin history tour
Day 1 Follow the walk in Kreuzberg (see WALK 2) as far as the BERLIN-MUSEUM. Lunch in the museum's *Weissbierstube*. Visit the MÄRKISCHES MUSEUM in the afternoon. Take the U-Bahn to Kochstrasse to visit the HAUS AM CHECKPOINT CHARLIE (*open daily until 10pm*).
Day 2 Visit the REICHSTAG in the morning. Lunch in one of the museum's restaurants, then walk along the Spree (see WALK 1) to the MUSEUM FÜR DEUTSCHE GESCHICHTE.

Calendar of events

Like most German cities, Berlin has several yearly **music festivals**, while its **film** and **theater festivals** are major European events. For information on all festivals in Berlin, contact **Infoladen und Galerie der Berliner Festspiele** (*Budapester Strasse 50, Tiergarten ☎ (030) 254890*). Information on all the festivals is listed in *Berlin Programm*. See also *Public holidays* on page 12.

January
‡ Jan-Feb: **Berliner Musiktage**: 3wk festival of experimental music.

February
‡ Mid-Feb: **Festival des politischen Liedes**. Festival of Political Song.
‡ Late Feb: **Internationale Filmfestspiele Berlin**. Berlin Film Festival, the second-largest in the world, featuring new releases and classics. Films normally screened in original language with subtitles.

April
‡ Early Apr-early May: **Freie Berliner Kunstausstellung** (FBK). A major show of paintings by Berlin artists, at Messegelände exhibition center.

May
‡ May: **Theatertreffen Berlin**. Berlin Theater Festival: experimental German theater, pantomime, dance and circus at various venues. ‡ Whitsun: Early morning **classical music concerts**

Walks

in the zoo and at various parks.
‡ May-Sept: **Spandauer Sommerfestspiele**. Summer festival of theater and music at Spandau (*for information* ☎ *(030) 3316920*).
June
‡ All month: **International jazz** in the garden of the Neue Nationalgalerie. ‡ Early June: **Festival of Traditional Music**. ‡ Mid-end June: **Festival of classical music** in Sanssouci Park, Potsdam. ‡ End June: **Köpenicker Sommer**. Commemorative parade and festival at Köpenick.
July
‡ July-Aug: Open-air **classical concerts by the Berlin Philharmonic** at the Waldbühne amphitheater. ‡ July-Aug: **Organ concerts** in the chapel at Schloss Charlottenburg. (*Sat, Sun* ☎ *(030) 8173364 for dates*.) ‡ Early July: **Internationales Drehorgelfest**. Whimsical street festival of barrel organs from Berlin and elsewhere.
‡ Second week: **Berliner Bachtage**. Bach festival (*details from: Büro der Berliner Bachtage, Bismarckstrasse 73* ☎ *(030) 3123677*).
August
‡ End Aug: **Berliner Tierparkfest**. Events for children at Tierpark Friedrichsfelde.
September
‡ **Berliner Festwochen**. Berlin Festival. Extended festival celebrating the culture of a particular period through a varied program of opera, dance, classical concerts, theater, painting, film and literature.
October
‡ Oct: **Berliner Festtage**. Theater and film festival. ‡ First Sun in Oct: **Berlin Marathon**. ‡ End Oct-early Nov: **JazzFest Berlin**. International jazz festival held in the Philharmonie concert hall and the Delphi-Filmpalast.
December
‡ Dec: **Christmas markets** at Breitscheidplatz and under the Funkturm.

Walks and trips

Although the enormous size of Berlin discourages walking tours, several compact areas are fascinating to explore on foot. Described in the following walks are some of the best of these: the quiet quays along the Spree, the leafy residential districts of Kreuzberg, and the extensive lakes and forests of the Grunewald.

WALK 1: THE SPREE
See map below and maps 1-4A1-C10. Allow 3-4hrs.
Berlin first developed from a settlement on the River Spree, and several important buildings still overlook its quiet quays (*Ufer*), including the REICHSTAG, DOM cathedral and MUSEUMSINSEL. The tree-lined waterfront offers a peaceful and unusual route through the heart of Berlin, past historic buildings and handsome 19thC bridges.

Take the S-Bahn to Tiergarten, turn left along Strasse des 17.

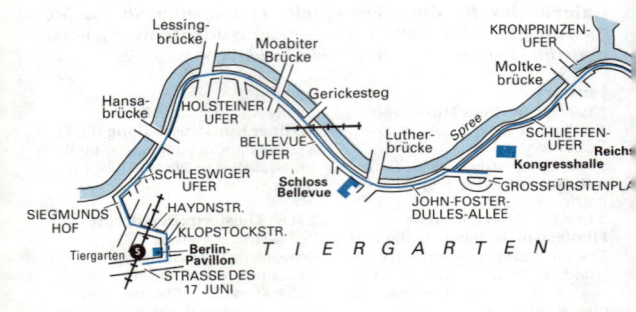

Walks

Juni, then left into Klopstockstrasse past the BERLIN-PAVILLON with its curious collection of Old Berlin street lamps. Now turn left into Haydnstrasse, walk under the elevated railroad, and continue down Siegmunds Hof to reach the Spree. Turn right along Schlesiger Ufer, an attractive quay shaded by weeping willows.

Just beyond the **Hansabrücke**, you see some handsome *Jugendstil* (Art Nouveau) houses on the opposite quay. Soon you reach the **Lessingbrücke**, a graceful iron structure with four red sandstone piers decorated with tragic scenes from such 18thC dramas as Lessing's *Emilia Galotti*. The parapet is adorned with figures of Neptune, frogs, and cats gnawing mice.

Continue along Holsteiner Ufer to the **Moabiter Brücke**, a low, black bridge built in 1894, decorated with four bears. Farther on, the **Gerickesteg** is an attractive *Jugendstil* footbridge with a sweeping staircase, built in 1914. Walk below the S-Bahn bridge and continue along Bellevue Ufer to the 18thC **Schloss Bellevue**, the German president's official Berlin residence. The nearby **Luther Brücke** — a stone bridge with obelisks at the corners — was built in 1892, bombed during World War II and rebuilt in 1951.

John-Foster-Dulles-Allee leads straight ahead through the Tiergarten to the semicircular **Grossfürstenplatz**. Four statues representing the great German rivers were moved here from the Königsbrücke in 1880. Damaged by shrapnel in the fierce fighting here in 1945, they have been left in ruins, the Rhine without a head, the Elbe riddled with bullet holes.

Continuing along the waterfront, you come to the KONGRESSHALLE, a now rather dated symbol of American-fired 1950s optimism. Beyond here, you may see obsolete signs warning that the end of the British Sector is approaching. The frontier between East and West Berlin lay just beyond the **Moltke Brücke**. Named after the general who commanded the victorious Prussian armies in 1866 and 1870, the red sandstone bridge is a rare relic of Prussian military pride, decorated with eagles poised on military trophies, and grief-filled women's faces. The street lamps on the bridge continue the military symbolism: cherubs laden with drums, swords and trumpets. Erected in 1886-91, the bridge was destroyed in 1945 and rebuilt in 1986.

Kronprinzen Ufer, once on the edge of the British sector, still remains an eerie wasteland. The land to the S of here was to have been the site of a vast Nazi assembly hall designed by Albert Speer. An overgrown footpath leads along the waterfront to the

Walks

REICHSTAG, an isolated, melancholy building, carefully repaired after the war with thousands of tiny blocks of stone. The Wall used to halt further progress along the Spree, but there is nothing now to stop you continuing along Reichstagufer to the **Marschallbrücke**. The decayed physics department of **Humboldt University** is to the right. **Bahnhof Friedrichstrasse** spans the Spree a short distance farther on. Cross the river by the footbridge, and turn right along Schiffbauerdamm. The **Köpjohan Stiftung** (*#8*) is a handsome Old Berlin charitable institution decorated with boat-building cherubs. The quay leads to the **Berliner Ensemble** at Bertolt-Brecht-Platz, the theater where Brecht's *Threepenny Opera* was first performed in 1928. The square opposite contains three pillars bearing lines from his works, and a statue of the affable playwright seated on a park bench.

Now cross **Weidendammer Brücke**, an elegant *Jugendstil* iron bridge decorated with Hapsburg eagles and ornate lamps. Turn left along Am Weidendamm until you come to the **Monbijou Brücke**, a small stone bridge named after the Hohenzollern palace that stood here, until its destruction in 1945. Continue along Am Kupfergraben, an arm of the Spree flowing along the S side of MUSEUMSINSEL. The S-Bahn elevated railroad runs noisily between the BODE-MUSEUM and the PERGAMON-MUSEUM, shaking the precious vases within.

Turn left at the **Eiserne Brücke**, a stone bridge built in 1914-16. It is named after Berlin's first iron bridge, which spanned the river in 1797. Bodestrasse leads past the NEUES MUSEUM and the NATIONALGALERIE on the left, and the ALTES MUSEUM on the right. At the handsome **Friedrichs Brücke**, designed in 1892 with four monumental flanking columns, turn right along the Spree. The DOM (cathedral) rises out of the water, rather like a Venetian church. Once through the tunnel under Karl-Liebknecht-Strasse, you see the bronze-windowed **Palast der Republik** on the right, formerly the seat of the East German parliament. It stands on the site of Schlüter's Baroque Stadtschloss, bombed in 1945 and demolished 5yrs later.

Beyond the **Rathausbrücke** (the statue of the Great Elector now at Schloss Charlottenburg once stood on this bridge), the Spreeufer runs along the S edge of the NIKOLAIVIERTEL, a moderately successful reconstructed quarter of Old Berlin. An interesting statue near the site of Berlin's first bridge shows a woman poring over a map of medieval Berlin, as if she were trying to make sense of the enormous changes that have occurred here.

Another underpass brings you to the quiet Rolandufer, lined with weeping willows. Benches are conveniently placed beside a large lock, the **Mühlendamm-Schleuse**, still used by huge Polish barges laden with gravel. A chart attached to the Neoclassical **lock-keeper's house** gives current water-levels on the Elbe, Oder and Havel rivers.

Continue to the **Jannowitzbrücke**, cross the Spree and turn right along the Märkisches Ufer, past the MÄRKISCHES MUSEUM. The Classical **Insel Brücke** leads you across the Spree to **Fischerinsel**, a drab East German housing development. From the quay, you obtain a good view of a row of restored 18thC buildings, including the OTTO-NAGEL-HAUS and the **Ermelerhaus**, which is described in RESTAURANTS on page 106.

At the next bridge, cross the river again, and continue along the waterfront to the **Gertrauden Brücke**. Numerous bronze rats scuttle around the base of a statue dedicated to Gertraud, the patron saint of travelers.

Oberwasserstrasse brings you to Berlin's oldest surviving bridge, the **Jungfernbrücke**, a curious wooden drawbridge built in 1798. The next bridge, the **Schleusenbrücke**, is an elegant Neoclassical design, decorated with medallions showing 17thC and 18thC views of Berlin. The last bridge you come upon is the **Marx-Engels-Brücke** (formerly the Schloss Brücke), a majestic structure designed by Schinkel in 1820-22. Decorated with a cast-iron frieze of sea-horses and figures of battling warriors, it terminates Unter den Linden in heroic style.

Continue along Am Zeughaus past the arsenal, which is decorated with giant plumed helmets. Several old cannon are lined up along the waterfront, including a weapon with the letters H and VOC symbolizing the Hoorn chamber of the Dutch East India Company. A Renaissance cannon bears the motto *Saturnus Frisst die Kind Allein, Ich Fress Sie Aller Gross und Klein* (Saturn devours only children, I devour everyone both large and small). Weapons such as this one (cast in 1617) were to devour one half of Berlin's population in the Thirty Years' War (1618-48). Go back to the Marx-Engels Brücke and turn right down Unter den Linden, then right up Friedrichstrasse, to board the U-Bahn or S-Bahn at Bahnhof Friedrichstrasse.

WALK 2: KREUZBERG
*See map on page 38 and map **4**. Allow 2-3hrs.*

Kreuzberg is interesting for its diverse architectural styles encompassing massive 19thC offices, fragments of war-damaged buildings and boldly experimental apartment blocks. A lively bohemian district, it is teeming with art galleries, cafés and bars.

Take the U-Bahn or M-Bahn to **Gleisdreieck**, then walk down Schönebergerstrasse and cross the Landwehrkanal. Curious fragments of statues damaged in the Battle of Berlin (1943-44) can be seen in the courtyard of the LAPIDARIUM (an old pumping house). Continue down Schönebergerstrasse to Askanischer Platz. The **Anhalter Bahnhof** once stood on this square. Badly damaged in 1945, it was demolished in 1961, leaving only a token fragment of dusty brown brick wall. You might notice a symbolic upturned railroad locomotive on the wasteland behind the station, and a massive concrete bunker dating from World War II.

Walk through the garden in front of the station ruin, turn left down Stresemannstrasse and right to reach the MARTIN-GROPIUS-BAU, a 19thC museum still surrounded by an eerie landscape of rubble and weeds. Cross the square to reach a concrete building containing the TOPOGRAPHIE DES TERRORS exhibition. Stand on the hill of rubble (once an art school), and look at the plan of the site to identify the location of prewar buildings such as the Prinz-Albert-Palais and the Hotel Excelsior. Encouraging signs of urban renewal can be seen all around, notably the 12-story tower built by Pietro Derossi (*Wilhelmstrasse 120*).

Turn left down Wilhelmstrasse; all that remains of the government offices of Imperial Germany that once lined this street is the massive **Air Ministry**. Now turn right along Zimmerstrasse, once a front-line street divided by the Wall. You may notice a few buildings on the left side of the street with their windows barred to prevent East Germans escaping. Turn right at Friedrichstrasse 990, past the HAUS AM CHECKPOINT CHARLIE, a fascinating museum devoted to the history of the Wall.

A left turn on Kochstrasse takes you through the prewar center of Berlin's newspaper publishing industry. A towering office

Walks

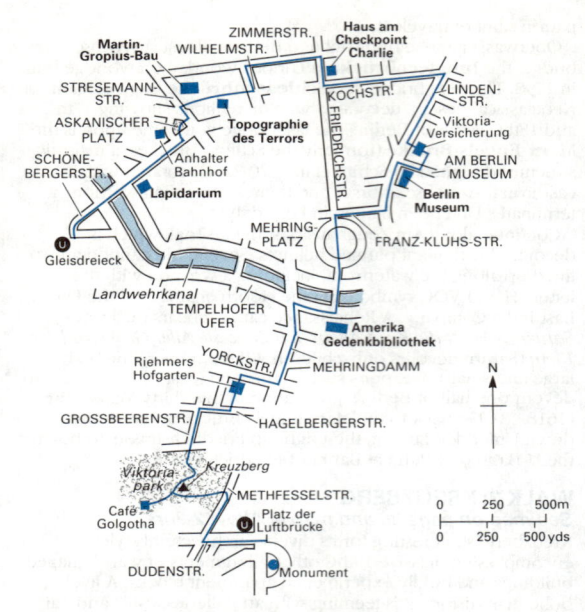

building (*Kochstrasse 50*) was built in 1961 by the Axel Springer publishing group as a defiant gesture aimed at the East German authorities just across the Wall.

Turn right at Lindenstrasse, where some of the most sensitive recent architecture in Berlin has been built under the guidance of the Internationale Bauausstellung (International Building Exhibition or IBA), sometimes incorporating fragments of old buildings. A striking modern apartment block is situated in the courtyard of the Viktoria-Versicherung, a massive rusticated insurance office laden with thick columns and heavy statues (*Lindenstrasse 20-25*). Completed in 1913, it seems to reflect the brutal strength of Berlin on the eve of World War I. A dark, menacing portal leads into the courtyard, where a colorful Post-Modern apartment block designed by Arata Isozaki provides a measure of the new spirit in Berlin architecture.

Walk into the second courtyard and turn right, then right again on Am Berlin Museum, an attractive street with compact Post-Modern apartment blocks loosely modeled on suburban Berlin villas. Back on Lindenstrasse, turn left past the Baroque BERLIN-MUSEUM, where you can sample good local cooking in a reconstructed old *Weissbierstube*.

Just beyond the museum, turn right along Franz-Klühs-Strasse, then left down Friedrichstrasse to reach **Mehringplatz**, one of the squares laid out in the early 18thC by the Soldier King. Walk under the elevated U-Bahn and across the Landwehrkanal, then turn right along Tempelhofer Ufer, past the **Amerika-Gedenkbibliothek**, a modern library built with US funding in 1952-54. Turn left along Mehringdamm, past a huge barracks with mock medieval towers (*#20-25*), built in 1850-53 for the Royal Prussian Regiment of Dragoon Guards.

Now cross Yorckstrasse, a broad tree-lined boulevard, and turn

38

Walks

right to reach **Riehmers Hofgarten** (*Yorckstrasse 83*). Built by Wilhelm Riehmer in 1881-1900, the unusual complex consists of 20 mansions overlooking leafy gardens. Walk through the courtyard and leave by the entrance on Hagelbergerstrasse, beside an attractive-looking Old Berlin restaurant. Turn right, then left up Grossbeerenstrasse, where you have a splendid, almost surreal view of the artificial waterfall that cascades down the slopes of the VIKTORIAPARK. Enter the park and climb one of the romantic paths that wind up the Kreuzberg. The view from the summit is a typical Berlin panorama of chimneys and spires, industry and culture. You might be tempted by a café called **Golgotha** (☎ *(030) 7852453*), situated on the slope behind the war memorial, where from 10pm you can dance to disco music on summer evenings.

Leave by the path beside the **Schultheiss brewery** to get to Methfesselstrasse, then turn left along Dudenstrasse to reach U-Bahnhof Platz der Luftbrücke. Before leaving, notice the **Airlift monument** opposite Tempelhof Airfield symbolizing the three air corridors used during the Berlin Airlift. A famous photograph is reproduced on a nearby information sign showing Berlin schoolboys scrambling up a mountain of rubble to cheer on the fully-loaded Douglas Dakota DC-3s.

WALK 3: GRUNEWALD
See map on page 40 and map 5. Allow 3-4hrs.

The extensive woods, lakes and nature reserves of the Grunewald are within easy reach of the city by public transportation. The route described below follows the shores of four lakes, from S-Bahnhof Grunewald to S-Bahnhof Nikolassee, a distance of about 8km (5 miles).

At S-Bahnhof Grunewald, an attractive rural station, take the exit signposted **Hundekehlesee** and turn right along Auerbacher Strasse, a leafy suburban street. Descend the cobbled lane to the left (beside some tennis courts) to reach the Hundekehlesee (dog-neck lake), a peaceful stretch of water lined with reeds and water lilies.

At the end of the lake, cross the Koenigs Allee, turn left and then right into the **Hundekehlefenn nature reserve**. The path follows a stream through a typical Brandenburg landscape of woods and marshes. Soon you come to the **Grunewaldsee**, a pleasant lake fringed with sandy beaches. Take the lakeside path to the left to reach the JAGDSCHLOSS GRUNEWALD, an old Hohenzollern hunting lodge on the waterfront. For a lunch of trout with a glass of dry Frankish wine, head to the **Chalet Suisse restaurant** (*Im Jagen 5, off Chalet-Suisse-Weg* ☎ *(030) 8326362*), a rustic Alpine chalet set amid flowers and fountains: follow the sign to Dahlem, then Clayallee.

Continue along the lakeside, past the **Forsthaus Paulsborn**, a rural restaurant, and cross Hütten Weg. A narrow path winds through the undulating sand hills of the **Langes Luch** (long lynx) **nature reserve**. The path emerges on a main road in the forest where you see a totally unexpected sign pointing to a U-Bahn station named Onkel-Toms-Hütte (Uncle Tom's Cabin). The *Hütte* is now on the edge of a housing estate designed by Bruno Taut during the Weimar Republic.

The footpath plunges into the woods again, skirting the edge of the **Riemeisterfenn**, a dark, eerie marsh populated by ducks and swans. The path emerges eventually on the edge of the **Krumme Lanke**, an attractive lake popular with swimmers. Take the fork along the right shore, cross the bridge at the end of

39

Trips

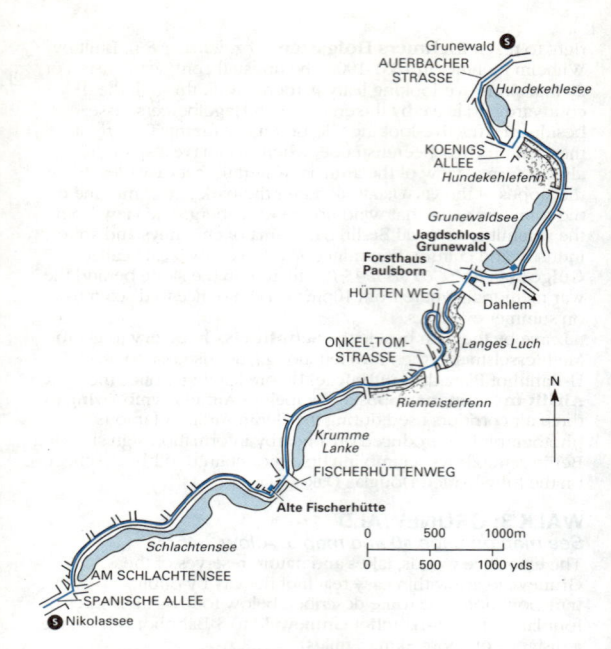

[Map showing route with locations: Grunewald, AUERBACHER STRASSE, Hundekehlesee, KOENIGS ALLEE, Hundekehlefenn, Grunewaldsee, Jagdschloss Grunewald, Forsthaus Paulsborn, HÜTTEN WEG, Dahlem, ONKEL-TOM-STRASSE, Langes Luch, Riemeisterfenn, Krumme Lanke, FISCHERHÜTTENWEG, Alte Fischerhütte, Schlachtensee, AM SCHLACHTENSEE, SPANISCHE ALLEE, Nikolassee. Scale: 0–1000m / 0–1000 yds]

the lake and climb the steps to reach the Fischerhüttenweg.

Once across the road, you disappear into the woods again to reach the shores of the ominous-sounding **Schlachtensee** (lake of slaughter), the subject of a romantic painting by Walter Leistikow which is on display in the Berlin-Museum. The **Alte Fischershütte**, a long-established tavern, has a tempting lakeside terrace for summer days.

Now follow the right bank to the end of the lake, then turn right along Am Schlachtensee and straight ahead along Spanische Allee to reach **S-Bahnhof Nikolassee**, a magnificent Neo-Gothic station, built in 1901, which looks almost like a Hohenzollern hunting lodge. Return by S-Bahn in the direction of Erker for Bahnhof Zoo, or Frohnau for Friedrichstrasse.

BERLIN BY S-BAHN
It's worth reading the route description before departing. Choose a quiet time of day, such as 9am-noon. Allow 2hrs.

The Stadtbahn (city railroad), begun in 1875, links Berlin's outer suburbs with the city center. Built on high brick viaducts with consecutively numbered arches sometimes containing cafés or shops, the S-Bahn became a symbol of modernity for such Berlin Impressionist painters as Lesser Ury. After World War II, the S-Bahn was administered by the East Germans, and the trains and stations became rather dilapidated, although the network has improved greatly since it was merged with *BVG*, the Berlin transportation authority. Traveling by S-Bahn, you may sometimes catch unusual views of the city as the train rumbles along the elevated lines.

Quiet Savignyplatz station is a good departure point, with its walls decorated with provocative works of art highlighting global

Trips

pollution. Take the S-Bahn in the direction of Friedrichstrasse, if possible sitting on the side opposite the doors for the best view. Soon you'll see (on the left) the **Theater des Westens**, built in 1896. With its flamboyant turrets and medieval German details, it looks totally out of place in the otherwise modern quarter. The **zoo** is on the right after Bahnhof Zoologischer Garten. On the left, overlooking an idyllic stretch of the Landwehrkanal, is a striking modern blue building on stilts with a giant pink water duct. Designed by Ludwig Leo in 1971, it is the site of fluid mechanics experiments carried out by Berlin technical university.

Now look right down the Strasse des 17. Juni and you'll see the SIEGESSÄULE, a Prussian victory column placed at the Grosser Stern intersection. The apartment blocks to your right beyond Tiergarten station are part of the 1950s-built HANSAVIERTEL quarter. After Bellevue station, you may see the 19thC **Luther Brücke** on the right as the S-Bahn crosses the Spree. The somber former parliament building, the REICHSTAG, rises above the woods on the right, while in the distance you can see the winking lights of the television tower (FERNSEHTURM) built by the East Germans near Alexanderplatz. Just beyond Lehrter station, the line crosses a canal that used to form the border between East and West Berlin. Shortly afterward, the train draws into the bustling Bahnhof Friedrichstrasse.

The elevated railroad then cuts across MUSEUMSINSEL, passing between the BODE-MUSEUM and the PERGAMON-MUSEUM. You may spot the statue heads of Greek warriors through the windows of the Pergamon Museum on the right. After crossing the Spree again, the S-Bahn follows the line of the medieval city walls, stopping at **Marx-Engels-Platz**, a dusty old brick station. The next halt, **Alexanderplatz**, is bright and modern, with glass walls looking out on the rather bleak square. Beyond here, the railroad skirts the NIKOLAIVIERTEL; it is on the right, an area of reconstructed houses painted in pastel colors. Farther S, the MÄRKISCHES MUSEUM is the striking brick building on the opposite bank of the Spree.

Leave the train at **Jannowitzbrücke**, an elevated iron station built above the Spree. You now have to take the S-Bahn back to Friedrichstrasse, and change to the *Nord-Süd S-Bahn* (north-south), following signs for *Anhalter Bahnhof*. Again, sit opposite the doors if possible. The line runs through a tunnel built in 1934-39, emerging at Grossgörschenstrasse station in Schöneberg district. You might decide to break the journey here and look at KLEISTPARK, a 5min walk from the station.

Soon you pass dusty Old Berlin blocks with *Hinterhöfe* (back courts), alternating with well-designed modern apartments — a typical Berlin mixture. Farther S, the S-Bahn stops at several former villages, now leafy suburbs, such as **Steglitz**, **Lichterfelde** and **Zehlendorf**. The BOTANISCHER GARTEN is a 10min walk from the station of the same name. Later, the train stops at S-Bahnhof **Mexicoplatz**, a curious *Jugendstil* rotunda surmounted by a dome, built in 1905. A 2min walk from S-Bahnhof **Schlachtensee** brings you to the shores of an attractive Grunewald lake.

The line terminates at **Wannsee**, where you can stroll to the beach or take a boat trip on the Havel. Line S3 to S7 then takes you back to the city through the forest, stopping at S-Bahnhof **Grunewald**, an excellent center for walking. The elevated railroad then passes through **Charlottenburg** district to S-Bahnhof **Savignyplatz**, a good place to get off the train to avoid the crush at Zoologischer Garten station.

Trips

BERLIN BY BUS
Allow 1hr to complete the trip.

A trip on bus 100 from the Zoologischer Garten to Alexanderplatz provides a fascinating glimpse of historic Berlin. Introduced in 1991, the bus route crosses the former frontier between the west and east sectors. It passes many famous buildings and lets you see some recent developments that have followed upon reunification.

The bus leaves from Hardenbergplatz, opposite Bahnhof Zoologischer Garten. Look right to see the splintered profile of the **Gedächtniskirche**, now surrounded by modern buildings. The **zoo** and AQUARIUM are on the left.

After crossing the Landwehrkanal, you head into the TIERGARTEN, a romantic park in the city centre. The SIEGESSÄULE victory column stands in the middle of the Grosser Stern traffic intersection. The bus then turns down Spreeweg past Schloss Bellevue (over to the left).

On John-Foster-Dulles-Allee, you will notice a semicircle of ruined statues on **Grossfürstenplatz** (to the right), a relic of the fierce fighting in the Tiergarten in 1945. The bus makes a sharp left turn to drop passengers beneath the soaring roof of the KONGRESSHALLE, and continues to the REICHSTAG.

Now the bus follows the former course of the BERLIN WALL to the BRANDENBURGER TOR, which once stood within the Soviet sector. You travel along the length of UNTER DEN LINDEN, passing the **Humboldt-Universität** (to the left) and the **Staatsoper** (on the square to the right). Look left to see Schinkel's **Neue Wache**, modeled on a Greek temple, and the huge Baroque **Zeughaus**, a former arsenal.

The bus crosses the Marx-Engels-Brücke, built by Schinkel, to reach the island in the Spree where the village of Cölln was founded. At the far end of the **Lustgarten** (the square on the left) stands Schinkel's ALTES MUSEUM, one of five museums forming the MUSEUMSINSEL complex. The DOM stands on the same square. The Stadtschloss, a huge Baroque palace demolished in 1950, occupied the square to the right.

The bus now crosses the Spree to the site of the original settlement of Berlin. The brick **Marienkirche** (on the right) is one of the last relics of Hanseatic Berlin. The route terminates near the FERNSEHTURM on ALEXANDERPLATZ, where you can pick up the S-Bahn or U-Bahn.

BOAT TRIPS
From Tegel to the Glienicker Brücke; daily, Apr-Oct. For sailing times ☎ (030) 8100040. Allow 6-8hrs for the entire trip.

Berliners in search of *Lebensraum* (living space) tend to flock to the lakes, rivers and canals around Berlin. Several Berlin companies run boat trips on the Havel and Spree rivers, on the Potsdam lakes, and on the canals that run through the old city (see USEFUL ADDRESSES on page 15). The main departure points are **Tegel**, **Wannsee**, **Spandau**, the **Kongresshalle**, the Schlossbrücke at **Schloss Charlottenburg**, and **Treptow harbor**. When the frontiers opened in 1989-90, boat operators lost no time in introducing new routes from West Berlin to East Berlin, and from Wannsee to Potsdam.

To take full advantage of convenient ticket combinations, buy a BVG *Kombi-Tageskarte*, a day-pass covering S-Bahn, U-Bahn, bus and tram services in Berlin, plus regular Havel river services (*Linienverkehr*) operated by **Stern und Kreisschiffahrt**. The pass can also be used on *Havel Queen* paddle steamer cruises.

Take the U-Bahn to Tegel and walk down Alt-Tegel to the pier at **Greenwichpromenade**. **Line 1** (*normally departs 10.25am*), weaves between some small islands in the **Tegeler See** to reach the Havel. The boat continues past the **Eiswerder**, an island with movie studios, then through a lock, to arrive at the **Lindenufer** pier on the SPANDAU waterfront.

The cruise continues down the Havel to the **Freybrücke** pier, a 5min walk from a strange area of marshes and lakes known as the *Tiefwerder*. To the S of here, the boat enters a broad expanse of the Havel bordered on the E by the GRUNEWALD. You'll see the 19thC **Grunewaldturm** rising above the trees on the left and, farther S, **Lindwerder** island, which has a small restaurant. The boat moors at **Kladow**, a former fishing village in the dunes, then continues to the Pfaueninsel pier, where you should disembark. Take the ferry to PFAUENINSEL to wander among King Friedrich Wilhelm III's Gothic follies.

Back on the mainland, take a **Line 2** boat to **Wannsee** via **Glienicker Brücke**. The boat stops at **Moorlake** pier, where you might decide to get off to visit the curious Russian wooden cabin at NIKOLSKOE, a 10min walk from here. The boat continues to the **Glienicker Brücke**, the main bridge between Berlin and Potsdam, which remained virtually closed to traffic throughout the Cold War. Disembark to visit the **Volkspark Klein-Glienicke** (next to the pier), a romantic park with a *Schloss* designed by Schinkel. **Park Babelsberg** (see POTSDAM excursion on pages 124 and 129), once cut off by the Wall, is now just a 10min walk from Klein-Glienicke.

The boat rounds the headland and turns into the **Griebnitzsee**, which once marked the frontier. Three stops later, the boat ties up at **Wannsee** pier, a 2min walk from the S-Bahnhof.

Sights and places of interest

No visit to Berlin would be complete without exploring the treasures housed in a few of the 100 or so serious museums in the city. Afterward, you can unwind in the marvelous parks, beach resorts, woods and zoos with which the city is so well endowed.

The museums, palaces, picture galleries and gardens of Berlin have even now not fully recovered from the *Sturm und Drang* of World War II. Works of art were irreparably damaged or looted, while bombs destroyed many buildings. The postwar division of Berlin created an unhappy situation in which the main 19thC museums lay in East Berlin, while most of the art treasures were in West Berlin, shipped by the Americans from remote hiding places in southern Germany. New museums were built in the West to hold masterpieces of painting and sculpture, whereas the monumental Old Berlin museums in the East remained empty and neglected.

The construction of the Wall added a further complication, as West Berliners could no longer visit the historical museum or the opera, while people living in the Soviet sector were cut off from the zoo. Two independent cultural cities developed, each with a historical museum (the MÄRKISCHES MUSEUM and the BERLIN-MUSEUM), a national gallery (the NATIONALGALERIE and the NEUE NATIONALGALERIE), a Classical art museum (the PERGAMON-MUSEUM and the ANTIKENMUSEUM), an Egyptian collection (the BODE-MUSEUM and the ÄGYPTISCHES MUSEUM) and a zoo (the TIERPARK FRIEDRICHSFELDE and

Sights and places of interest

Major sights classified by type

CHURCHES
Dom
Französischer Dom ☗ ⋖⋗
Friedrichswerdersche Kirche ☗
Kaiser-Wilhelm-Gedächtniskirche
Maria Regina Martyrum
Marienkirche
Neue Synagogue
Nikolaikirche

DISTRICTS, SQUARES, STREETS
Alexanderplatz
Breitscheidplatz
Britz
Charlottenburg
Dahlem
Hansaviertel ☗
Karl-Marx-Allee ☗
Köpenick
Kreuzberg
Kultur-Forum
Kurfürstendamm
Lübars
Mitte
Museumsinsel ★ ☗
Nikolaiviertel
Platz der Akademie ☗
Potsdamer Platz
Prenzlauer Berg
Spandau
Tegel
Unter den Linden ★

FORESTS, RIVERS, PARKS, BEACHES
Botanischer Garten ★
Grunewald
Havel ✱
Kleistpark
Pfaueninsel ★ ☗
Spree
Tiergarten ✱
Treptower Park
Viktoriapark ⋖⋗
Volkspark Friedrichshain
Wannsee ✱

GENERAL INTEREST
Berlin Wall
Berliner Flohmarkt ★
Berlin-Pavillon

Brandenburger Tor ☗
Brecht-Weigel-Haus
Dorotheenstädtischer Friedhof
Fernsehturm ⋖⋗
Funkturm ⋖⋗
Gedenkstätte Deutscher Widerstand
Gedenkstätte Plötzensee
Hamburger Bahnhof
Kongresshalle ☗
Lapidarium
Neptunsbrunnen
Nikolskoe
Olympia-Stadion
Panorama ✱
Reichstag
Siegessäule ⋖⋗
Topographie des Terrors

MUSEUMS & GALLERIES
Ägyptisches Museum ‡ ★
Altes Museum ☗
Antikenmuseum ‡
Bauhaus-Archiv
Berlin Museum ★
Bode-Museum ★ ☗
Brecht-Weigel-Haus
Bröhan-Museum
Brücke-Museum ★
Deutsches Rundfunk-Museum
Ephraimpalais ☗
Galerie der Romantik ‡ ★
Gemäldegalerie ‡ ★
Georg-Kolbe-Museum
Haus am Checkpoint Charlie
Käthe-Kollwitz-Museum
Knoblauchhaus
Kunstgewerbemuseum ‡
Kunstgewerbemuseum Schloss Köpenick ☗
Märkisches Museum
Martin-Gropius-Bau ☗
Museum für Deutsche Geschichte ☗

Museum für Deutsche Volkskunde ‡
Museum für Indische Kunst ‡
Museum für Islamische Kunst ‡
Museum für Naturkunde
Museum für Ostasiatische Kunst ‡
Museum für Verkehr und Technik ★ ✱
Museum für Völkerkunde ‡
Museum für Vor- und Frühgeschichte ‡
Museumsdorf Düppel
Musikinstrumenten-Museum ‡
Nationalgalerie ★
Neue Nationalgalerie ‡ ★ ☗
Neues Museum ☗
Otto-Nagel-Haus
Pergamon-Museum ★
Postmuseum
Reichstag
Schloss Charlottenburg ★ ☗
Skulpturengalerie ‡
Topographie des Terrors
Zille-Museum

PALACES & CASTLES
Jagdschloss Glienicke
Jagdschloss Grunewald ☗
Schloss Charlottenburg ★ ☗
Schloss Friedrichsfelde
Schloss Klein-Glienicke ★ ☗
Schloss Köpenick ☗
Schloss Tegel
Zitadelle Spandau ⋖⋗

ZOOS
Aquarium ✱
Tierpark Friedrichsfelde ✱
Zoologischer Garten ★ ✱

‡ indicates museums run by the **Staatliche Museen Preussischer Kulturbesitz** (SMPK). These postwar West Berlin museums are open free of charge, and provide excellent documentation, sometimes in English.

If you only know the name of a museum in English and cannot find it up in SIGHTS AND PLACES OF INTEREST, try looking it up in the INDEX. Other sights that do not have their own entries may be included in a district entry; look these up in the INDEX too. Look for the ★ against the most important sights and ☗ for buildings of great architectural interest. Good views (⋖⋗) and places of special interest for children (✱) are also marked.

44

the ZOOLOGISCHER GARTEN). The reunification of Berlin will lead inevitably to some sweeping and as yet unpredictable changes, as collections are moved or amalgamated. Collections that were split 50 years ago may be reunited, although the logistics of such an exercise, not to mention the funding needed, will make this a plan for the medium rather than the short term.

Berlin's main museums and galleries are currently concentrated in four major clusters. The oldest group of buildings is the MUSEUMSINSEL complex, comprising five institutions holding some 12 separate collections. Six more museums and galleries are located at SCHLOSS CHARLOTTENBURG, while eight modern museums form the DAHLEM complex. The recently built KULTUR-FORUM (S of the Tiergarten) now has three museums, with a further four planned.

Opening hours in East Berlin and Potsdam are likely to become more harmonized with those in the West. The vast majority of sights are closed on public holidays. Ticket discount schemes have not yet been developed, and the only combined ticket currently available in Berlin is the *Sammelkarte* sold at SCHLOSS CHARLOTTENBURG, which gives reduced-rate admission to the sights in the palace grounds.

Words in SMALL CAPITALS indicate a **cross-reference** to another section of the book or to a full entry in SIGHTS AND PLACES OF INTEREST. For a full explanation of symbols see page 5.

ÄGYPTISCHES MUSEUM *(Egyptian Museum)*
Schlossstrasse 70, Charlottenburg ☎ (0372) 320911. Map 1B2. Open Mon-Thurs 9am-5pm; Sat, Sun 10am-5pm. ⚹ (☎ in advance). U-Bahn to Richard-Wagner-Platz or Sophie-Charlotte-Platz; bus 121, 145, 204 to Schloss Charlottenburg.

A remarkable collection of Egyptian antiquities is currently housed in a handsome Neoclassical building opposite Schloss Charlottenburg. One of two identical guard houses (the other contains the ANTIKENMUSEUM) built by Friedrich August Stüler in 1851-59, the eastern Stüler building (*Ostlicher Stülerbau*) boasts a beautiful round stairwell with a domed roof. A darkened room on the first floor contains the hauntingly beautiful painted limestone **bust of Nefertiti** (or Nefretete), the aunt of Tutankhamen, discovered by a Berlin archeologist in 1912. The exquisite skin tones and vivid tints of blue and red have been untouched since c.1340BC, and virtually the only damage to the head is the missing left eye, making the right profile now the more striking. A damaged bust of her husband, King Echnaton, shows the same jutting profile and elegant features. Across the stairwell from Nefertiti is the **Berlin Green Head**, carved a millennium later. Influenced by Greek art, the gnomic green head (depicting an unknown Egyptian priest) has a sinister look.

The adjoining **Marstall** (stables) is an impressive gallery, with slender iron columns supporting a vaulted roof. The **Kalabsha temple gate**, built in 20BC, now provides a handsome entrance to the exhibition area. After admiring the antiquities, you might be tempted to visit the nearby **Gipsformerei** (see SHOPPING) to buy a plaster cast bust of Nefertiti to ship home.

ALEXANDERPLATZ
Mitte. Map 4C8. U-Bahn or S-Bahn to Alexanderplatz.
The bleak and windswept Alexanderplatz is a sad legacy of Soviet planning in Berlin. Named after Czar Alexander I — who visited Berlin in 1805 — Alexanderplatz was one of prewar

Altes Museum

Berlin's busiest squares. Alfred Döblin's 1929 novel *Berlin Alexanderplatz* captured the feverish vitality of the square under the Weimar Republic, but Alexanderplatz had already begun to lose its cosmopolitan allure by 1933 when Nazis attacked the Jewish-owned Wertheim department store. There is little left nowadays of the former vitality, although Alexanderplatz may change as Soviet influences recede.

ALTES MUSEUM 🏛
Lustgarten, Mitte ☎ (0372) 203550. Map 4B8. Open Wed-Sun 10am-6pm. U-Bahn or S-Bahn to Friedrichstrasse or S-Bahn to Marx-Engels-Platz.

Berlin's oldest museum, the Altes Museum was built in 1824-30 by Karl Friedrich Schinkel in a handsome Neoclassical style modeled on Greek temples (see illustration on page 24). The lofty rotunda, with its busts of philosophers and poets, was, like St. Hedwigs-Kathedrale, inspired by the Pantheon in Rome. A polished granite basin was made for the center of the rotunda, but it could not be lifted into place, and remains in front of the museum, where it still mirrors the DOM on its dazzling surface.

Originally called the Museum am Lustgarten, the Altes Museum stands on the Spree island facing the former Lustgarten (pleasure garden) of the Prussian kings. Built to display a collection of paintings donated by King Friedrich Wilhelm III, the building eventually became too small, and the pictures were rehoused in the BODE-MUSEUM.

Much of the gallery space is currently occupied by postwar East German works from the Nationalgalerie's collection, but it seems unlikely that this memento of the old order will remain for much longer. The Altes Museum also holds the **Kupferstichkabinett**, a collection of old prints and drawings which may soon be reunited with the Dahlem print collection in a new museum at the KULTUR-FORUM.

The main attraction at present is the **Sammlung Ludwig**, a large collection of postwar international art which includes works by Beuys, Picasso, and the Cobra group.

ANTIKENMUSEUM
Schlossstrasse 1, Charlottenburg ☎ (030) 320911. Map 1B2. Open Mon-Thurs 9am-5pm; Sat, Sun 10am-5pm ♿ (☎ in advance). U-Bahn to Richard-Wagner-Platz or Sophie-Charlotte-Platz; bus 121, 145, 204 to Schloss Charlottenburg.

Slender Cretan vases, Etruscan mirrors, and a Roman gladiator's helmet smashed in combat are among the antiquities displayed in one of two identical guard houses facing Schloss Charlottenburg (the other contains the ÄGYPTISCHES MUSEUM).

The collection once formed part of the Antiquarium, a department of the Neues Museum dispersed during World War II. Now divided between the PERGAMON-MUSEUM and the Antikenmuseum, the Antiquarium may eventually be reunited in the NEUES MUSEUM, when restoration is completed. Until then, the western Stüler building (*Westlicher Stülerbau*) provides a handsome setting for an important collection of **Greek vases** painted with black-figure and red-figure designs representing mythological gods and heroes. Look out in particular for the Greek classroom scenes on a unique red-figure Athenian drinking cup painted by Duris in the 5thC BC, and the slender satyr on a red-figure amphora decorated by the anonymous artist known as the "Berlin painter."

The **Schatzkammer** (treasure chamber) contains the Silberschatz von Hildesheim, a collection of Roman silver discovered in 1868. Probably made at the end of the 1stC BC, the treasure includes a gilded silver dish embossed with the goddess Minerva. Notice the curious clay figure of the *Dornauszieler*, a Negro boy carefully removing a thorn from his foot.

AQUARIUM
Budapester Strasse 32, Tiergarten ☎ (030) 254010. Map 2D5. Open daily 9am-6pm; last Sat in month, 9am-9pm ♣ U-Bahn or S-Bahn to Zoologischer Garten.

Established in 1869 on Unter den Linden, the Berlin aquarium moved in 1913 to a large new building next to the ZOOLOGISCHER GARTEN. Destroyed in World War II, the aquarium has been rebuilt and restocked with rare fish, reptiles and insects from every continent. It is now one of the world's largest and most modern collections of aquatic animals.

BAUHAUS-ARCHIV
Klingelhöferstrasse 13-14, Tiergarten ☎ (030) 2540020. Map 3D6. Open 11am-5pm; closed Tues ⓵ Bus 106, 129, 219, 341 to Lützowplatz.

Bauhaus teapots from the 1920s, sleek steel chairs, architectural plans, paintings and models are displayed in a white, functional museum overlooking the Landwehrkanal. The building was designed by Walter Gropius, the Berlin architect whose methods of teaching revolutionized the Bauhaus school of design in Weimar. Originally a private collection, the archives are full of works by Gropius, Kandinsky, Klee, Schlemmer and Moholy-Nagy, and only a small number can be displayed at any one time.

BERLIN-MUSEUM ★
Lindenstrasse 14, Kreuzberg ☎ (030) 25862839. Map 4D8. Open 10am-10pm; closed Mon ⓵ ⇌ U-Bahn to Hallesches Tor or Spittelmarkt.

One year after the Berlin Wall was built, a group of local history enthusiasts set up a museum in West Berlin as a substitute for the old MÄRKISCHES MUSEUM in the Soviet sector. The Berlin Museum moved in 1971 to the law courts (*Kammergericht*), a handsome yellow and white Baroque building commissioned in 1735 by King Friedrich Wilhelm I to embellish Friedrichstadt new town. Badly damaged in World War II, the building was restored to almost perfect condition, while the rest of the neighborhood was torn down and reconstructed in Post-Modern style.

Although the MÄRKISCHES MUSEUM still owns the most important historical relics, the Berlin-Museum has rapidly amassed an impressive alternative collection of maps, paintings, models, porcelain, toys and furniture. You can even sample Berlin's culinary history in the Old Berlin **Weissbierstube** (*open Tues-Fri 11am-6pm, Sat, Sun 11am-4pm*). A friendly Berliner with a handsome moustache pours you a glass of Berliner *Kindl Weisse* with a dash of *röt* or *grün* (see page 110 for an explanation of this custom). You then help yourself at the antique buffet to Berlin specialties such as *Boulette* (cold hamburger), *Rollmops* (pickled herring) and *Soleier* (pickled eggs). The nostalgic Berlin atmosphere is sometimes rounded off by a tape of Marlene Dietrich singing husky 1930s songs.

One room in the museum contains a fascinating **collection of maps and plans of the city**, including a detailed scale model from 1688. The only two buildings to have survived from this

Berlin-Pavillon

period are the Nikolaikirche and the Marienkirche. A glance at the maps shows that the explosive growth of Berlin has happened only in the last 100yrs. Before then, the area between Charlottenburg and Tiergarten was open countryside, as Carl Oesteld's 1786 map shows, while Kurfürstendamm was just a winding country lane as late as Major Sineck's 1856 plan.

The period rooms offer a chance to glimpse changing styles of interior decoration. The restrained elegance of early 19thC Berlin is reflected in a Neoclassical interior and a Biedermeier room from the 1830s, while the more pompous style of the *Gründerzeit* — when Berlin became capital of the Second Reich — can be seen in the 1870s Neo-Renaissance interior rescued from a Kreuzberg mansion. Notice a photograph of a stern-faced Johann Kranzler, who in 1830 opened the famous Café Kranzler at the corner of Friedrichstrasse and Unter den Linden. A wartime photograph elsewhere in the museum shows the café in flames.

The Berlin-Museum has built up an excellent collection of paintings to reflect the changing character of the city. The harmonious scale of the early 19thC Prussian capital is illustrated by Eduard Gaertner's panoramic views painted in 1832 from the roof of Schinkel's Friedrichswerdersche Kirche. But the elegant Neoclassical city was ruptured by modern industrialism, as is clear from the paintings by the Berliner Secession artists Lesser Ury, in his view of *Bahnhof Friedrichstrasse* (1888), and Curt Herrmann, in his study of Savignyplatz in 1912.

Nollendorfplatz particularly appealed to *fin-de-siècle* Berlin artists such as Max Beckmann, who painted an attractive Impressionist view of the elevated station (now the BERLINER FLOHMARKT) in 1911. An Expressionist work by Ernst Kirchner shows yellow trams converging on the square. The relentless industrialization is reflected in Lyonel Feininger's *Gasometer in Berlin-Schöneberg* (1912), a dramatic Cubist painting by an American artist who later taught at the Bauhaus.

The wild Expressionism that flourished in the final years of Imperial Berlin resurfaced in the postwar period. A favorite subject was the Berlin Wall, as in Rainer Fetting's *Mauer* (wall). When the Wall started to come down in 1990, the Berlin-Museum lost no time in salvaging two concrete sections from Kreuzberg decorated with expressive graffiti by Kiddy Citny.

The Berlin-Museum boasts an extensive collection of KPM porcelain, including some large Neoclassical amphorae decorated with landscape paintings of the Spree and the Potsdam lakes. The museum's attic contains the sort of dusty curiosities you might expect to come upon in an abandoned Prussian mansion. There is a delightful collection of toys made in Berlin, including angelic Biedermeier dolls, a stuffy Gründerzeit dollhouse, some well-thumbed children's books, a miniature theater, complex working machines, a miniature grocery store, and a regiment of tin soldiers marching along Unter den Linden. Note too the reconstructed 1870s intarsia workshop and antique Kaiserpanorama with stereoscopic views of Imperial Berlin.

BERLIN-PAVILLON
Strasse des 17. Juni, Tiergarten ☎ (030) 8676911. Map 2C5 ⇌ Open 11am-7pm; closed Mon. S-Bahn to Tiergarten.
Built at the same time as the nearby HANSAVIERTEL, the Berlin-Pavillon is a rather neglected relic of the 1957 International Building Exhibition. The little white pavilion on the edge of the Tiergarten is now used for temporary exhibitions on modern Berlin architecture, town planning and ecology.

Bode-Museum

The pavilion contains a curious Old Berlin *Kneipe* where you can lunch on typical Berlin specialties such as *Boulette* and *Sülze*. In the summer, tables are set out in the courtyard amid a clutter of 19thC fire alarms and gas lamps.

The sidewalks around the pavilion are lined with a bizarre collection of 22 historic gas lamps which are lit at twilight. The lamppost from Riehmers Hofgarten in Kreuzberg (*#16*) is a superb example of Berlin ironwork, while a rather eccentric invention (*#11*) was designed by Franz Schwechten, the architect of the Grunewaldturm.

BERLIN WALL
Site of Berlin Wall shown on map 6.
The double concrete wall that once divided Berlin has almost vanished, although a strip of wasteland still cuts through the city like an operation scar. Single sections of the graffiti-daubed Wall were auctioned to art collectors in 1990, while smaller lumps of concrete were patiently chipped off by souvenir-hunters.

Local historians have pleaded for sections of the Wall to be preserved, but they seem to have been overruled by those wanting all traces of the past obliterated. You may, however, still see the wall crossing open fields or running along the Havel shore (see POTSDAM *Lakes Walk* on page 124). Some painted sections of the Wall have been preserved for posterity in the BERLIN-MUSEUM and the MUSEUM FÜR DEUTSCHE GESCHICHTE.

BERLINER FLOHMARKT (Berlin Flea Market) ★
At U-Bahnhof Nollendorfplatz, Schöneberg ☎ (030) 2167546. Map 2D5. Open 11am-7pm; closed Tues. U-Bahn to Nollendorfplatz.
A bizarre flea market set up in 1973 in a disused elevated railroad station. Sixteen mustard-colored 1920s U-Bahn carriages have been converted into shops selling tin train sets, ancient typewriters, faded postcards of Old Berlin sights, and cheap jewelry. Many dealers have huge stocks of banknotes printed during the inflation years: a 2 million Mark note dated 1923 is now worth a mere 15DM. There's also a photographer's studio where you can have your portrait done wearing period costume, while an artist in another railroad carriage will cut your silhouette in one minute flat. The ZILLE-MUSEUM is another nostalgic attraction at the flea market.

The Old Berlin atmosphere spreads to the friendly café **Zur Zolle** (*open 11am-7pm; closed Tues* ☎ *(030) 2167546*), situated in the abandoned station. A few tables have been squeezed into one of the disused U-Bahn carriages, while a spacious adjoining room is decorated with festive strings of lights and tin signs advertising Berlin Kindl beers and Dr Dralle's patent shampoo. You can also sit in the old iron and glass station waiting room, which resembles a conservatory with its exotic palms and ferns.

An old Berlin tram runs along the disused tracks to the next station down the line, which is now occupied by a Turkish market. Tram enthusiasts might enjoy the 2min trip, but the market is rather disappointing, filled with drab shops selling cheap electronic equipment.

BODE-MUSEUM ★ 🏛
Monbijou Brücke, Mitte ☎ (0372) 203550. Map 4B8. Open 10am-6pm; closed Mon, Tues. U-Bahn or S-Bahn to Friedrichstrasse or S-Bahn to Marx-Engels-Platz.
The handsome dome of the Bode-Museum rises above the River

Bode-Museum

Spree at the W tip of the MUSEUMSINSEL. Built in 1897-1904 by Ernst von Ihne, the Bode was originally called the Kaiser-Friedrich-Museum, but the imperialistic overtones of its name clashed with East German ideology, and in 1956 the museum was renamed after Wilhelm von Bode, the first director. The museum once boasted one of Europe's greatest collections of paintings by Flemish and German Old Masters, but most of the works were dispersed during World War II to end up in the Dahlem GEMÄLDEGALERIE.

Although the collection may never return, the Bode is worth a visit just to savor the Neo-Baroque interior, with its two monumental staircases surmounted by lofty domes. Damaged by wartime bombardment, the museum was lovingly restored by the East German government.

The museum currently contains five collections, although major changes are probable in the coming years. The first room of the **Skulpturensammlung** (Sculpture Collection) contains a haunting collection of war-damaged Baroque sculpture. The Greek philosophers and plump cherubs were dug from the rubble in the nearby Dorotheenstrasse (now Clara-Zetkin-Strasse) after World War II. They are all that remain of Schlüter's final architectural masterpiece, the Villa Kamecke, built in 1711 in what was then a leafy Berlin suburb. The same room contains fragments of Baroque sculpture salvaged from the gutted shell of the Stadtschloss on the Lustgarten.

The collection of Late Gothic and Renaissance sculpture was also depleted when a bomb hit the bunker at the zoo, where many of the works had been hidden. Many of the works that survived the war are now in the SKULPTURENGALERIE at Dahlem, but the Bode still owns some remarkable medieval German carvings from Swabia and Franconia, including a delicately carved Late Gothic Adoration by Tilman Riemenschneider.

The highlight of the **Frühchristliche-byzantische Sammlung** (Early Christian and Byzantine Collection) is a vibrant 6thC Byzantine mosaic removed from the apse of San Michele in Africisco, a ruined church in Ravenna. Sold in 1843 to King Friedrich Wilhelm IV, the work was damaged during shipment to Berlin, and again in 1945, but it has been restored to its original luster.

Created in 1850 as part of the Neues Museum, the spectacular Ägyptisches Museum was gutted in World War II. The best part of the collection is now at the ÄGYPTISCHES MUSEUM in Charlottenburg, but several beautiful works are to be seen in the rather old-fashioned cabinets in the **Egyptian rooms** at the Bode-Museum, including the serene head of a queen thought to be Nefertiti. The large collection of mummies includes an embalmed crocodile and even an egg. A small study room devoted to the **Papyrus Collection** reflects the profound German scholarship encouraged by Wilhelm von Bode. The Egyptian collection may eventually be returned to the NEUES MUSEUM when restoration work is completed there in the late 1990s.

Once Germany's greatest picture gallery, the **Gemäldegalerie** (picture gallery) of the Bode-Museum lost many works in World War II, including almost all the Rubens paintings it owned, which were too large to move to safety. The masterpieces that survived are currently in the GEMÄLDEGALERIE at Dahlem, leaving the magnificent rooms at the Bode filled with minor works that had not been considered worth shipping out of the city. The most interesting works left here are the 17thC Dutch and Flemish

Brandenburger Tor

Masters, hung in a series of intimate picture cabinets.

With few masterpieces left to admire, the gallery has a profoundly melancholy atmosphere, especially as several of the sculptures on view are still blackened by smoke from the wartime firestorms. The scarred marble faces in Donatello's *Virgin and Child* are a moving testament to the savagery of war. You will also see a 15thC angel by Antonio Rizzo which has lost both its arms, and the head of a cupid by the Flemish sculptor François Duquesnoy, which was shattered by a stray bullet.

Founded in the 16thC by Elector Joachim II, the **Münzkabinett** (Coin Cabinet) is the oldest collection in Berlin. A small room is devoted to temporary exhibitions of coins and medallions, but most of the collection remains locked away. Among the exhibits in the **Museum für Vor- und Frühgeschichte** (Museum of Prehistory and Early History) is a collection of Trojan finds donated by the German archeologist Heinrich Schliemann.

Be sure not to miss the museum **café** (*open Wed-Sun 10am-5pm*). Situated amid palms on the balcony below the airy dome (*Grosse Kuppel*), the café is one of the last spots in Mitte where you can savor the grandeur of Old Berlin.

BOTANISCHER GARTEN ★
Königin-Luise-Strasse 6 (N gate) or Unter den Eichen 5 (S gate), Zehlendorf ☎ (030) 830060. Map 6E4. Open daily May-Aug 9am-8pm; Apr, Sept 9am-7pm; Mar, Oct 9am-5pm; Nov-Feb 9am-4pm. Greenhouses close Apr-Sept 5.15pm; Mar, Oct 4.15pm; Nov-Feb 3.15pm ♿ (☎ (030) 83006119 in advance). U-Bahn to Dahlem-Dorf; S-Bahn to Botanischer Garten.

Rolling lawns and exotic trees make Berlin's botanical garden one of the most romantic spots in the city. The first botanical garden in Germany (now the KLEISTPARK) was laid out in the 17thC to supply Frederick the Great's court with flowers, medicinal herbs, vegetables, and hops for brewing beer.

This new botanical garden, laid out at Dahlem in 1897, now boasts one of the world's largest botanical collections, with more than 18,000 different types of plants and flowers systematically arranged according to geographical regions. Sections are devoted to the vegetation of the Alps, the Steppes, the Balkans, the Himalayas and North America. But perhaps the most striking features are the vast greenhouses landscaped with artificial waterfalls and exotic lily ponds.

BRANDENBURGER TOR *(Brandenburg Gate)* 🏛
Tiergarten. Map 3C7. S-Bahn to Unter den Linden.

The Brandenburger Tor was built in 1789-91 by Carl Gotthard Langhans at the W end of Unter den Linden in order to provide an imposing Neoclassical entrance to the city. Modeled on the

Brecht-Weigel-Haus

Propylaea on the Athens Acropolis, the Doric gate was surmounted by a copper *quadriga* (a chariot drawn by four horses) designed by Gottfried Schadow. Although the figure in the chariot symbolizes peace, the Brandenburg Gate has long been associated with militarism. The armies of Napoleon, Prussia, Imperial Germany and the Third Reich have all marched in triumph beneath the bronze chariot.

With the construction of the Berlin Wall, the gate became isolated in no-man's-land. Immediately after the Wall was breached in 1989, the Brandenburg Gate became the scene of immense celebrations marking the end of the Cold War. The postwar grime has now been scraped off, and the Brandenburger Tor seems set to become a symbol of peace once more.

BRECHT-WEIGEL-HAUS
Chaussestrasse 125, Mitte ☎ (0372) 2829916. Map 3A7. Open Tues-Fri 10am-noon; Sat 9.30am-noon, 12.30-2pm. U-Bahn to Nordbahnhof.

The East Berlin house where Bertolt Brecht (1898-1956) spent the last 3yrs of his life has been turned into a small museum. The rooms are stocked with memorabilia of the German Communist playwright and theater director who fled from Hitler in 1933 and spent 15yrs in exile before returning to the Soviet sector of Berlin. There he worked with the Berliner Ensemble in the theater where his first major success, *Der Dreigroschenoper* (The Threepenny Opera) opened in 1928.

The house now contains a small bookstore stocked with Brecht's works, and a basement restaurant (*open Mon-Fri 7.30-11pm ☎ (0372) 2823843*) where the cooking sometimes follows German recipes used by Brecht's wife, Helene Weigel. On leaving, wander down the lane next to the house to enter the romantic cemetery, the DOROTHEENSTÄDTISCHER FRIEDHOF, where Brecht and Weigel are buried.

BREITSCHEIDPLATZ
Charlottenburg. Map 2D4. U-Bahn to Kurfürstendamm.

The open space below the broken spire of the KAISER-WILHELM-GEDÄCHTNISKIRCHE became West Berlin's main square after World War II. The huge **Europa-Center** complex was built in the 1960s, on the site of the destroyed Romanische Café, as a glittering symbol of West Berlin's prosperity, with shops, restaurants and a nightclub set amid landscaped ponds and waterfalls. Perhaps the most captivating feature is a thermal clock, which resembles a huge chemistry experiment, with water bubbling through glass pipes and jars to mark the hours and minutes.

The square outside contains the bizarre **Weltkugelbrunnen** (world fountain), designed by Joachim Schmettau. Every hour, some 400,000 liters of water cascade over polished bronze statues representing crocodiles, apes, trees, and a sunbathing woman with a bottle of beer by her side.

BRITZ
Neukölln. Map 7E6. U-Bahn to Hermannplatz, then bus 144 to Alt-Britz.

The old village of Britz has been absorbed into Berlin, but there are still attractive buildings such as a 13thC village church next to a pond (*Backbergstrasse 40*), and a castle, **Schloss Britz** (*Alt-Britz 73 ☎ (030) 6066051*), built in the 18thC and reconstructed in 1880-83. But the main attraction is the **Britzer**

Brücke-Museum

Garten (*entrances at Mohriner Allee or Buckower Damm, open daily 9am-8pm* ☎ *(030) 7009060*), Berlin's newest park, created by Wolfgang Miller for the 1985 National Garden Show.

Ingeniously landscaped to give an impression of open fields, the park features three hills and an artificial lake. Open-air concerts are staged by the lakeside throughout the summer, ranging from police brass bands to pop music. Children can clap at puppet shows or clowns at the playground (*Spiellandschaft*) or in the milk bar (*Milchbar*). The **Café am See** (*open 10am-6pm* ☎ *(030) 7036087*), a bizarre concrete grotto overlooking the lake, offers a family Sunday brunch.

BRÖHAN-MUSEUM
Schlossstrasse 1a, Charlottenburg ☎ (030) 3214029. Map 1B2. Open Tues-Sun 10am-6pm ♿ (☎ in advance). Bus 121, 145, 204 to Schloss Charlottenburg.

A small museum near Schloss Charlottenburg, filled with fragile Art Nouveau and Art Deco vases and furniture. Although mainly of specialist interest, the museum conveys something of the spirit of early 20thC Berlin, and the virtually deserted rooms provide a restful retreat from the crowded Schloss.

Formerly a private collection belonging to Karl Bröhan, the museum owns some exceptional Art Nouveau vases, mostly from France, although a few were manufactured in the KPM factory in Berlin. Several rooms are furnished in 20thC styles, including the **Salon Hector Guimard**, which is filled with Art Nouveau works, and the **Salon Henry van de Velde** containing furniture by the Belgian director of the Weimar school of design (which became the Bauhaus under Walter Gropius).

The museum owns a collection of 20thC Berlin paintings, ranging from the placid Impressionism of Karl Hagemeister's 1902 *Seerosen* (water lilies), to the restless urban Expressionism in Willy Jaeckel's *Im Café* (1912), which shows the seething interior of the Romanische Café (situated where the Europa-Center now stands).

BRÜCKE-MUSEUM ★
Bussardsteig 9, Dahlem ☎ (030) 8312029. Map 6E4. Open 11am-5pm; closed Tues ♿ (☎ in advance). Bus 115 to Pücklerstrasse, then a 5min walk.

One of Berlin's most appealing art galleries stands in a quiet cul-de-sac on the edge of the Grunewald. Devoted to the artists of *Die Brücke* (see ART IN BERLIN), the Bauhaus-style museum was built in the 1960s, and has large windows opening onto the pine woods. The setting is perfect for paintings such as Otto Mueller's *Zwei badende Mädchen* (1921), a powerful work of primitive energy depicting two naked girls beside a lake.

Founded in Dresden in 1905 by Erich Heckel, Ernst Ludwig Kirchner and Karl Schmidt-Rottluff, *Die Brücke* represented the first wave of German Expressionism. The jagged outlines and vibrant colors of the movement were inspired by artistic rebels such as Van Gogh, Gauguin and Munch, but there were also hints of primitive art and German Renaissance woodcuts in the style. The group was officially disbanded in 1913, and many of their paintings perished at the hands of the Nazis.

Heckel's works illustrate the evolution of his style from the tranquil *Laute spielendes Mädchen* (Girl playing a lute) of 1913 to harrowing paintings executed during World War I. Many artists never recovered from the two World Wars, but Heckel regained his early lyrical style in an exquisite still life painted in 1949.

Charlottenburg

Kirchner's 1913 *Berlin Street Scene* is a somber, almost primitive portrait of a crowded Berlin street on the eve of World War I. Struck down by a nervous breakdown during this war, Kirchner was sent to Davos to convalesce. He continued to live in the Swiss resort after the war, and his painting became more calm and abstract. But the serenity was apparently deceptive, for in 1938 he committed suicide. The bizarre yellow sheep of *Schafherde* were painted shortly before his death.

Karl Schmidt-Rottluff used vivid colors: blood red in *Dreidurchbruch* (1910), bright green in a 1911 portrait of Rosa Schapire, and a melancholy blue in *Weinstube* (1913).

Although off the beaten track, the Brücke-Museum is an essential place to visit if you want to understand one of the most exciting periods in German art. Afterward, you can wander through the GRUNEWALD to discover earlier German artists in the JAGDSCHLOSS GRUNEWALD.

CHARLOTTENBURG
Center west. Maps 1C2 and 5-6C3-4.

Named after the Baroque palace built for Sophie Charlotte, Charlottenburg is an elegant quarter of spacious tree-lined boulevards and solid 19thC apartments. Most of Berlin's best hotels, restaurants, stores, cafés and cinemas are located in this district. After World War II, numerous archeological relics and paintings from the MUSEUMSINSEL ended up at SCHLOSS CHARLOTTENBURG.

KURFÜRSTENDAMM, the main artery, is a bustling street from early morning until long after midnight, but it sometimes pays to explore streets "Off-Ku'damm" for intimate restaurants and original shops. The area around Savignyplatz is dotted with attractive modern cafés that begin to buzz around 10pm.

DAHLEM
In the SW suburb of Zehlendorf. Map 5E3. U-Bahn to Dahlem-Dorf.

The leafy suburb of Dahlem still has something of the character of a north German village, especially around the 14thC brick church of **St. Annen** (*Königin-Luise-Strasse 55*). Shaded by old yew trees, the romantic churchyard contains decayed Neoclassical tombs of scientists, opera singers, sculptors, actresses and World War I soldiers. A map at the entrance lists the most important occupants.

The U-Bahnhof at Dahlem-Dorf adds to the rural atmosphere, with its half-timbered walls and thatched roof. Built in 1913 in the style of a Lower Saxony farmhouse, the station has a painted wooden ceiling and a rustic station clock.

A major museum complex was built at Dahlem after 1945, to display works of art displaced from the MUSEUMSINSEL. The museums currently at Dahlem are the GEMÄLDEGALERIE (Germany's greatest collection of Old Masters), the SKULPTURENGALERIE (German and Italian sculpture), the KUPFERSTICHKABINETT (prints and drawings), the MUSEUM FÜR VÖLKERKUNDE (a modern ethnography collection), the MUSEUM FÜR DEUTSCHE VOLKSKUNDE, and museums of Indian, Islamic and Far Eastern Art.

The **Freie Universität** is a large, modern university campus at Dahlem. Originally established in a building on Unter den Linden in the winter of 1945, the Free University sought to restore intellectual freedom, which had been crushed by the Nazis. But the early idealism quickly faded as the university came increasingly under Communist party control, and a group of

Ephraimpalais

disillusioned lecturers and students eventually moved to the new campus at Dahlem in 1948.

DEUTSCHES RUNDFUNK-MUSEUM *(German Broadcasting Museum)*
Hammarskjöldplatz 1, Charlottenburg ☎ (030) 3028186. Open 10am-5pm; closed Tues ♿ (ground floor only). U-Bahn to Theodor-Heuss-Platz; S-Bahn to Westkreuz.

Radio hams might enjoy the small German museum of broadcasting situated in a former studio at the foot of the FUNKTURM. Polished wood wirelesses from the 1920s are displayed in a period room amid potted plants, while a mock 1930s radio shop is crammed with radios once used to pick up Hitler's speeches or Marlene Dietrich songs.

DOM
Marx-Engels-Platz, Mitte ☎ (0372) 2125722. Map 4B9. Open Mon-Sat 10am-noon, 1-5pm, Sun noon-5pm. S-Bahn to Marx-Engels-Platz.

The blackened hulk of Berlin's Baroque Dom (cathedral) stands on the site of an old Dominican church on the Spree island. Begun next to the royal palace during the reign of Frederick the Great, the cathedral was finally completed by Schinkel in 1822. But the building was not grand enough for Kaiser Wilhelm II, who commissioned the present edifice in Italian High Baroque style. Blasted by bombs in 1944, the cathedral was left a ruin until 1975. The interior is still being restored, but you can visit a small exhibition in a side chapel, which documents the destruction and rebuilding of the Dom.

DOROTHEENSTÄDTISCHER FRIEDHOF *(Dorotheenstadt Cemetery)*
Chausseestrasse 126, Mitte. Map 3A7. Open daily 8am-6pm (May-Sept until 7pm). S-Bahn to Friedrichstrasse; U-Bahn to Nordbahnhof.

Many eminent Berliners are buried in a picturesque old cemetery hidden down a narrow lane near Bahnhof Friedrichstrasse. Founded in 1762 for the new towns of Dorotheenstadt and Friedrichswerder, it contains the overgrown tombs of famous Berlin writers, philosophers, architects, artists, scientists, politicians and industrialists.

A plan at the entrance pinpoints the graves of the sculptor Johann Gottfried Schadow, the architect Karl Friedrich Schinkel, the author Heinrich Mann and the industrialist August Borsig. A striking monument of glazed Neo-Renaissance tiles commemorates the inventor Friedrich Hoffmann, while the philosopher Hegel is buried, as he requested, next to his colleague Fichte. The tombs of Marxist dramatist Bertolt Brecht and his wife, actress Helene Weigel, are also side by side. John Heartfield, the radical photomontage artist, is commemorated by a simple monument marked with his monogram, an H. The adjoining **Französischer Friedhof** is an old burial-ground of Berlin's Huguenot community.

EPHRAIMPALAIS 🏛
Poststrasse 16, Mitte ☎ (0372) 21713302. Map 4C9. Open 10am-6pm, closed Mon. U-Bahn or S-Bahn to Alexanderplatz.

An elegant Rococo palace on the edge of the NIKOLAIVIERTEL was built in 1760 for Veitel Heine Ephraim, the court jeweler to

Fernsehturm

Frederick the Great. The house used to stand farther E, but it had to be demolished in 1935 during the construction of the Mühlendamm-Schleuse, a large lock. The city authorities carefully stored about 2,000 blocks of masonry, and many years later the palace was rebuilt to something approaching its former splendor.

A restaurant currently occupies the ground floor, while the elegant upstairs rooms contain a department of the MÄRKISCHES MUSEUM. Once you have put on enormous felt slippers to protect the precious floors, you can glide through the palace looking at maps, plans and paintings covering the history of Berlin from the 17thC to the 19thC.

FERNSEHTURM *(Television Tower)*
Alexanderplatz, Mitte ☎ *(0372) 2123333. Map 4B9. Open daily, May-Sept, 8am-11pm, Oct-Apr 9am-11pm* 🍴 🍺 ◁€ *U-Bahn or S-Bahn to Alexanderplatz.*

Built in the 1960s in the center of East Berlin, the 1,187ft (362m) Fernsehturm (television tower) is one of the city's landmarks. Long lines wait to take the high-speed elevator up to the observation deck and revolving restaurant, situated in a steel-clad sphere resembling a Soviet Sputnik. Perched 670ft (204m) above Alexanderplatz, you can (on a clear day) gaze across the apartment roofs of Berlin to the flat Prussian plains beyond.

FRANZÖSISCHER DOM *(French Cathedral)* 🏛
Platz der Akademie 5, Mitte ☎ *(0372) 2292042. Map 4C8* ◁€ ⚒ *U-Bahn to Französische Strasse.*

Built in 1701-8 for the French Protestant community, the Französischer Dom now contains a small museum of Huguenot mementoes (*open Tues, Wed, Sat 10am-5pm, Thurs 10am-6pm, Sun 11.30am-5pm*).

A lofty tower was added to the church in 1780-85 by Karl von Gontard. Berliners toil up the spiral stair to the balustrade (*open daily 10am-6pm*) to admire the heart of their reunited city. The view back down the stairwell is not for the faint-hearted.

One last flight of steps leads up to the **Glockenspiel**, where you can sit on benches to listen to the *carillon* chime automatically each day (*noon, 3pm and 7pm*). Twice a week (*Tues 2pm, Sat 3pm*), the *carillonneur* climbs a spiral stair and crosses a narrow iron bridge to reach the keyboard, which is enclosed in an iron structure suspended from the dome.

FRIEDRICHSWERDERSCHE KIRCHE 🏛
Werderstrasse, Mitte ☎ *(0372) 2081323. Map 4C8* ⚒ *(ground floor only). Open 10am-6pm; closed Mon, Tues. U-Bahn to Hausvogteiplatz.*

The Friedrichswerdersche Kirche (1824-30) was built by Schinkel in an elegant Late Gothic style inspired by English Perpendicular churches. Blasted by shrapnel during World War II, the red-brick building was expertly restored in 1982-87.

The slender Neo-Gothic arches now provide an elegant backdrop for a collection of Neoclassical sculptures from the NATIONALGALERIE on Museumsinsel. The works include Johann Gottfried Schadow's model for the *Two Princesses*, and Christian Tieck's statue of Schinkel holding a plan of the Altes Museum. Notice Rudolf Schadow's statue of a spinner unwinding an imaginary thread.

Situated on the wooden gallery, the **Schinkelmuseum** contains architectural plans and photographs of Schinkel's

Gedenkstätte Deutscher Widerstand

principal buildings. Although interesting, the exhibition does not possess the same wealth of material as the **Schinkel-Pavillon** at SCHLOSS CHARLOTTENBURG.

Another small exhibition in the gallery shows the ruined church after the war. A photograph showing the neighborhood of the church after a bombing raid reveals that the only building left intact was a newsstand.

Schinkel enthusiasts should not miss the ornate doorway on a building N of the church, leading into the **Café Schinkel-Klause**. The door was designed in 1836 by Schinkel for the Bauakademie (Academy of Architecture), an imposing Neoclassical building that once stood on the Spree waterfront near the church. Bombed during World War II, the academy was razed to the ground by the East Berlin authorities in 1961 — the same year that West Berlin tore down the gutted shell of the Anhalter Bahnhof.

FUNKTURM *(Radio Tower)*
Messedamm, Charlottenburg ☎ (030) 30381. Open daily 10am-11pm ◁€ U-Bahn to Theodor-Heuss-Platz; S-Bahn to Westkreuz.

Not far from the **Messe** (exhibition center), the Funkturm is an impressive radio mast built in 1925. The steel tower is redundant now, but you can still take the elevator to the observation deck 410ft (125m) above street level for a dizzying view of tangled roads and railroad lines.

GALERIE DER ROMANTIK *(Gallery of Romantic Painting)* ★
Neuer Flügel (new wing) at Schloss Charlottenburg ☎ (030) 2662650. Map 1B2. Open Tues-Fri 9am-5pm; Sat, Sun 10am-5pm & Bus 121, 145, 204 to Schloss Charlottenburg.

Romantic 19thC German paintings of jagged peaks and solitary abbeys are currently displayed in the E wing of Schloss Charlottenburg. Formerly displayed in the NATIONALGALERIE on Museumsinsel, the works found a home in Charlottenburg after World War II. The collection is scheduled to move eventually to a new gallery near the NEUE NATIONALGALERIE.

The main glory of the Galerie der Romantik is a collection of 23 works by Caspar David Friedrich. Paintings such as *Solitary Tree* and *Monk Beside a Lake* illustrate the German Romantic love of solitude and nature, while the 19thC nostalgia for the Middle Ages can be seen in a painting of the gloomy moonlit ruins of Eichwald Abbey.

The gallery owns a sizeable collection of moody Romantic paintings by Karl Friedrich Schinkel, the architect of Neoclassical Berlin. His early Neo-Gothic architectural aspirations are mirrored in an emotional study of an imaginary medieval church perched on a rock by the sea, painted in 1815. The Classical world seized his imagination in later life, as in *Golden Age of Greece*.

The stately elegance of 19thC Berlin is captured in the panoramic view of *Unter den Linden* painted by Eduard Gaertner in 1853. A curious painting by Johann Hummel shows the highly polished granite basin still standing in front of the ALTES MUSEUM in the Lustgarten.

GEDENKSTÄTTE DEUTSCHER WIDERSTAND *(German Resistance Memorial)*
Stauffenbergstrasse 13, Tiergarten ☎ (030) 26042202. Map

Gedenkstätte Plötzensee

3C6. Open Mon-Fri 9am-6pm; Sat, Sun 9am-1pm. Bus 129 to Stauffenbergstrasse.
A memorial to Graf von Stauffenberg and other army officers who attempted to assassinate Hitler on July 20, 1944 stands near the site of the German army headquarters where many of the conspirators were summarily executed. An exhibition of photographs and documents gives an insight into the history of the unsuccessful coup, which led to thousands of people being arrested on the slightest suspicion of involvement. A new exhibition, opened in 1989, charts the tragic history of resistance in Nazi Germany.

GEDENKSTÄTTE PLÖTZENSEE
Hüttigpfad, Charlottenburg ☎ (030) 3443226. Open daily Mar-Sept 8am-6pm; Feb, Oct 8.30am-5.30pm; Jan, Nov 8.30am-4.30pm; Dec 8.30am-4pm. Bus 123 from S-Bahnhof Tiergarten to Plötzensee.
A cobbled lane leads past a modern prison to the site of Plötzensee prison, where thousands were tortured and murdered by the Nazis from 1933-45. Many of those involved in the Von Stauffenberg Plot died here in 1944. The dimly lit shed where the executions took place has been kept as a memorial, and a small exhibition of official documents provides a harrowing glimpse of the Nazi period.

If you take bus 123 from S-Bahnhof Tiergarten to Plötzensee, you pass a **memorial** on the left side of Levetzowstrasse (just after the Hansabrücke). Not marked on any maps, the monument stands on the site of the building where many of Berlin's Jews were brought before deportation. A large iron monument lists the destinations and dates of the trains from Berlin. The MARIA REGINA MARTYRUM, another monument to Nazi victims, can also be reached by bus 123.

GEMÄLDEGALERIE *(Picture Gallery)* ★
Arnimallee 23, Dahlem ☎ (030) 83011. Map 6E4. Open Tues-Fri 9am-5pm; Sat, Sun 10am-5pm ⚹ ⇌ U-Bahn to Dahlem-Dorf.
The Prussian royal collection of paintings was fused in the 19thC with several private collections, including that of Edward Solly, a British merchant in Berlin, to form the Gemäldegalerie, one of the world's finest collection of Old Masters. Originally housed in the Altes Museum, the works were later transferred to the Kaiser-Friedrich-Museum (now the BODE-MUSEUM). The Gemäldegalerie at the Bode-Museum still contains a few minor paintings from the original collection, but most of the masterpieces were dispersed in World War II. Some paintings were lost when fire swept the bunker in which they were stored, but the rest survived the war in deep salt mines. They were returned to Berlin from the US army's art collection depot at Wiesbaden in 1957, and hung in the former Asiatic Museum at Dahlem. A new building to house the Gemäldegalerie was planned to be constructed at the KULTURFORUM, though the unification of the city has now cast some doubt upon the project.

The **medieval Italian collection** (wing A) contains attractive works by Botticelli (rm 114) and Raphael (rm 111), while two exquisite miniature 16thC Renaissance portraits are hung on red velvet walls (rm 109a). Paintings by Altdorfer and Dürer in the **medieval German department** (wing B) are displayed on green velvet walls that match the background in Dürer's portrait of Friedrich III of Saxony (rm 138). Dürer might have appreciated

Gemäldegalerie

such painstaking display, as he selected background colors carefully: his 1501 portrait of a young German girl is set against a dark, northern background, while a portrait of a Venetian girl stands out against a blue sky.

Lucas Cranach the Elder (rm 134), the court painter to the Electors of Saxony in Wittenberg, reflects the spirit of the German Renaissance in such strange mythological works as *Venus and Amor*, and the *Jungbrunnen* (fountain of youth), in which wrinkled old women are transformed into lithe maidens. Hans Holbein the Younger's *Georg Gisze* (rm 133) is a vigorous Renaissance portrait of a German Hanseatic merchant standing in a room cluttered with bills and ledgers.

The German art critic Max Friedländer played a major role in building up the magnificent collection of works by 15thC **Flemish Primitives** (Wing C). After World War I, two wings from Jan van Eyck's Ghent altarpiece were sent to Belgium as part of Germany's war reparations, but the Gemäldegalerie still boasts three exquisite miniature works by Jan van Eyck (rm 143). The *Virgin in the Church* is an early work, painted in the 1420s with typical Eyckian precision. A striking portrait of the Italian merchant Giovanni Arnolfini, wearing a curious turban of red cloth, was executed in Bruges at about the same time as Van Eyck's famous Arnolfini wedding portrait, which now rests in London's National Gallery.

Baudouin de Lannoy, the subject of a later Van Eyck portrait, wears the collar on the order of the Golden Fleece, and a large green hat. De Lannoy was appointed Governor of Lille in 1423, and later accompanied Van Eyck on a diplomatic mission to Portugal. The slightly sinister *Man with the Carnation* was once believed to be by Van Eyck, but a recent study of the wood on which it is painted proves that it came from a tree felled after the artist's death. A painting of Christ on the Cross has also been dropped from Van Eyck's *oeuvre* on stylistic grounds.

Petrus Christus, a pupil of Van Eyck, painted the *Exeter Madonna*, an exquisite miniature barely larger than a postcard, showing a detailed view of tiny figures crossing the bridge over the Minnewater in Bruges. Christus' skills at portraiture are seen in his *Portrait of a Young Girl*, a marvelous study of a young, slightly irritated girl wearing fashionable Burgundian clothes. The *Madonna of Jan Vos* could almost be a Van Eyck, except that the faces are softer, more in the style of Raphael.

The museum owns three great altarpieces by the Brussels painter Roger van der Weyden (rm 144). The *Bladelin Altarpiece* includes a portrait of the donor, Pieter Bladelin, kneeling at prayer before the Nativity. Bladelin, an official at the court of Philip the Good in Bruges, amassed sufficient private wealth to found the new town of Middelburg in Flanders, seen in the background. The *Miraflores Altarpiece* is a more complex work, with a picture frame that seems almost part of the Gothic church. The *St John Altarpiece* features a lovingly-painted landscape of wheatfields and rocky outcrops, with three scenes from the life of John the Baptist. The statues of saints with swords poised behind the executioner suggest the inevitability of retribution. The *Portrait of a Young Lady* depicts an intelligent, aristocratic woman in a rather heavy Burgundian costume. A melancholy portrait of Charles the Bold, son of Philip the Good, is a copy of a lost work by Roger van der Weyden.

Hugo van der Goes's ambitious *Monforte Altarpiece*, named after a Spanish monastery where it once hung, has superb portraits of the Magi and a giant cluster of lilies that might have

Georg-Kolbe-Museum

been painted by an Impressionist (rm 146). The painting of *John the Baptist in the Wilderness* by Geertgen tot Sint Jans of Haarlem shows the melancholy saint in an unexpectedly lush landscape filled with rabbits and deer.

The Flemish Renaissance is represented by Quinten Metsys' *Throned Madonna* and Joachim Patenir's *Rest on the Flight to Egypt*, which is full of minuscule details such as soldiers attacking a village. Pieter Bruegel the Elder's *Netherlandish Proverbs* (rm 148) is a bizarre pictorial compendium of familiar expressions such as hitting one's head against a brick wall (bottom left), and the blind leading the blind (top right). Notice also a man armed to the teeth, and busily belling the cat. Recent research on Bruegel's enigmatic study of *Two Chained Monkeys* (rm 150) has established that the long-tailed African monkeys in the painting were introduced to Antwerp (the city in the background) by 16thC Portuguese traders.

Flemish and Dutch Baroque paintings occupy a series of handsome rooms on the first floor. Although many large canvases by Rubens perished in World War II, there are still a few Baroque works by the Antwerp master in the yellow-walled *Rubenshalle* (rm 240), including a portrait of his frail first wife, Isabella Brant (rm 241), and Hélène Fourment, his second wife, posing as Andromeda.

Dutch interiors by Vermeer and De Hoogh (rm 242) are attractively hung on a dark green cloth that matches the wall in the background of Vermeer's *Couple Drinking Wine*. Vermeer's superb handling of light is illustrated by *Young Girl with Pearl Necklace*, while Pieter de Hoogh's *Mother* is an appealing scene of Dutch domestic calm.

Low-horizon Dutch landscape paintings (rm 237) are hung against a pale blue background that matches the sky in Esaias van de Velde's 1618 view of *Zierikzee*. There are views of *Haarlem* and *Amsterdam* by Jacob van Ruisdael, and a prospect of *Arnhem* by Jan van Goyen.

Two entire rooms are filled with works by Rembrandt (rms 235-6), including portraits of Saskia, his first wife, painted the year after she died, and Hendrickje Stoffels, his voluptuous second wife, painted in 1659. Other portraits by Rembrandt include a striking *Head of Christ* and a youthful self-portrait wearing a fur coat and black hat. The collection's famous *Man in the Golden Helmet* was recently exposed as a fake.

GEORG-KOLBE-MUSEUM
Sensburger Allee 25, Charlottenburg ☎ *(030) 3042144. Map 5D3. Open Tues-Sun 10am-5pm* ♿ *(*☎ *in advance). Bus 149 to Raussendorffplatz.*

A collection of bronze nudes and sketches by Georg Kolbe (1877-1947) and other 20thC Berlin sculptors. The works are attractively displayed in the atelier and garden of a villa built for Kolbe in the 1920s.

GRUNEWALD
E of the Havel. Wilmersdorf and Zehlendorf. Map 5D3. S-Bahn to Grunewald or Schlachtensee; U-Bahn to Onkel-Toms-Hütte; bus 218 from Theodor-Heuss-Platz to the Grunewaldturm.

The mystical Germanic love of forests has ensured the preservation of the extensive Grunewald on the w edge of Berlin. Christopher Isherwood described the Grunewald as a "dank, dreary pinewood" in *Goodbye to Berlin*, but much of the old forest was felled for firewood after the war, and the pines have been replanted with a more agreeable mixture of oak and ash. You can wander for hours through the dark woods, disturbed only by the roar of traffic on the Avus, Germany's oldest race track, now an autobahn, built through the Grunewald in 1912-21.

The ancient forest, known as the *Grünen Wald* (Green Forest), was a favorite hunting ground of Elector Joachim II, who built a handsome Renaissance hunting lodge on the edge of a dark lake. The JAGDSCHLOSS GRUNEWALD now contains a somber collection of German Renaissance paintings depicting Hohenzollern rulers and hunting scenes.

A 19thC Romantic urge led to the construction of the **Grunewaldturm** (*Havelchaussee* ☎ *(030) 3041203, open daily 10am-6.30pm; closes at dusk in winter* ⬤ ▬). Designed in 1897 by the architect of the KAISER-WILHELM-GEDÄCHTNISKIRCHE, the Neo-Gothic tower was built in memory of Kaiser Wilhelm I. Perched on a hill overlooking the Havel, the 180ft-high (55m) balcony offers a view of thick forests and vast expanses of water.

You can also climb to the top of the **Teufelsberg** (devil's mountain) for a different view of the forest (*Teufelsseechaussee, S-Bahn to Grunewald, then a 20min walk through the woods* ⬤). The 377ft (115m) Teufelsberg is one of eight artificial hills built in Berlin from the rubble left behind after World War II. Most of the laboring was carried out by women (*Trümmerfrauen*), due to a chronic shortage of able-bodied men. An American radar station at the summit strangely resembles some extravagant castle built by King Ludwig of Bavaria.

The Grunewald is easily reached by S-Bahn (S3 and S5), or U-Bahn (line 2). S-Bahnhof Grunewald is a good starting point for rambles in the forest. You can follow a string of lakes to the S (see WALKS on page 39), or wander along one of the meandering paths that lead to the Grunewaldturm — about 1hr's walk. Areas designated as nature reserves (*Naturschutzgebiet*) are worth exploring, while the low hills rising E of the Havel provide some marvelous panoramic views.

The woods are dotted with rustic country inns (*Wirtshäuser*) offering good beer and basic German food, and many are situated in historic buildings overlooking the lakes or the Havel.

HAMBURGER BAHNHOF
Invalidenstrasse 50-51, Tiergarten ☎ (030) 3941438. Map 3A7 ▬ *S-Bahn to Lehrter Bahnhof or U-Bahn to Nordbahnhof.*

Constructed in 1845-47 as one of five great terminus stations on the edge of the old city, the Hamburger Bahnhof was closed down in 1884 when the more modern Lehrter Bahnhof began operating. The handsome Neo-Renaissance station was converted in 1906 to a museum of transportation and building (the forerunner of the MUSEUM FÜR VERKEHR UND TECHNIK). Bombed in World War II, it reopened in 1987 as an art center. Excellent temporary exhibitions of mainly 19thC painting and sculpture are staged in the vaulted station hall where trains once departed for Hamburg. A café is situated in the Neo-Renaissance waiting room.

HANSAVIERTEL ⋒
Altonaer Strasse, Klopstockstrasse and environs, Tiergarten. Map 2C5. S-Bahn to Tiergarten or Bellevue; U-Bahn to Hansaplatz.

Situated on the N edge of the Tiergarten, the Hansaviertel was

Haus am Checkpoint Charlie

once one of Berlin's most elegant districts. Devastated in World War II, it was rebuilt in 1957 as West Berlin's response to the acclaimed Stalinallee (now KARL-MARX-ALLEE) in the Soviet sector. A team of 53 international architects was commissioned to design a modern residential quarter, with shops, a cinema and a day nursery. Set in landscaped grounds, the buildings range in height from 1-15 stories. The architecture may now look slightly dated, but the apartment blocks are still an interesting compendium of postwar styles. A rusted enamel sign outside U-Bahnhof Hansaplatz gives the locations of the 36 projects and the names of the architects.

HAUS AM CHECKPOINT CHARLIE
*Friedrichstrasse 44, Kreuzberg ☎ (030) 2511031. Map **4D8***
🍴 Open daily 9am-10pm. U-Bahn to Kochstrasse.

Now that most of the Berlin Wall has been knocked down, the Haus am Checkpoint Charlie has lost its dramatic impact. During the Cold War, the Wall could only be crossed at three posts, named Alpha, Bravo and Charlie. Checkpoint Charlie, situated in the American sector, was the most volatile of the border posts, where US and Soviet tanks occasionally stood ready for war. But the military checkpoint became redundant in 1990 and the guard post was shipped to the MUSEUM FÜR VERKEHR UND TECHNIK, turning the Haus am Checkpoint Charlie into something of an anachronism.

Originally set up in a café near the border post, the Haus am Checkpoint Charlie (or Mauermuseum) charts the history of the 102-mile (165km) concrete wall built around West Berlin in 1961. The museum acquired a curious collection of makeshift vehicles constructed by inventive East Berliners to escape to the West, including a tiny bubble car, two hot-air balloons, a radiogram (a radio-cum-phonograph) in which a lithe 24yr-old girl curled up, and a welding machine with a compartment hidden by coils of wire.

Now dusty and dated, the museum somewhat resembles a 1970s student apartment that hasn't been cleaned up in a long time. Newspaper cuttings glued to the walls, threadbare carpets and a scruffy café create an air of nonchalant anarchy intended perhaps to appeal to the young visitors who flock here from all over the world.

A newly-created section covers the events of 1989-90. There are banners carried by protesting East Berliners, and some impressive works of East European art, including Daniel Mitlijanskij's *Requiem for Sacharov*, which features a procession of mourners carved from solid tree trunks.

HAVEL
*W suburbs, Zehlendorf and Spandau districts. Map **5B3-E2***
✱ S-Bahn to Wannsee; U-Bahn to Altstadt-Spandau.

The river Havel creates an attractive landscape of lakes fringed with dunes and woods, in the W suburbs of Berlin. Rising in an area of lakes to the N of the city, the Havel flows through a lock at the old town of **Spandau**, then widens into a broad lake with the GRUNEWALD on the E bank and the former fishing villages of Gatow and Kladow on the quiet W bank. Farther S, the river laps the shores of PFAUENINSEL, then flows under the **Glienicker Brücke** to **Potsdam**. After passing through the town of **Brandenburg**, the Havel finally enters the River Elbe.

Stern line steamers first began operating on the Havel in 1888, and the **Stern und Kreisschiffahrt** line now runs regular

Kaiser-Wilhelm-Gedächtniskirche

summer sailings between TEGEL (on the Tegeler See inlet), SPANDAU, WANNSEE (on the Grosser Wannsee inlet), PFAUENINSEL and the Glienicker Brücke.

The w bank of the Havel (*reached by bus 134 from U-Bahnhof Rathaus Spandau*) is dotted with old villages and quiet nature reserves. The former village of **Gatow** boasts a 14thC church with a wooden roof.

The only landing stage for steamers on the w bank is at **Kladow**, which has an attractive tree-lined waterfront with an extensive Biergarten in the summer. A leafy country lane climbs up to the old village church.

JAGDSCHLOSS GLIENICKE
s of Königstrasse, Zehlendorf. Map 5E3 **☞** *Park open daily, dawn-dusk. S-Bahn to Wannsee, then bus 116 to Glienicker Brücke, or line 1 boat to Glienicke Brücke.*

A 17thC Baroque hunting lodge erected by the Great Elector near the SCHLOSS KLEIN-GLIENICKE was rebuilt in the 19thC by Prince Friedrich Karl. The Jagdschloss (now a college) is not open to the public, but you can wander in the 19thC gardens on the banks of the Havel. Like so many parks in sw Berlin, it was landscaped by Lenné in the informal style of English country house gardens. A good view of Potsdam is seen from a little promontory to the w.

JAGDSCHLOSS GRUNEWALD ▥
Am Grunewaldsee 29, Zehlendorf ☎ *(030) 8133597. Map 5D3. Open Apr-Sept, 10am-6pm; Mar, Oct 10am-5pm; Nov-Feb 10am-4pm; closed Mon. Bus 115 to Pücklerstrasse, then a 10min walk through the woods.*

The Renaissance Jagdschloss Grunewald, designed in 1542 by Caspar Theiss for Elector Joachim II, stands on a lake in the depths of the woods. The former hunting lodge was altered by later Prussian rulers, but the original 16thC **Grosse Saal** (Great Hall) on the ground floor has survived intact. With red sandstone floors and painted ceilings, this is now the sole surviving Renaissance interior in Berlin.

The Jagdschloss was one of several royal palaces in Berlin to be seized by the state after Kaiser Wilhelm II fled to the Netherlands in 1918. The rooms are now hung with landscape paintings from various royal palaces, including some from the now demolished Schloss Monbijou.

Dappled sunlight falls on 16thC paintings by Lucas Cranach the Elder. The mystical Germanic attachment to dark forests is revealed in *The Water Nymph*, while a painting of Judith with the head of Holofernes shows Cranach's obsession with female cruelty.

A room overlooking the lake contains nine paintings from a Passion Cycle, painted for the Berlin Dom. The upstairs rooms contain some 17thC Dutch landscapes by the Haarlem School, and a painting showing the elderly Kaiser Wilhelm I arriving at the Jagdschloss in 1887. Don't miss the 19thC *trompe l'oeil* rusticated stonework as you leave, or the painted hunting scene underneath interlocked antlers above the door.

KAISER-WILHELM-GEDÄCHTNISKIRCHE
Breitscheidplatz, Charlottenburg ☎ *(030) 245023. Map 2D4. Open Tues-Sat 10am-6pm, Sun 11am-6pm. U-Bahn and S-Bahn to Zoologischer Garten.*

The E end of Kurfürstendamm is dramatically terminated by the shattered spire of the Kaiser-Wilhelm-Gedächtniskirche, one of

Karl-Marx-Allee

ten Berlin churches gutted by fire during a single air raid on November 22, 1943. The church was built in 1891-95 in the Romanesque style of the Rhine as a memorial to Kaiser Wilhelm I. Most of the church was demolished after the war, leaving just the jagged spire, and a portico decorated with glinting mosaics illustrating episodes of Hohenzollern history. Intended as a somber reminder of World War II, the church in recent years has been irreverently nicknamed the *hohler Zahn* (rotten tooth).

A modern hexagonal church, bathed inside with mysterious blue light, was constructed in 1959 where the nave of the Gedächtniskirche once stood. Impish Berliners call it "the makeup box," while a modern bell tower erected nearby is colloquially known as the "lipstick tube."

KARL-MARX-ALLEE ⅲ
Map 4B10. U-Bahn to Alexanderplatz or Frankfurter Tor.
The route along which the Soviet army marched into Berlin in 1945 became the first planned socialist avenue in East Berlin. Originally called the Frankfurter Allee, the 3km street was renamed Stalinallee. But in 1961, when the Soviet dictator fell from grace, the avenue became Karl-Marx-Allee (a name that is itself unlikely to survive much longer).

Stalinallee was designed in 1952 by Hermann Henselmann, who had already built an impressive tower block just s on the Weberwiese. The monumental building blocks were intended to mirror the Neoclassical style of Schinkel's Berlin, and they incorporated elegant arcades, and loggias with slender columns on the top floor. Two matching tower blocks on the Stausberger Platz (modeled on Karl von Gontard's two church towers on the PLATZ DER AKADEMIE) provide an impressive entry to the street. The project included a children's store — **Das Haus des Kindes** — and a restaurant — **Haus Berlin**. Bertolt Brecht, a close friend of Henselmann, was inspired to compose a verse which now adorns the Haus Berlin entrance.

The prestigious project later ran into difficulties; by the time work began at the Frankfurter Tor, the East Berlin authorities were beginning to complain about the high cost of the design. Labor relations worsened when production quotas on the project were raised, and on June 16, 1953, the Stalinallee workers staged a strike, which quickly turned into a general demonstration for democratic rights in East Germany. The next day, the Soviet Union sent in the army to crush the revolt.

KÄTHE-KOLLWITZ-MUSEUM
Fasanenstrasse 24, Charlottenburg ☎ (030) 8825210. Map 2D4. Open 11am-6pm; closed Tues. U-Bahn to Kurfürstendamm.
A museum devoted to the graphic art and sculpture of Käthe Kollwitz (1867-1945) occupies several rooms of a palatial Charlottenburg mansion built in 1897. As a doctor's wife in the

impoverished district of Prenzlauer Berg, she sketched harrowing scenes such as *Woman with Dead Child* (1903). Kollwitz continued to portray the suffering of women and children during World War I and into the 1920s. Her poster *Nie wieder Krieg* (Never Again War) was an attempt to combat growing militarism in 1923, while *Brot* highlighted poverty in the inflation-ridden years between the wars.

In 1922-23, Kollwitz produced the cycle of woodcuts titled *Krieg* in memory of her son, Peter, who had died in World War I. A second cycle of eight woodcuts entitled *Tod* was produced in the early years of Nazi rule.

KLEISTPARK
Schöneberg. Map 3E6. Open dawn-dusk. U-Bahn to Kleistpark.

A small formal park named after the German Romantic dramatist Heinrich von Kleist. Originally a hop garden for the royal brewery, the site became Berlin's first botanical garden in 1679.

Two Baroque colonnades lend elegance to an otherwise rather dull quarter of Schöneberg. Designed by Karl von Gontard in 1777 for Frederick the Great, they originally flanked the Königstrasse (now the Rathausstrasse), which led from the royal palace to Alexanderplatz. Removed in 1910 to improve traffic flow along the important artery, the 18thC Königskolonnaden (king's colonnades) were rather confusingly renamed the **Kleist Colonnades**.

Two statues that depict men taming wild horses are copies of works on the Anitschkoff Bridge in Leningrad/St Petersburg. A gift from Czar Nicholas I to his brother-in-law Friedrich Wilhelm IV, they stood in the Lustgarten before being moved here in 1945.

The park is overlooked by the imposing Neo-Baroque **Kammergericht**, the former German supreme court of appeal, built in 1913 to replace the 18thC court in Lindenstrasse (now the BERLIN-MUSEUM). The Allied Control Authority was established here in 1945, and the flags of the four powers flew from the balcony until 1948, when the Soviet Union withdrew from the alliance following a dispute about currency controls. Three flags have flown since then, all probably to disappear when the Allies finally quit Berlin.

KNOBLAUCHHAUS
Poststrasse 23, Mitte ☎ (0372) 21713392. Map 4C9. Open 10am-5pm; closed Mon. U-Bahn or S-Bahn to Alexanderplatz.

A Baroque house built for Johann Knoblauch in 1760 has been carefully reconstructed in the NIKOLAIVIERTEL. Rebuilt in 1835 Neoclassical style, the house boasts handsome rooms furnished in Biedermeier style. The building now contains a collection of family mementoes including relics of Eduard Knoblauch, architect of the NEUE SYNAGOGUE, and Armand Knoblauch, founder of Berlin's Böhmische brewery.

KONGRESSHALLE 🏛
John-Foster-Dulles-Allee 10, Tiergarten ☎ (030) 397870. Map 3B6. Open Tues-Thurs 2-6pm; Fri, Sun 10am-8pm; closed Mon, Sat. Bus 100 to Kongresshalle.

Situated in a corner of the Tiergarten overlooking the Spree, the Kongresshalle was built in 1957 as America's contribution to the International Building Exhibition (IBA). Designed by Hugh Stubbins as a symbol of international friendship, the Kongress-

Köpenick

halle is a striking example of 1950s futuristic design, with a remarkable concrete roof that inspired wry Berliners to dub the edifice the *Schwangere Auster* (pregnant oyster).

Surrounded by a bleak, windswept promenade deck, the Kongresshalle is now rather melancholy, although the 1950s chairs and lamps may appeal to design enthusiasts. Recently renamed the **Haus der Kulturen der Welt** (House of World Culture), it currently stages temporary exhibitions on aspects of life in the Third World, plus occasional concerts and plays.

A gaunt black tower stands near the Kongresshalle. Built in 1987 by the Daimler Benz company, it contains a 68-bell **carillon** (*concerts daily at noon and 6pm*).

KÖPENICK
SE Berlin. Map 7E7. S-Bahn to Köpenick, then tram 25 to Alt-Köpenick.

Surrounded by lakes and forests, Köpenick is a wistful old town standing on a peninsula at the confluence of the Dahme and Spree rivers. The old quarter of Alt-Köpenick still has the neglected look of most former East German towns, with dusty brick churches and derelict Baroque houses, but once the grime has been scraped off, it could well be as attractive as Spandau.

A fortress was erected on this strategic site in the 12thC, and by the 13thC the town was important enough to receive a charter. The **castle** was rebuilt in Renaissance style by Joachim II, but only the foundations now remain. The present edifice was built in an intimate Dutch Baroque style for a son of the Great Elector, and currently houses a museum of decorative arts, the KUNST-GEWERBEMUSEUM SCHLOSS KÖPENICK. The attractive **Rathaus** (town hall) on Alt-Köpenick was built in 1903-5 in the style of a northern German brick church.

The annual *Köpenicker Sommer* festival in June commemorates the events chronicled in Carl Zuckmayer's play *Der Hauptmann von Köpenick* (The Captain of Köpenick). The play tells of a shoemaker disguised as a captain, who orders a group of soldiers to travel by train to Köpenick to arrest the Bürgermeister.

The **Grosser Müggelsee** to the E of the old town is an extensive lake with several beaches. **Weisse Flotte** steamers depart from the Luisenhain pier on the Dahme for a 3hr tour of the inland lake. You can also take a creaky East Berlin tram (#25) from Platz des 23 April to **Rahnsdorf** on the edge of the Berliner Stadtforst. The tram rumbles past crumbling country villas surrounded by apple orchards, and down the main street of **Friedrichshagen**, a pleasant old town with dusty 18thC Neoclassical dwellings. There are convenient S-Bahn stations at Rahnsdorf (a 10min walk through the woods from the tram terminus) and at Friedrichshagen.

KREUZBERG

Named after a natural hill (now the VIKTORIAPARK), Kreuzberg district is a 19thC quarter s of Mitte. Parts of the district are heavily industrialized, such as **Gleisdreieck**, with its railroad yards, pump house (now the LAPIDARIUM) and factories, but elsewhere you can find attractive tree-lined avenues with solid Old Berlin apartments.

Kreuzberg was badly damaged in World War II, and remained largely derelict afterward. Its vast, dilapidated apartments were settled by a cosmopolitan mix of Turkish immigrant workers, avant-garde artists and students. With the construction of the Berlin Wall, the quarter developed something of a frontier spirit, providing an exciting setting for social experiments, radical art galleries, cafés and theaters. Many flourished briefly, but a few, such as the **Künstlerhaus Bethanien** (*Mariannenplatz*), have become Berlin institutions. This is an ornate Neo-Gothic hospital converted into an alternative center and containing artists' studios and craft workshops. The stretch of Oranienstrasse between Oranienplatz and Heinrichplatz has several bars for wild nights, while the waterfront cafés along Paul-Lincke-Ufer are quiet places for a late breakfast.

In recent years, Kreuzberg has looked less shabby, as old apartment blocks such as Riehmers Hofgarten have been renovated. Some of Germany's best modern architecture has been recently constructed in areas of Kreuzberg bordering the Wall, in an attempt to repair the urban fabric. The demolition of the Wall is likely to make the district increasingly desirable, although hopefully a few green and purple spotlights will continue to glow in apartment windows to symbolize Kreuzberg's radical edge.

KULTUR-FORUM
S of Tiergarten. Map 3C6. U-Bahn to Gleisdreieck, then M-Bahn (when running) to Kemperplatz; bus 129, 148, 187, 248, 341 to Kultur-Forum.

The cluster of museums and concert halls on the S edge of the Tiergarten was planned as a center of the arts by Hans Scharoun in 1960-63. The buildings are grouped rather randomly around the **St Matthäi-Kirche**, designed by August Stüler in 1844. The isolated Byzantine-style church is all that remains of an old neighborhood destroyed in World War II.

Scharoun set the tone for the Kultur-Forum with his controversial PHILHARMONIE concert hall design. He later added the **Kammermusiksaal** and the nearby **Staatsbibliothek** to the scheme. The MUSIKINSTRUMENTEN-MUSEUM and the KUNSTGEWERBE-MUSEUM subsequently fueled local wrath with their brutal style. A new GEMÄLDEGALERIE (incorporating an 1895 villa that survived the war) and a KUPFERSTICHKABINETT are being built, although the plans may be altered radically now that the city is unified.

Although still rather bleak and disconnected, the Kultur-Forum has several excellent museums run by the Staatliche Museen Preussischer Kulturbesitz (see page 44 for an explanation). The Musikinstrumenten-Museum stages occasional jazz concerts, while the nearby NEUE NATIONALGALERIE boasts a lively café.

KUNSTGEWERBEMUSEUM *(Museum of Arts and Crafts)*
Tiergartenstrasse 6, Tiergarten ☎ *(030) 2662911. Map 3C6. Open Tues-Fri 9am-5pm; Sat, Sun 10am-5pm; closed Mon* ♿ ▣ *U-Bahn to Gleisdreieck, then M-Bahn (when running) to Kemperplatz; bus 129, 148, 187, 248, 341 to Kultur-Forum.*

Inspired by the Victoria & Albert Museum in London, the Kunstgewerbemuseum was founded in 1867 as a museum of decorative arts. A magnificent building (now the MARTIN-GROPIUS-BAU) was built in 1881 to house the collection of ceramics, tapestries, furniture, glass and metalwork. In 1920, the museum moved to the Stadtschloss on the Spree, vacated after the Kaiser fled to the Netherlands. Dispersed during World War II, the works are now divided between the Kunstgewerbemuseum and the KUNSTGEWERBEMUSEUM SCHLOSS KÖPENICK.

Built in 1978-85 near Scharoun's Philharmonie, the Kunst-

Kunstgewerbemuseum Schloss Köpenick

gewerbemuseum forms part of the unfinished KULTUR-FORUM. The bleak, virtually windowless concrete design deters all but the most determined of visitors, yet it is worth penetrating the bunker-like building, as it contains an exceptional collection of European arts and crafts. Although the concrete-walled rooms are brutally sterile, the display techniques are generally excellent.

A small **Medieval collection** (Rm I) includes ornate reliquaries and other religious works. The more extensive **Renaissance rooms** (Rms II and III) are hung with large Brussels tapestries depicting Classical legends and Biblical stories. Cabinets filled with Venetian glass, Nuremberg silverware and Florentine majolica show 16thC craftsmen's skills. Don't miss the ornate objects belonging to the **Lüneburger Ratssilber**, a collection of 15th-16thC silver vessels bought to symbolize the wealth of the Hanseatic port of Lüneburg. The sale of the town silver to the Berlin-Museum in 1874 sadly reflects the decline of the proud merchant town situated SE of Hamburg.

The **Baroque collection** (Rm IV) contains a fascinating collection of 17thC "cabinets of curiosity" (*Kunstkammern*). Crammed with secret boxes and drawers and encrusted with silver and precious stones, the **Pommersche Kunstschrank** was assembled in Augsburg in 1610-16 for the duke of Pommern-Stettin. Although the cabinet was destroyed in World War II, the contents survived, and they now fill three glass cases in the museum. The objects include erudite games, miniature books, medical instruments, razors, hair brushes, tools and even a tiny Renaissance fruit press.

A display of elegant **18thC porcelain** manufactured in Meissen, Nymphenburg and Berlin — including a magnificent KPM amphora vase painted in 1840 with a view of the Russian Orthodox church in Potsdam — is on view in Rm V. The **Chinesenzimmer**, an intimate 18thC room decorated with chinoiserie motifs, comes from the Palazzo Graneri in Turin. Rm VI is devoted to Biedermeier and Art Nouveau works, while Rm VII has sleek Art Deco vases.

KUNSTGEWERBEMUSEUM SCHLOSS KÖPENICK 🏛
Schloss Köpenick, Schlossinsel, Köpenick ☎ *(0372) 6572651. Map 7E7. Open 10am-6pm; closed Mon, Tues* 🚆 *S-Bahn to Köpenick or Spindlersfeld.*

Tucked away on a wooded peninsula at the confluence of the Spree and Dahme rivers, the old Schloss at Köpenick now contains an attractive museum of decorative arts. The intimate Baroque palace was built in 1678-90 for Prince Friedrich, the Great Elector's son, by the Dutch architect Rutger van Langevelt. A **chapel** on the opposite side of the courtyard was added by Johann Nering in 1682.

With its ornate ceilings and creaking wooden stairs, the former Hohenzollern palace makes an idyllic setting for a collection of Renaissance cabinets, Nuremberg pewter, Augsburg gold chalices and Berlin porcelain. The works came from the old Kunstgewerbemuseum, founded in 1867. Originally housed in a former panoramic picture gallery, the collection was moved to an abandoned porcelain factory, then to a custom-built museum of decorative arts (now the MARTIN-GROPIUS-BAU). After the 1918 Revolution, the ever-growing collection moved to the Baroque royal palace facing the Lustgarten. Shipped out in crates during World War II, the collection was reassembled in the KUNSTGEWERBEMUSEUM in the western sector and Schloss Köpenick in the Soviet zone. The Köpenick museum is much smaller than its counterpart near the Tiergarten, but the intimate Baroque setting is more pleasing. The only disappointment is that the museum café overlooking the river has not yet shaken off its dour Eastern Bloc atmosphere.

A dark **Renaissance room** from Schloss Haldenstein, near the Swiss town of Chur, was acquired by the Berlin museum in 1884. Built in 1548 by a craftsman who signed himself H.S., the room is decorated with elaborate *intarsia* representing perspective views of Renaissance cities.

The Baroque **Wappensaal** (coats-of-arms chamber) on the second floor was added to Schloss Köpenick in the late 17thC. Designed as a ballroom by the Italian architect Giovanni Carove, it is lavishly decorated with huge coats-of-arms of the Prussian provinces. The fireplaces are surmounted by masked savages supporting helmets laden with feathers and bizarre beasts. It was in this room bristling with Prussian pomp that Friedrich Wilhelm I conducted the court-martial of his son, the future Frederick the Great, for desertion.

The adjacent room contains relics of the **Silberbuffet**, a collection of gold and silver vessels. Commissioned by Elector Friedrich III, the ornate pieces were made in Augsburg in 1695-98 by the Biller family of goldsmiths. The works were shown to the public for the first time in 1982 in a room modeled on the Rittersaal at the Stadtschloss (where they were originally displayed). Some of the objects in the room were made by Berlin silversmiths, such as an overscaled 18thC silver tankard decorated with several hundred coins.

KUPFERSTICHKABINETT *(Engravings Collection)*
Arnimallee 23-27, Dahlem ☎ *(030) 83011. Map 6E4. Open Tues-Fri 9am-5pm; Sat, Sun 10am-5pm. U-Bahn to Dahlem-Dorf.*

The Great Elector's collection of drawings and watercolors formed the basis of Berlin's print cabinet. Moved to the Altes Museum in 1831 and later to the Neues Museum, the collection ended up after the war split between the Kupferstichkabinett at Dahlem and the Altes Museum. The two collections are likely to be reunited in the coming years in a new building at the KULTUR-FORUM.

The print collection has major works by Dürer, Grünewald, Cranach, Pieter Bruegel the Elder, Rubens, Rembrandt, Kandinsky and Dix. The prints are normally kept in storage, but you can ask to look at particular works. The museum shows a selection of prints taken from the collection in a permanent exhibition called *Im Blickpunkt* (At a Moment's Glance).

KURFÜRSTENDAMM
Charlottenburg. Map 1-2E1-D4. U-Bahn to Kurfürstendamm.

Extending 2 miles (3.5km) from the KAISER-WILHELM-GEDÄCHTNISKIRCHE to the Halensee, the Kurfürstendamm (Ku'damm to Berliners) is a broad, leafy avenue modeled on the Avenue des Champs-Elysées in Paris. Created in 1882 by Otto von Bismarck to connect the city with the Grunewald, Kurfürstendamm follows an old route from the Stadtschloss on the Spree to the Grunewald hunting lodge used by Electors (*Kurfürsten*). Wealthy Berliners began building opulent villas on the avenue in the 1880s, and fashionable cafés and restaurants later sprung up, rivaling those on Unter den Linden. The avenue was shortened in 1886 at the time when the Kaiser-Wilhelm-

Lapidarium

Gedächtniskirche was built, and the final stretch became Budapester Strasse.

Most of the hotels and cafés on Kurfürstendamm were bombed during World War II, and only a handful of prewar buildings are still standing, such as the former Chinese embassy (# *218*), and the ornate 1905 *Jugendstil* corner block (# *59-60*). A few buildings preserve something of the flavor of Old Berlin, notably the **Hotel Bristol Kempinski** and the **Café Möhring**, but most of the avenue has been rebuilt in a sober modern style.

Kurfürstendamm is still Berlin's liveliest street, with cafés, hotels, stores, theaters and cinemas stretching along its entire length. The flamboyant street lamps, large clocks and Neo-classical newsstands (the best two, located at the corner of Uhlandstrasse, are tiny Neoclassical buildings) create a distinctive Berlin atmosphere that draws crowds from dawn until long after midnight.

LAPIDARIUM
Hallesches Ufer 78, Kreuzberg. Map 3D7. Open only during temporary exhibitions. U-Bahn or M-Bahn to Gleisdreieck.

A curious collection of war-damaged Berlin sculpture has been abandoned in the courtyard of a former 19thC pumping house on the Landwehrkanal. Known as the Lapidarium, it is rarely open, but you can peer through the iron gate to the right of the building to see a row of damaged statues striking preposterous poses. They are all that remain of a double avenue of 27 statues of Prussian rulers, commissioned by Wilhelm II to line the Siegesallee (Victory Avenue) in the Tiergarten. Most Berliners considered the Siegesallee merely comic, and dubbed it the *Puppenallee* (dolls' avenue). But the writer Sybille Bedford, born in Charlottenburg, was quite taken with the figures. "I would stand before each Margrave of Brandenburg or King of Prussia upon his pedestal and study his countenance and dates," she recalled in her semi-autobiographical *Jigsaw*. "Here then was history in the round, history visible, as well as in nice order, for the statues began at one end of the avenue with the remotest Brandenburg and culminated with Kaiser Wilhelm I. Sometimes I was intrigued by an appearance, sometimes by a name; my favorites were an epicene youth leaning upon his shield, Heinrich the Child, and a mysterious personage covered in chain-mail, Waldemar the Bear."

The Siegesallee stood in the path of a much grander avenue planned by Albert Speer, and the statues were removed to the perimeter of the Grosser Stern. Here, they were shelled in World War II, losing fingers, arms and even heads. Now abandoned in a damp courtyard, the Prussian dolls are rather melancholy symbols of Berlin's history.

LÜBARS
In the N district of Reinickendorf. Map 6A5. Bus 222 from U-Bahnhof Tegel to Alt-Lübars.

Surrounded by flat fields and farmhouses, the former village of Lübars is a surprisingly rural corner of Berlin. The Wall used to cut across the fields just N of the village, but life in the farming community is now back to normal. The village church — a modest Baroque edifice — was rebuilt in the 1790s after a fire.

The little village gets rather crowded in the summer, but out of season it still has a rural air. You can lunch on Lübars ham, the local specialty, at an old village inn, the **Dorfkrug zum lustigen Finken** (*Alt-Lübars 20* ☎ *(030) 4027845*), which has a terrace.

MARIA REGINA MARTYRUM *(Martyrs' Memorial)*
Heckerdamm 230, Charlottenburg ☎ (030) 3826011. Open daily 9am-5.30pm (Nov-Mar, closes 4.30pm). U-Bahn to Jacob-Kaiser-Platz; bus 121, 123, 221 to Heckerdamm.

Built in the middle of a postwar housing estate in 1960-63, a bleak Catholic church commemorates victims of the Nazis. The empty courtyard hemmed in by concrete walls is meant to recall the concentration camps, as is the menacing Glockenspiel tower, where the church bells are hung.

MARIENKIRCHE
Neuen Markt, Mitte ☎ (0372) 2124467. Map 4B9. Open Mon-Thurs 10am-noon, 1-5pm; Sat noon-4.30pm; closed Fri, Sun. S-Bahn or U-Bahn to Alexanderplatz.

The attractive 13thC Marienkirche, now stranded in the middle of a bleak square, was the second church to be built in Berlin. Destroyed by a fire in 1380, the red brick edifice was rebuilt in a simple, north German Late Gothic style. The elegant Neoclassical spire was added in 1790 by Carl Gotthard Langhans, architect of the BRANDENBURGER TOR.

A large 15thC *Totentanz* (dance of death) fresco was uncovered in the 19thC. The church has some striking tombs, including a 17thC memorial to Feldmarschall Otto von Spar. Laden with flags and cannon, the tomb was designed by Artus Quellien the Elder.

Restored after World War II, the Marienkirche now contains a collection of religious paintings and sculptures dug from the rubble of bombed Berlin churches.

MÄRKISCHES MUSEUM
Am Köllnischen Park 5, Mitte ☎ (0372) 2700514. Map 4C9. Open Wed-Sun 10am-6pm; closed Mon, Tues. U-Bahn to Märkisches Museum; S-Bahn to Jannowitzbrücke.

The Märkisches Museum was founded in 1874 as a historical museum for Berlin and the Mark of Brandenburg. It now occupies an eccentric early 20thC building based on copies of historical buildings in the Mark of Brandenburg.

The brick choir is modeled on the 15thC Katharinenkirche in Brandenburg, W of Berlin, while the tower is copied from the Bischofsburg in Wittstock, NW of Berlin. The colossal figure by the entrance is modeled on the medieval Roland statues that symbolize municipal liberty in many Brandenburg towns.

Virtually destroyed in World War II, the museum has been carefully rebuilt by the East Germans. Boasting a large collection of historical relics from prehistoric times to the 20thC, the museum has a rather melancholy air, with empty, echoing cloisters and cold stone stairs. The atmosphere may well improve, however, once the texts throughout the museum have been purged of their hectoring Marxist tone.

The **prehistoric collection** in the basement includes conjectural reconstructions of ancient northern German dwellings. The first documents to refer to Berlin and Cölln are displayed here; Cölln is mentioned in a 1237 document, while the name Berlin crops up for the first time in a deed penned in 1244.

Neoclassical monuments by Gottfried Schadow are displayed in a gloomy corridor. There is a tomb of a 6yr-old boy, and a memorial to Marianne Schadow, the sculptor's wife. Several rooms are filled with Berlin porcelain, including sentimental Rococo figures modeled on Meissen ware, imitation Delftware faience of the 1770s, and handsome Neoclassical *Ansichtsporzellan* (porcelain decorated with miniature landscapes and townscapes) produced at the KPM works in 1815-32.

The Industrial Revolution in Berlin is symbolized by a powerful series of four large **murals** that once decorated the Villa Borsig. The works were commissioned by the German industrialist to illustrate iron production. Two more panels from the series are displayed in the MUSEUM FÜR VERKEHR UND TECHNIK.

The museum has some attractive **paintings** of Berlin, including views of the Tiergarten, Treptow, Unter den Linden and a remarkable rural view of *Kreuzberg* (1847) by Adolph Menzel. Eduard Gaertner's view of the Garrison Church in Potsdam shows the church, destroyed in World War II, where the Nazis staged a sham parliament in 1933. *Monday Morning* (1898) by Hans Baluschek is a sad, sensitive study of four young Berlin women on the morning after a riotous night. The Norwegian Edvard Munch, a leading Berlin Expressionist, painted a striking portrait of Walther Rathenau, the Jewish government minister murdered by extremists in the summer of 1922.

The most delightful room contains a collection of **antique mechanical musical instruments** (*played on Wed and Sun 11am-noon*), which includes curiosities disguised as wardrobes, clocks or cabinets to blend in with Berliners' Biedermeier furniture. A Neoclassical *Flöttenuhr* plays Mozart melodies with a rather tinny sound, but the Polyphone from Leipzig has a marvelous liquid tone. A street organ made in the Schönhauser Allee in Prenzlauer Berg emits lusty, nostalgic tunes.

The park behind the museum stands on the site of a Renaissance bastion, but, confusingly, contains an 18thC round turret moved here from another part of the city defenses in 1893. Dotted among the trees are odd, old statues, including one of Hercules wrestling with a lion.

MARTIN-GROPIUS-BAU 🏛
Stresemannstrasse 110, Kreuzberg ☎(030) 254860. Map 3D7. Open 10am-10pm; closed Mon ☎ (☎ in advance) U-Bahn to Kochstrasse or Otto-Grotewohl-Strasse; S-Bahn to Anhalter Bahnhof.

Surrounded by eerie wasteland, the Martin-Gropius-Bau once housed Berlin's museum of decorative art (now in the KUNST-GEWERBEMUSEUM). Built in 1877 by Martin Gropius (uncle of Walter Gropius), the museum closely resembles Schinkel's 1836 Bauakademie (bombed in 1945 and demolished in 1961). The ornate Italian Renaissance museum incorporates an airy, glazed courtyard surrounded by arcades, and heavy ceilings decorated with war-damaged mosaics and frescoes (including one ironically entitled *Pax*).

Reconstructed in 1979-81, the building currently houses the modern art collection of the Berlin Gallery, the archives of the Werkbund movement and the Jewish historical museum. Temporary exhibitions are sometimes staged in the museum's palatial rooms.

The **Berlinische Galerie** on the first floor exhibits a selection of works from its extensive collection of 19th and 20thC Berlin painting, sculpture, photography and architecture. Lesser Ury's *Leipziger Strasse* (1898) depicts a rainy night on one of Berlin's fashionable arteries, while a sinister 1920s atmosphere is reflected in Conrad Felixmüller's *Boxer at a Fairground Booth*. The devastating impact of World War II haunts postwar works such as Hans Scheib's harrowing statue of *Christ in Torment*, and Wolf Vostell's giant canvas covered with bones and severed limbs titled *Die Schlacht* (Slaughter). But there's a kind of impish Berlin humor, too, in Ines Berger's *Picnic for Vincent*, showing Van Gogh in a wood with three naked prostitutes.

A trip to the attic (simplest by elevator) lets you see the impressive double-skin roof above the courtyard. The **Werkbund-Archiv** found there contains a collection of works of the *Deutscher Werkbund*, a federation of architects and craftsmen formed at Munich in 1907 to promote high-quality industrial design. The museum organises stimulating temporary exhibitions based on the Werkbund collection, and other 20thC artifacts.

The **Jüdische Abteilung des Berlin Museums** is a rather forgotten and forlorn collection of Jewish mementoes. Founded in 1933, the museum illustrates the role of Jews in Berlin's history. There is a gravestone from Spandau's Jewish quarter dating back to 1320, found during excavations at ZITADELLE SPANDAU, and a 19thC map showing the 30 different synagogues in Berlin.

Sobering statistics reveal that Berlin's Jewish population dropped from 170,000 in 1933 to just 5,000 in 1945. The stories of a few of the victims can be pieced together from several files crammed with personal documents.

MITTE
Center E. Map 4C8.
Mitte (middle) is the old center of Berlin, covering the settlements of Berlin, Cölln, Dorotheenstadt and Friedrichswerder. Berlin's principal museums, theaters, government buildings and churches were built here from the 18th-20thC.

Bombed in World War II, Mitte became the center of East Germany's capital after 1945. The buildings of the Second and Third Reich were demolished, and much was rebuilt in a cold official Socialist style, although some handsome 18th and early 19thC buildings were restored, such as Schinkel's ALTES MUSEUM and FRIEDRICHSWERDERSCHE KIRCHE. Several quarters were rebuilt in Old Berlin style, including the PLATZ DER AKADEMIE, the NIKOLAIVIERTEL and the MUSEUMSINSEL.

With the collapse of the old order in 1989, the character of Mitte is rapidly changing. The district boundary to the S and W is still clearly defined by a broad strip of wasteland, but nearby streets such as Friedrichstrasse and Unter den Linden have become increasingly fashionable.

An interesting area of Mitte to explore lies just N of the S-Bahn viaduct. From Bahnhof Friedrichstrasse, follow the Schiffbauerdamm quay, cross the bridge and continue along Weidendamm, then head left across the Monbijou Brücke. Turn left at the end of Monbijoustrasse to look at the NEUE SYNAGOGUE. Retrace your steps and turn left up Krausnickstrasse, which leads to the **Sophienkirche**, an elegant Baroque church built in 1712.

Turn left up Grosse Hamburger Strasse, lined with dusty apartments still pock-marked with shell holes, then right into Sophienstrasse, a renovated street with attractive Old Berlin apartments painted in pinks and pale yellows. Cross the road and continue along Neue Schönhauser Strasse, turn right into Münzstrasse, then left into Almstadtstrasse. This was once the heart of the **Scheunenviertel**, a riotous working-class quarter whose two main streets were renamed after the leaders of the 1918 revolution.

Turn right along Hirtenstrasse and left down Kleine Alexanderstrasse to get to the U-Bahn and S-Bahn stations at Alexanderplatz.

Museum für Deutsche Geschichte

MUSEUM FÜR DEUTSCHE GESCHICHTE (Museum of German History) ⌘
Unter den Linden 2, Mitte ☎ (0372) 2000591. Map 4B8. Open Mon-Thurs 9am-7pm (closes Oct-Mar 6pm); Sat, Sun 10am-5pm; last entry 1hr before closing time. S-Bahn to Marx-Engels-Platz or Friedrichstrasse.

Currently occupying the massive Baroque Zeughaus (arsenal) on Unter den Linden, the Museum of German History has been in turmoil since the fall of the old regime in 1989. Founded in 1952, the museum provided a blunt Marxist interpretation of German history from the Stone Age to the Nazi years. The rooms dealing with the Soviet period were closed soon after the Communist government fell, to be purged of exhibits such as Russian tractors and Vietnamese peasants' hats.

Begun by Johann Nering in 1695, the Zeughaus was completed by the architect and sculptor Andreas Schlüter in 1699. The courtyard known as the **Schlüterhof** (where concerts take place in the summer) is surrounded by 22 arches whose keystones bear Schlüter's expressively carved heads of dying warriors. In the 1880s, the building was turned into a bombastic Military Museum, complete with a Hall of Fame of the Prussian Army.

The collection still has a strong military bias, with menacing pikes from the Peasants' Revolt, moldering red and blue Prussian uniforms, and dioramas of battles modeled with tin soldiers. Some of the old exhibits, such as a detailed reconstruction of the Bastille made by an enthusiastic East German, and a model of Karl Marx's house in London, are liable to be discarded. But it is to be hoped that the museum authorities will hold on to the battered suitcase carried by the left-wing leader Karl Liebknecht on his journey to America in 1886.

The most interesting rooms at present deal with 19thC Berlin history, with exhibits such as scientific equipment, an early automobile built in 1900, and a model of a grim *Mietskaserne* (tenement) of the 1880s.

Several rooms on the Nazi period contain a harrowing collection of documents, photographs and relics, revealing that many East German leaders were active opponents of Hitler. A small section is devoted to the history of postwar Germany, and pride of place is given to three concrete slabs from the Berlin Wall, bearing the lament "13 August 1961 — Walled in for 28 years!"

MUSEUM FÜR DEUTSCHE VOLKSKUNDE (Museum of German Folklore)
Im Winkel 6, Dahlem ☎ (030) 8390101. Map 6E4. Open Tues-Fri 9am-5pm; Sat, Sun 10am-5pm ♿ U-Bahn to Dahlem-Dorf.

Northern German folk costumes and painted farmhouse furniture are displayed in a modern museum in Dahlem. Inspired by the Norse Museum in Stockholm, the Museum of German Folklore was founded in 1889, but much of the original collection was lost during World War II. Some of the surviving works are now in the PERGAMON-MUSEUM, but the majority are displayed in this rather sterile environment at Dahlem.

MUSEUM FÜR INDISCHE KUNST (Museum of Indian Art)
Lansstrasse 8, Dahlem ☎ (030) 83011. Map 6E4. Open Tues-Fri 9am-5pm; Sat, Sun 10am-5pm ♿ ▣ U-Bahn to Dahlem-Dorf.

Spotlit Buddhas, miniature paintings and bronze figures of gods are dramatically displayed in this museum, which forms part of the complex at Dahlem. Founded in 1963, the museum boasts an acclaimed collection of ancient Hindu and Buddhist statues from India, Tibet, Nepal, Indonesia, Thailand and Burma.

MUSEUM FÜR ISLAMISCHE KUNST *(Museum of Islamic Art)*
Lansstrasse 8, Dahlem ☎ *(030) 83011. Map 6E4. Open Tues-Fri 9am-5pm; Sat, Sun 10am-5pm* ♿ 🚇 *U-Bahn to Dahlem-Dorf.*

The Islamic Art Museum at Dahlem has a rich collection of miniature paintings, ceramic bowls, carpets and books. Other Islamic treasures are currently displayed in the PERGAMON-MUSEUM.

MUSEUM FÜR NATURKUNDE *(Museum of Natural Science)*
Invalidenstrasse 43, Mitte ☎ *(0372) 28972540. Map 3A7. Open Tues-Sun 9am-5pm. U-Bahn or S-Bahn to Friedrichstrasse; S-Bahn to Lehrter Stadtbahnhof or U-Bahn to Nordbahnhof.*

Berlin's natural history museum was built in 1875-89 by August Tiede to display the Humboldt University's collection of minerals and fossils. The East Germans allowed the building to become rather dusty and dilapidated, and many of the rooms have been closed for years.

The collection is still worth a glance, particularly for the dinosaur skeletons in the lofty main hall. Excavated in East Africa in 1909-12, they include the world's largest assembled skeleton: a Brachiosaurus that fills much of the hall. The mineral collection is housed in beautiful antique wooden cases.

MUSEUM FÜR OSTASIATISCHE KUNST *(Museum of Oriental Art)*
Lansstrasse 8, Dahlem ☎ *(030) 83011. Map 6E4. Open Tues-Fri 9am-5pm; Sat, Sun 10am-5pm* ♿ 🚇 *U-Bahn to Dahlem-Dorf.*

Chinese porcelain, red lacquered furniture and Japanese woodcuts are among the treasures currently in Dahlem's Museum of Oriental Art. Founded in 1906, this was the first museum in Germany devoted to the art of the Far East, and it gradually assembled a small but exquisite collection of works from China, Japan and Korea. Berlin's Oriental collection was split in two by the war, however, and many of the works must now be viewed in the PERGAMON-MUSEUM.

MUSEUM FÜR VERKEHR UND TECHNIK *(Museum of Transportation and Technology)* ★
Trebbiner Strasse 9, Kreuzberg ☎ *(030) 254840. Map 3D7* 🚇 *Open Tues-Fri 9am-6pm; Sat, Sun 10am-6pm* ✱ ♿ 🚇 *U-Bahn to Gleisdreieck or Möckernbrücke.*

Berlin's vast museum of transportation and technology displays a fascinating and varied collection of trains, cars, bicycles, steam engines, model ships, typewriters, printing presses and computers. The museum was opened in 1983, within a complex of 19thC industrial buildings in the war-torn Gleisdreieck quarter, and incorporates several prewar collections, including that of the Museum of Transportation and Building which was formerly in the HAMBURGER BAHNHOF. As befits a science museum, the complex is constantly improving and expanding, although it still

Museum für Verkehr und Technik

does not quite measure up to the exciting center portrayed on the mural facing the Landwehrkanal. Allow 2hrs.

The **Eingangsgebäude** (entrance building) was built in 1908 as an ice-storage depot. Horse-drawn wagons were kept in the *Hof* (courtyard), where a door marked *Ausgang 6* leads to the *Pferdetreppe*, an old spiral ramp that gave access to the stables on the upper floors. Tethering rings can still be seen in the second-floor room that contains old printing presses.

The ground floor is a marvelous clutter of old technology. A collection of historic planes includes a rare 1917 Fokker triplane and a 1941 Junkers Ju 52. Among the many vintage vehicles (some of them parked in the basement garage) are several gleaming German automobiles built by Karl Benz and Gottlieb Daimler, and a smart 1904 fire engine.

A demonstration of suitcase manufacture is staged in a reconstructed 19thC factory, while the technology of housework is illustrated by an old German kitchen. The museum even has a reconstructed ladies' hairdressing salon full of menacing gadgets used to create the sleek permanent waves of the 1920s.

The **Versuchsfeld** (experiment room) on the first floor allows children to play with prisms, pulleys and other gadgets, while the computer gallery has several demonstration models programmed to play chess or compose music. One floor up, an 1835 Scottish printing press can sometimes be seen working.

The former locomotive works of Anhalter Bahnhof accommodate another department of the museum complex. A magnificent collection of old German steam trains and scale models is displayed in two huge 19thC **Lokomotivschuppen** (locomotive sheds). These are entered through the *Fürstenportal*, a monumental gateway saved when the Anhalter station ruins were demolished in 1961.

Two large murals showing a locomotive assembly works and a railroad bridge were painted in 1876 for the Villa Borsig in the suburb of Moabit. They formed part of a cycle of seven works commissioned by August Borsig, Imperial Germany's foremost locomotive manufacturer. The MÄRKISCHES MUSEUM has four more panels salvaged from the villa.

Several railroad coaches (including a well-padded Prussian model from 1898) are ranged around two locomotive turntables outside the sheds. The nearby open land is a bomb-site that has been left in its wild state as an ecological museum. Experiments on wind and solar energy are carried out in this romantic urban wilderness. Two historic windmills have been reconstructed nearby, while an abandoned water tower to the s adds an eerie note.

Most visitors are worn out by the time they reach the manager's office (*Beamtenwohnhaus*) situated between the two locomotive sheds, but it's worth climbing the stairs to explore the handsome wood-paneled rooms crammed with models of German ships, many of which were constructed in Berlin, including Germany's first steamship and iron steamship. The collection also includes superb scale models of Berlin locks and bridges, such as the Charlottenburger Brücke and the Oberbaumbrücke. A curious scale model of medieval Berlin in ruins incorporates trickling water to represent the Spree. The FERNSEHTURM has been added as a useful if anachronistic orientation point.

Energetic travelers who reach the third floor will find a bizarre collection of 19thC stereoscopes, including an antique *Kaiserpanorama* fitted with a row of binoculars for viewing three-dimensional scenes of European capitals.

Museum für Vor- und Frühgeschichte

The museum has a technical bookstore with a large stock of nostalgic prewar Berlin postcards. The old-fashioned museum café recalls a vanished era, with its clutter of antique tin signs and other relics.

MUSEUM FÜR VÖLKERKUNDE *(Museum of Ethnography)*
Lansstrasse 8, Dahlem ☎ (030) 83011. Map 6E4. Open Tues-Fri 9am-5pm; Sat, Sun 10am-5pm ↔ U-Bahn to Dahlem-Dorf.

A 17thC "cabinet of curiosities" created by the Great Elector was merged with numerous 19thC private collections of German folk art to form the Museum für Völkerkunde. Originally housed in a museum on Stresemannstrasse, the collection was moved to Dahlem in 1912. Some of the exhibits were later moved back to the former museum, and many of the treasures were destroyed by wartime bombing. The main collection is now housed in this modern complex at Dahlem, but a few objects rescued from the Stresemannstrasse museum are occasionally shown in the basement of the PERGAMON-MUSEUM.

Now one of the world's largest ethnographic collections, the museum in Dahlem covers Africa, America, Polynesia, the Near East, South Asia and the Far East. The Africa collection, built up during Germany's brief colonial period, contains beautifully lit masks and sensual wooden statues. The South Asia department has a marvelous display of Burmese and Indonesian puppets. A superb Polynesian collection includes several reconstructed houses, and a basement hall is filled with replica boats, including a catamaran built from a sketch made on Tonga by Captain James Cook.

MUSEUM FÜR VOR- UND FRÜHGESCHICHTE
(Museum of Prehistory and Early History)
Schloss Charlottenburg (w wing), Spandauer Damm, Charlottenburg ☎ (030) 320911. Map 1B2. Open Mon-Thurs 9am-5pm; Sat, Sun 10am-5pm ↔ Bus 145, 204 to Klausener Platz.

Berlin's museum of prehistory and early history is more interesting than its ponderous name might suggest. A "cabinet of curiosities" owned by the Hohenzollern family formed the nucleus of the original museum, established in Schloss Monbijou in 1829. Almost 100yrs passed before a permanent museum of prehistory and early history was opened in 1930. The new building was gutted by fire in World War II, and the collection ended up split between Schloss Charlottenburg and the BODE-MUSEUM. The collection is superbly displayed and lit, with occasional humorous touches such as the toilets labeled *homo sapiens*.

The **prehistoric collection** at Charlottenburg has relics from Germanic tribes, including a heap of ornamental buttons found at a Bronze Age site in the Berlin district of Lichterfelde. The metalworking skills of the Bronze Age are illustrated by the exquisite spiral necklaces and swords found in the Carpathian Mountains.

The centerpiece of the old museum was a collection of almost 10,000 Trojan antiquities gifted in 1880 by the German archeologist Heinrich Schliemann. While excavating the site of Homeric Troy (near Hisarlik, Turkey) in the 1870s, Schliemann uncovered a hoard of gold jewelry which he called Priam's treasure. Schliemann smuggled the collection of gold necklaces,

Museumsdorf Düppel

earrings and beads back to Berlin, where it was displayed in the Museum of Early History, but an equally unscrupulous World War II looter stole many of the works. The objects now on display are mostly copies, while, according to a recent discovery, the originals gather dust in a government bank vault in Moscow.

MUSEUMSDORF DÜPPEL
Clauertstrasse 11, Zehlendorf ☎ (030) 8026671. Map 5E3. Open Sun. and holidays only, May-Sept 10am-1pm ₳ Bus 211 to Clauertstrasse from S-Bahnhof Wannsee.

A stray bomb that fell on the Krummes Fenn in World War II revealed the remains of a lost medieval village. A group of archeologists resolved to reconstruct the 13thC village using replica medieval axes and local wood. On Suns in the summer, the smoke rises from the cluster of wooden huts, as volunteers clad in medieval skins demonstrate primitive techniques of spinning, weaving, pottery and bread-making.

MUSEUMSINSEL ★ 🏛
In Mitte. Map 4B9. S-Bahn to Marx-Engels-Platz.

The Museumsinsel was conceived in 1841 by the romantically-inclined Friedrich Wilhelm IV as an island devoted to the arts and sciences. Occupying the w tip of the Spree island, the "museum island" was designed as a harmonious assembly of five buildings filled with an extraordinary wealth of paintings and antiquities from Hohenzollern and private bequests.

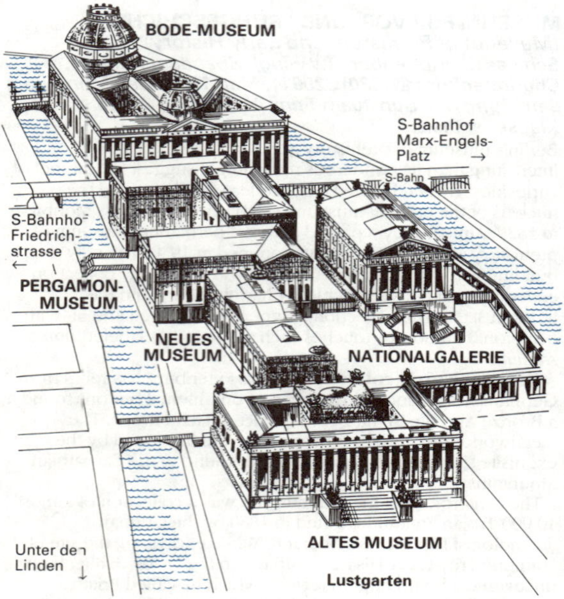

The oldest of the museums is the ALTES MUSEUM, built by Schinkel in 1824-30, long before the idea of a Museumsinsel had taken shape. August Stüler's NEUES MUSEUM rose to the W in 1843-59, in a Neoclassical style that blended with Schinkel's building. The NATIONALGALERIE was added to the N in 1867-76, modeled on a Classical temple. The fourth museum, the Kaiser-Friedrich-Museum (now the BODE-MUSEUM), broke the pattern, with its Neo-Baroque pomp, and gave the Museumsinsel a striking dome at the W tip of the island. The PERGAMON-MUSEUM, begun in 1909, was not completed until 1930, exactly 100yrs after the Altes Museum opened.

Friedrich's Museumsinsel was then complete, but it did not survive intact for long. Many modern paintings in the Nationalgalerie were removed in the 1930s as "decadent," and when war broke out, the principal treasures were shipped to secure hiding places in the Bavarian Alps. Some paintings and sculptures that were too large to move were destroyed during the wartime bombing.

The Museumsinsel was reduced to a melancholy shambles of gutted buildings after 1945, but the East German government began reconstruction almost at once, and by 1949 several rooms of the Nationalgalerie had reopened. The task was enormous, however, and the Neues Museum was still in ruins when the East German government collapsed in 1989. Many of the major works from the Museumsinsel are now in collections at DAHLEM, SCHLOSS CHARLOTTENBURG or the KULTUR-FORUM in West Berlin, but some treasures may eventually be returned to the island site. For the time being, the Pergamon-Museum and the Bode-Museum offer the most interesting collections.

MUSIKINSTRUMENTEN-MUSEUM
Tiergartenstrasse 1, Tiergarten ☎ (030) 254810. Map 3C7. Open Tues-Fri 9am-5pm; Sat, Sun 10am-5pm ♿ 🚇 U-Bahn to Gleisdreieck, then M-Bahn (when running) to Kemperplatz; bus 148 to Philharmonie, or bus 129, 248, 341 to Kultur-Forum.

Situated next to the **Philharmonie**, the museum of musical instruments is an airy, modern building forming part of the controversial KULTUR-FORUM. Designed in 1979-84 by Edgar Wisniewski, the museum owns a collection of rare lutes, clavichords, violins and pianos. Many of the instruments come from Hohenzollern palaces, including two boxed flutes owned by Frederick the Great.

You may find the museum rather lifeless unless you go when there is live music. A gaudy Wurlitzer organ built in 1929 fills the concert hall with lusty tunes (*Sats at noon*). But the best time to go is during one of the occasional performances of chamber music, jazz or folk, held amid the cases of precious instruments.

NATIONALGALERIE ★
Bodestrasse, Mitte ☎ (0372) 20355305. Map 4B8. Open Wed-Sun 10am-6pm ♿ S-Bahn to Friedrichstrasse or Marx-Engels-Platz.

Der Deutschen Kunst (For German Art), declares a ponderous inscription on the pediment of the Nationalgalerie. The stern Neoclassical art gallery was built in 1867-76 on the MUSEUMSINSEL to house a collection of 19thC German art donated by Joachim Wagener, a Berlin merchant. The gallery became rather less Germanic in the early 20thC when it acquired a small number of works by Chagall, Goya, Rodin and Cézanne. But in the 1930s, the Nationalgalerie became fiercely nationalistic once more. Its collection of 20thC German paintings — displayed in the

Neptunsbrunnen

Kronprinzenpalais (now the **Operncafé**) on Unter den Linden — was purged of many works vilified by the Nazis as decadent art.

The Nationalgalerie was rapidly repaired after the war, and reopened in 1949. Although many of its finest works have been destroyed or dispersed, the gallery is still worth visiting, both for its elegant Neoclassical interiors, and its 19th-20thC collection of painting and sculpture.

The lobby contains the attractive 18thC *Prinzessinnengruppe* (The Two Princesses), set in a gilded niche. Modeled on a Classical work, this early stone sculpture by Johann Gottfried Schadow shows Princesses Luise and Friederike, the daughters of Herzogs von Mecklenburg-Strelitz. The drapery is beautifully folded, although the girls' faces are rather idealized. There is a more convincing bust of Friederike elsewhere in the collection. Notice, too, the *Victory* statue by Christian Rauch, blackened from the fires of World War II.

The contented glow of the 19thC Biedermeier period is reflected in the portrait of Wilhelmine Begas by Johann Erdmann Hummel, and the portrait of Marie, wife of Karl von Preussen. Early 20thC paintings are hung in galleries whose dark green walls are decorated with Classical motifs. Von Lenbach's portraits of Richard Wagner and Otto von Bismarck are somewhat stiff and somber, but there are delightful Impressionist portraits including Max Liebermann's *Wilhelm von Bode* (1904), depicting the first director of the Bode-Museum, and Franz Skarbina's *Woman on a Sofa* (1881).

Several paintings by the Austrian Expressionist Oscar Kokoschka reflect the shifting mood of Berlin, from the edgy, jagged *Portrait of Wilhelm Hunt* (1909), to the dark, morbid intensity of *The Hunt* (1918). The vibrant colors and nervous brush-strokes of *Pariser Platz* (1926) capture the surging crowds and roaring vehicles in Berlin at the height of the Weimar years. The view was painted from Kokoschka's bedroom at the fashionable Hotel Adlon, showing the Brandenburger Tor, the Siegessäule (which had not yet been moved to the Grosser Stern), and the dark mass of the Reichstag.

The blue and green interior in Lesser Ury's *Woman at a Writing Desk* (1898) reflects the mood of the late Empire, while *Nollendorfplatz at Night* (1925) shows the incessant movement of the 1920s. Painted from the artist's studio window (a popular vantage point in the 1920s), it shows cars and trams speeding along the rainswept boulevards, while couples stroll beneath the trees. The elevated station at Nollendorfplatz is now used as a flea market. Ury's *Verkehrsturm at the Potsdamer Platz* shows Berlin's busiest square in 1925.

Otto Nagel's *Park Bench in Wedding*, painted in 1927, is a more melancholy Berlin scene illustrating the grim poverty of a Berlin working-class district. The first clashes between Nazis and Communists took place in Wedding in the same year as this painting was executed.

The remainder of the Nationalgalerie collection can currently be tracked down in the ALTES MUSEUM, the FRIEDRICHSWERDERSCHE KIRCHE, the OTTO-NAGEL-HAUS, the NEUE NATIONALGALERIE and the GALERIE DER ROMANTIK.

NEPTUNSBRUNNEN *(Neptune Fountain)*
Rathausstrasse, Mitte. Map 4B9. U-Bahn or S-Bahn to Alexanderplatz.

The Neptune fountain facing the MARIENKIRCHE once stood opposite the now destroyed Stadtschloss. The elaborate structure, built by Reinhold Begas in 1891, is adorned with four female figures representing the Rhine, Elbe, Oder and Weichsel rivers. Water gushes out of vases, and spurts from crocodiles' mouths, making the fountain one of the coolest spots in town.

NEUE NATIONALGALERIE ★ 🏛
Potsdamer Strasse 50, Tiergarten ☎ (030) 2666. Map 3D6 🚇 Open Tues-Fri 9am-5pm; Sat, Sun 10am-5pm ♿ U-Bahn to Kurfürstenstrasse; bus 129, 148, 248, 341 to Kultur-Forum.

Situated on windswept wasteland near the Landwehrkanal, the Neue Nationalgalerie perfectly expresses the spirit of postwar Berlin. With its low, hovering roof and almost black exterior, the art gallery is a beautiful example of modern German architecture (see illustration on page 25).

The steel and glass building was constructed in 1965-68 by Mies van der Rohe, the last director of the Bauhaus, who had fled to the US in 1938. It was the only building he executed in Germany after the war.

The basement level of the art gallery houses a small, permanent collection of modern paintings removed from the NATIONAL-GALERIE on the Museumsinsel during World War II, and returned to West Berlin by the Allies in 1953-57.

The 19thC German works include Arnold Böcklin's dark, romantic *Die Toteninsel* (The Island of the Dead), and tranquil, domestic paintings by Adolph von Menzel such as *Das Balkonzimmer, Das Flötenkonzert* (Frederick the Great playing the flute at Schloss Sanssouci), and the *Palaisgarten des Prinzen Albrecht* (showing the garden of the Prince Albrecht Palace, now reduced to a desolate wasteland next to the MARTIN-GROPIUS-BAU).

The Neue Nationalgalerie has a small but excellent collection of 19thC French art, including Manet's *In the Winter Garden*, Courbet's *Wave* and Monet's vibrant *St Germain l'Auxerrois*.

Much of the Nationalgalerie's prewar collection of 20thC art was disposed of by the Nazis under their barbaric policy of banning allegedly "decadent art," but a few condemned paintings survived, such as Erich Heckel's *Village Dance*, Otto Dix's 1926 portrait of the art dealer Alfred Flechtheim, and Max Beckmann's grim 1938 painting *Tod*.

Temporary exhibitions of painting and sculpture usually occupy most of the gallery space. The museum bookstore has a wide range of art books and postcards, while the crowded basement café serves hearty north German food, including bowls of thick potato soup.

NEUE SYNAGOGE
Oranienburger Strasse 30, Mitte. Map 4B8. S-Bahn to Oranienburger Strasse; U-Bahn to Friedrichstrasse.

The Neue Synagogue is one of the few surviving synagogues in Berlin. Attacked by Nazis on *Kristallnacht* in November 1938 and gutted in an air raid in 1943, the domed building, designed by Eduard Knoblauch and built by Friedrich August Stüler in 1859-66, remained derelict until recently. A center for Jewish Studies (*Zentrum Judaicum*) is scheduled to open here in 1995.

NEUES MUSEUM 🏛
Museumsinsel, Mitte. Map 4B8. S-Bahn to Friedrichstrasse or Marx-Engels-Platz.

The Neues Museum remained a bombed ruin until a few years ago. The Neoclassical building (built by Stüler in 1843-59) is now

Nikolaikirche

slowly being restored and its murals painstakingly retouched, although the future role of the museum remains uncertain.

Commissioned by Friedrich Wilhelm IV as the first phase of his MUSEUMSINSEL plan, the "New Museum" housed a remarkable Egyptian collection in a colossal reconstructed temple.

The works once displayed there are now divided between the BODE-MUSEUM and the ÄGYPTISCHES MUSEUM, although it is possible that the museum's former treasures (including the famous bust of Nefertiti) will one day be returned to the island in the Spree.

NIKOLAIKIRCHE
Nikolaikirchplatz, Mitte ☎ (0372) 21713146. Map 4C9. Open Tues-Fri 9am-5pm; Sat 9am-6pm; Sun 10am-5pm; closed Mon & S-Bahn or U-Bahn to Alexanderplatz.

Founded early in the 13thC, the Nikolaikirche is Berlin's oldest surviving edifice, dedicated to St Nicholas, the patron saint of merchants and children. The church was rebuilt in the 15thC as a Late Gothic hall church with nave and aisles of equal height. Destroyed in World War II, the twin-towered ruin was painstakingly restored, and reopened recently as a branch of the MÄRKISCHES MUSEUM.

The airy, white interior contains several old tombs, including a monument to the Berlin goldsmith Daniel Männlich, which was designed in 1699 by Andreas Schlüter. The exhibits from the Märkisches Museum cover the history of Berlin up to the end of the Thirty Years' War in 1648.

You can hear the *carillon* playing automatically every day (*noon, 3pm and 6pm*), and a *carillonneur* also gives a weekly concert (*Sat 11am*).

NIKOLAIVIERTEL
In Mitte. Map 4C9. S-Bahn or U-Bahn to Alexanderplatz.

A waterfront district of old houses clustered around the NIKOLAIKIRCHE was carefully rebuilt after World War II to provide a whiff of Old Berlin. Some of the houses are exact copies of Berlin buildings destroyed in World War II, such as the *Zum Nussbaum* tavern on Poststrasse, but most were built from prefabricated concrete sections designed to evoke Hanseatic gable houses.

There are new museums in the EPHRAIMPALAIS and the KNOB-LAUCHHAUS, while other houses contain shops, cafés and restaurants. Some may dismiss the entire quarter as kitsch, but it does at least provide an escape from the bleak concrete buildings nearby.

NIKOLSKOE
Nikolskoer Weg, Zehlendorf. Map 5E3 ⇌ Bus 216 from S-Bahnhof Wannsee.

Two curious Russian-looking buildings overlooking the river Havel are souvenirs of the marriage between Charlotte, a daughter of Friedrich Wilhelm III, and the future Czar Nicholas I. The romantic spot in the Düppel woods became generally known by the familiar Russian name of Nikolskoe (property of Nicholas).

A picturesque wooden chalet known as the **Blockhaus Nikolskoe** was built by the Prussian king in 1819, when the couple visited Berlin. Modeled on a log cabin near St Petersburg (Leningrad) where Friedrich Wilhelm had been guest at a feast, the Blockhaus now contains a rustic restaurant (described in WHERE TO EAT on page 105).

Perched on a nearby wooded hill, the **Kirche St Peter und Paul** was built in 1834-37 by Friedrich August Stüler. The building is a scaled-down version of a church in St Petersburg admired by Friedrich Wilhelm during a visit to his daughter Charlotte in 1817.

When Charlotte (Czarina Alexandra) died in 1860, her brother Prince Carl (who lived nearby in SCHLOSS KLEIN-GLIENICKE) erected a memorial pavilion, the *Loggia Alexandra*, on the summit of the Böttcherberg.

OLYMPIA-STADION
Olympischer Platz, Charlottenburg ☎ (030) 3040676. Map 5C3. U-Bahn to Olympia-Stadion.
Familiar from Leni Riefenstahl's heroic propaganda films, the Olympic stadium was built as a Nazi showpiece for the 1936 Berlin Olympics. Modeled on the architecture of Classical Greece, the elliptical arena is an awesome edifice, with massive stone columns and rugged male statues. To Hitler's dismay, the Black American athlete Jesse Owens beat the apparently invincible German runners and won four gold medals at the games.

Rising to the w, the **Glockenturm** (bell tower) (*Am Glockenturm ☎ (030) 3058123, open Apr-Oct, daily 10am-5.30pm* ◆) offers a panoramic view of the Olympic site and the Grunewald. A lane runs through the woods to the **Waldbühne**, an open-air amphitheater built on a sloping site for the Olympics. The amphitheater was restored after its wartime bomb damage, and is now used in the summer for classical concerts and films (see NIGHTLIFE AND THE PERFORMING ARTS on page 111).

OTTO-NAGEL-HAUS
Märkisches Ufer 16-18, Mitte ☎ (0372) 2791402. Map 4C9 ▣ Open Sun-Thurs 10am-6pm (Wed 8pm). U-Bahn to Märkisches Ufer; S-Bahn to Jannowitzbrücke.
Two reconstructed Baroque houses overlooking the Spree now house part of the NATIONALGALERIE collection. Named after the radical Berlin artist Otto Nagel (1894-1967), the museum is currently devoted to Communist artists and photographers from the November Revolution to the present day, including Otto Nagel, John Heartfield, Käthe Kollwitz and Otto Dix. The museum was once an important forum for temporary exhibitions of East European and Soviet art, but this role is likely to change in the future.

The potent Turkish coffee served in the museum café may likewise soon be a thing of the past.

PANORAMA
Budapester Strasse 38, Tiergarten ☎ (030) 2628004. Map 2D5. Screenings daily, on the hour, 11am-10pm ✱ ▣ U-Bahn or S-Bahn to Zoologischer Garten.
A large blue sphere beside the zoo contains a high-tech cinema where a specially-shot 360° film about Berlin is projected onto a dome. The main drawback is that you have to sit on the floor with your head tilted back so as to get the full three-dimensional effect.

Teenagers might perhaps be impressed by the realism of scenes depicting a Nazi parade or an air raid on Berlin, but older movie-lovers might just prefer to see a screening of Fassbinder's *Berlin Alexanderplatz* (see FILM IN BERLIN on page 29) at a conventional movie theater.

Pergamon-Museum

PERGAMON-MUSEUM ★
Am Kupfergraben, Museumsinsel, Mitte ☎ (0372) 203550. Map 4B8. Open Wed-Sun 10am-6pm & S-Bahn to Friedrichstrasse or Marx-Engels-Platz.

Extraordinary architectural relics from ancient civilizations are displayed in the Pergamon-Museum. Opened in 1930, the museum contains four important collections of antiquities, covering Classical Greece and Rome, the Middle East, Islam and the Far East. There is also a small collection covering German folklore.

A vast hall in the **Classical collection** (*Antikensammlung*) is taken up with the **Pergamon Altar**, a colossal monument from the ancient Greek city of Pergamon (now Bergama in Turkey), the capital of the Attalid dynasty. Built in 180-159BC on a hillside above the Aegean Sea, the altar was one of the architectural masterpieces of the Hellenistic Age. Excavated in 1878-86 by the dashing German archeologist Carl Humann, the entire edifice was shipped back to Berlin for reconstruction, which took some 20yrs. Magnificent marble friezes of figures in high-relief decorate the bases, including Hercules being savaged by a lion, Eros entangled with a snake, and Athena clad in a flowing robe. One of the few incomplete figures is Aphrodite, whose head is now in a museum in Istanbul.

An interesting exhibition behind the altar displays old photographs of the ruined altar, showing buffalo being used to transport massive relics from the site. The city of Bergama recently appealed for the return of the altar to the bare hillside where it once stood, but for the time being, this exceptional work of art remains in Berlin.

A room of Roman relics includes the huge **Miletus Market Gate**, strikingly displayed against an azure background. The gate was built in the reign of the Emperor Hadrian at the entrance to one of the markets in Miletus, a prosperous port on the W coast of Asia Minor. A detailed scale model shows the former location of the gate.

The **Vorderasiatisches Museum** (Middle East Museum) contains a remarkable reconstruction of the **Ishtar Gate**, based on fragments excavated in 1899. One of the eight city gates of Babylon, it was built c.580BC by King Nebuchadnezzar. Faced with glazed tiles adorned with enameled bulls and dragons, the gateway leads to a **Processional Way** flanked by high walls of glazed tiles decorated with lions. The ceremonial street originally led from the temple of the god Marduk through the Ishtar Gate to the Akitu House, where the golden image of Marduk was taken in procession every New Year. Nebuchadnezzar's throne room has been diligently reconstructed near the gateway.

Besides manuscripts, Persian carpets and ceramics, the **Islamisches Museum** (Islam Museum) contains the impressive facade of Mschatta, an 8thC castle in the Jordanian desert, SE of Amman, presented by Sultan Abdul Hamid to Kaiser Wilhelm II in 1903. The **Ostasiatische Sammlung** (Far East Collection) was founded by Wilhelm von Bode in 1906 and contains a rich collection of Chinese porcelain.

The **Museum für Volkskunde** (Folklore Museum) has never recovered from the devastation of World War II, when the old museum in Mitte was bombed and most of the collection destroyed. Now rather forgotten in the basement of the Pergamon, the museum valiantly tries to stage interesting temporary exhibitions based on a small selection of its surviving collection of German farmhouse furniture and folk costumes.

PFAUENINSEL ★ 🏛

Wannsee, sw Berlin ☎ (030) 8053042. Map 5E2. Open daily, May-Aug 8am-8pm; Apr, Sept 8am-6pm; Mar, Oct 9am-5pm; Nov-Feb 10am-4pm. Bus 316. S-Bahn to Wannsee, then take boat line 1 to Pfaueninsel, then a 5min ferry crossing.

A ferry plies across the narrow strait to Pfaueninsel (peacock island), a romantic island where the eponymous peacocks strut among mock ruins. Johann Kunckel rowed across here in the 17thC to carry out chemical experiments that led to the invention of ruby glass, but the island remained a wilderness until the late 18thC, when Friedrich Wilhelm II built a fantastic ruined castle there to amuse his mistress, the beautiful Countess Lichtenau (whose portrait hangs in the BERLIN-MUSEUM).

The island became dotted with curiosities built by Friedrich Wilhelm III in the 19thC, including a palm house, which provided 19thC painters with an exotic setting for Oriental fantasies. The glass building burned down in 1880, but most of the other follies have been zealously maintained.

Like many aristocratic parks on the Havel, Pfaueninsel was landscaped in 1822 by Lenné in a romantic English style. A few elderly Berliners still recall that the island provided the setting for a spectacular Nazi party organised by Dr Goebbels during the 1936 Olympics. The island is now a peaceful nature reserve, offering a rare opportunity to wander undisturbed by any noise except the screeching of peacocks. On arrival, look at the map near the pier to plan a route. Allow at least 1hr to walk around the island; follow the signs to the *Fähre* (ferry) if you lose your way.

The **Schloss** (pictured above) at the S end of the island is an eccentric folly constructed in 1794-99 by Johann Brendel for Friedrich Wilhelm II. Brendel was a cabinet-maker by trade, and he used his joinery skills to build a wooden ruined castle. It was expertly painted white with mock joints, so that many people mistake it for a stone edifice. The gateway contains a *trompe l'oeil* landscape to add to the deception. The wooden bridge that once linked the twin round towers was replaced in 1807 by Berlin's first iron bridge.

The Schloss (*open Apr-Sept, Tues-Sun 10am-5pm; Oct 10am-4pm; closed Nov-Mar*) contains rare 19thC furniture and faded murals installed by Friedrich Wilhelm III.

Brendel created another fantasy ruin at the N end of the island. Known as the **Meierei** (dairy farm), the building is adorned with Gothic arches and trefoil windows. Notice the chandelier glinting in a first-floor room. A nearby mock Gothic barn known as the **Rinderstall** (cattle shed) has real geese clucking in the yard.

The portal of the **Luisen-Tempel** standing to the N formed the original facade of Queen Luise's mausoleum at SCHLOSS CHARLOTTENBURG. When Schinkel constructed a more imposing temple front in 1829, the old portal was rebuilt amid the follies on Pfaueninsel.

Schinkel also designed the **Kavalierhaus** (gentleman's house) in the middle of the island in 1824. A six-story Late Gothic house bought in Danzig (Gdansk) by the Crown Prince is carefully

Platz der Akademie

fused into the fabric. King George IV of Britain presented Friedrich Wilhelm III with a miniature frigate for his fantasy island. It was moored in a little boat house known as the **Fregattenschuppen**, near the landing stage.

An 1830 map hanging in the house by the pier reveals that the island once had a zoo. The animals were moved in 1842 to the new ZOOLOGISCHER GARTEN in Charlottenburg, leaving only some exotic birds on Pfaueninsel. To track them down, follow the signs (or the screechings) to the **Vogelhaus**, a netted bird reserve with noisy parrots perched above artificial waterfalls.

PLATZ DER AKADEMIE 🏛
In Mitte, s of Unter den Linden. Map 4C8. U-Bahn to Französische Strasse.
A large square named the Gendarmenmarkt (where King Friedrich I built a guard house for his Gendarmes regiment) was laid out in the 17thC at the heart of the new town of Friedrichstadt. Gradually enhanced with grand Baroque and Neoclassical buildings, the square became one of Berlin's most handsome spots. Severely bombed in the Battle of Berlin, the Platz der Akademie (as it was renamed in 1950) remained in ruins until the 1980s.

Now carefully restored, the square is surrounded by graceful arcades sheltering academic bookstores and cafés.

Two identical churches were built on the square in the first decade of the 18thC. The FRANZÖSISCHER DOM to the N was built for the Huguenots, while the **Deutscher Dom** to the S served the German Lutherans. The two churches were later elevated to cathedral status, and lofty domed towers were added by Karl von Gontard.

A theater, the **Schauspielhaus**, was built between the two churches. Gutted by fire in 1817, it was replaced by an elegant Neoclassical edifice designed by Schinkel. This, in turn, was destroyed in World War II. The East German government carefully rebuilt the fabric, but converted the interior into a large hall for classical concerts and a small room for chamber music.

POSTMUSEUM *(Postal Museum)*
Leipzigerstrasse (on corner of Mauerstrasse), Mitte
☎ *(0372) 2312202. Map 4C8. Open Tues-Sat 10am-6pm*
♿ *(☎ in advance). U-Bahn to Otto-Grotewohl-Strasse.*
Built in 1839 around a vast Neo-Renaissance courtyard, the German postal museum was bombed in World War II, and remained a ruin for several decades. Recently restored, the building contains a nostalgic collection of jaunty antique mail boxes and franking machines.

POTSDAM   See pages 119-135.

POTSDAMER PLATZ
Map 3C7. S-Bahn to Potsdamer Platz.
There is currently almost nothing to see at Potsdamer Platz, yet to Berliners it is one of the most poignant spots in their city. Considered the busiest square in Europe in the 1930s, Potsdamer Platz was reduced by bombing to a bleak tract of wasteland overshadowed by the Berlin Wall. All traces of the concrete wall have now been removed, and the square seems likely to be redeveloped as a giant office complex and shopping center, to the chagrin of some Berliners, who would like Potsdamer Platz to remain wild.

PRENZLAUER BERG
Map 7C7. U-Bahn to Dimitroffstrasse.

The 19thC district of Prenzlauer Berg has scarcely changed since the end of the war and, even now, you can come across derelict breweries, neglected graveyards and crumbling apartment blocks riddled with shell holes. A few streets have been primly restored by the East German authorities, but the most interesting sights in Prenzlauer Berg are the streets that have not been touched for more than half a century.

To explore the district on foot, walk along Dimitroffstrasse from the U-Bahn station of the same name, then turn right into **Husemannstrasse**. While most of Prenzlauer Berg under East German rule was left to rot, Husemannstrasse was given the sort of lavish treatment usually reserved for Neoclassical opera houses. The tree-lined street has, as a result, an odd air of unreality, with its grand 19thC houses, handsome old street lamps and iron pumps. Here, you can stroll along a broad Berlin sidewalk as it used to be, with a wide strip of flagstones flanked by cobblestones.

The **Friseurmuseum** (hairdressers' museum) (*Husemannstrasse 8, open Tues, Wed 10am-noon and 1-5pm*) contains an eccentric assortment of gadgets that once cut and permed chic Berliners' hair. A few doors down (*#10*), there's a real barber's shop that looks as if it has been stocked from the museum collection. Berlin's working-class history is documented at the **Museum Berliner Arbeiterleben um 1900** (*Husemannstrasse 12, open Tues-Thurs, Fri 10am-3pm, Sat 11am-6pm*). You might pause for coffee at the *Kaffeestube* (*#6*), an attractive café formerly the haunt of serious-minded East Berliners.

Husemannstrasse leads into Käthe-Kollwitzplatz, a leafy triangular space with a few cafés where you can eat ice cream or sip a beer. The Berlin artist Käthe Kollwitz (see KÄTHE-KOLLWITZ-MUSEUM) lived in a nearby apartment from 1891 to 1943. A statue of *Die Mutter* (the mother) in the square is based on one of her many drawings of suffering women.

Now turn right down Wörther Strasse and left along Schönhauser Allee. The U-Bahn rattles along an elevated viaduct here, creating a rather dismal atmosphere. On the left, behind an iron gate that is normally locked, you will see a large Jewish cemetery packed with overgrown tombs that have not been tended for several decades. You can pick up the U-Bahn just beyond here at Senefelder Platz.

REICHSTAG
Platz der Republik, Tiergarten ☎ (030) 39770. Map 3B7 ⓺ ⚏ ▣ Open Tues-Sun 10am-5pm. Bus 100, 248 to Reichstag.

Curiously isolated at the E end of the Tiergarten, the Reichstag was built in 1884-94 by Paul Wallot as a parliament for the Second German Empire. Inscribed in 1916 with the bold motto *Dem Deutschen Volke* (For the German People), the Reichstag became a gloomy symbol of failed German democracy after an arsonist gutted the building in 1933. The construction of the Berlin Wall a few feet from the derelict parliament added a further note of foreboding.

Shell holes from the bitter last weeks of fighting in 1945 were carefully patched up with thousands of tiny blocks, which still remain clearly visible, and the echoing, defunct parliament was reconstructed; the reunited German parliament met there for the first time in Oct 1990. A permanent historical exhibition was

Schloss Charlottenburg

opened in 1971 to mark the centenary of the foundation of the Second Empire. Titled *Fragen an die deutsche Geschichte* (Questions on German History), the exhibition chronicles the development of democracy and the rise of fascism in Germany. As well as old documents and historic photographs, there are reconstructed street scenes showing wartime Berlin, when people chalked urgent messages to relatives on the walls of their burned-out homes. Other scenes show Berlin youths protesting in the 1960s.

The Reichstag has a typical Berlin cafeteria — stand eating *Bockwurst* (boiled sausage) and cold potato salad, while perhaps discussing the new political situation with your neighbor. Another café serves coffee and cake in a more elegant setting.

The square in front of the Reichstag was laid out by Schinkel in 1840 as a military parade ground, "to educate the Prussian people to be soldiers and loyal subjects." Hitler had much the same aim in mind when he planned to build a broad avenue across the square, lined with monumental buildings and including the world's largest assembly hall, two railroad stations and a triumphal arch. A new museum of German history designed by Aldo Rossi is scheduled to be built near the Reichstag, for completion by the year 2000.

SCHLOSS CHARLOTTENBURG ★ 🏛

Luisenplatz, Charlottenburg ☎ (030) 320911. Map 1B2. Open Tues-Sun 10am-5pm. Buy a combined ticket (Sammelkarte) to visit all the museums at a reduced rate ➡ (in grounds) 🚇 U-Bahn to Richard-Wagner-Platz or (armed with a good map) U-Bahn to Jungfernheide, then cross the Spree by the footbridge to enter the Schlosspark by the N gate; Bus 109, 121, 145, 204 to Schloss Charlottenburg.

An old stone pillar opposite Schloss Charlottenburg gives its location as *1 Meile von Berlin* (1 mile from Berlin). Originally named Schloss Lietzenburg, the palace was built in the old village of Lietzow to the w of Berlin, as a summer residence for Sophie Charlotte. The spirited wife of Friedrich III, and great-granddaughter of James VI of Scotland, Sophie Charlotte passed her days at Charlottenburg debating with Leibnitz on profound philosophical problems.

The emphasis in 17thC German philosophy on reason and harmony is neatly reflected in the architecture of Johann Nering's compact palace, built in 1695-99. From the palace gates you can see the original Schloss, measuring just 11 bays across. The growth of Prussian power is mirrored in the subsequent extensions to the building. Two wings enclosing the courtyard were begun in 1701, the same year that the Kingdom of Prussia was founded, while Eosander von Goethe later added the lofty cupola and the long **orangery** to the w. The composition was balanced by the **new wing** (*Neuer Flügel*) to the E, built in 1740-46 by Georg Wenzeslaus von Knobelsdorff for Frederick the Great, while a final Rococo flourish was added in 1787-91 by Carl Gotthard Langhans, who conceived the **theater** at the w end of the orangery. Facing the palace, two identical **guard houses** flanking the Schlossstrasse were constructed in 1851-59 by Friedrich August Stüler. The Schloss is illustrated on page 22.

Badly damaged in an air raid in November 1943, Schloss Charlottenburg underwent a massive postwar restoration, to emerge in the 1960s in almost mint condition as a major new museum complex for West Berlin. The GALERIE DER ROMANTIK

Schloss Charlottenburg

currently occupies the ground floor of the new wing, while the MUSEUM FÜR VOR- UND FRÜHGESCHICHTE is established in the Langhans wing to the W. The ÄGYPTISCHES MUSEUM and the ANTIKENMUSEUM are located in the two guard houses, and the BRÖHAN-MUSEUM in a former infantry barracks nearby.

The **equestrian statue** of the Great Elector was moved to the main courtyard in 1950. Designed by the architect Andreas Schlüter and cast in bronze by Johann Jacobi in 1700, the colossal work shows its subject in a heroic pose, with his frock-coat flying in the wind. The statue originally stood on the Lange Brücke (now the Rathausbrücke), but was moved during World War II. The boat on which it was being transported sank in the Tegeler See, and the statue was not recovered until 1950.

The **Neringbau und Eosanderbau** — the original Schloss — can be visited only on a guided tour. Totally reconstructed after World War II, the palace now contains only a few relics of Sophie Charlotte. The main attraction is an 18thC **Porzellanzimmer**, crammed to the ceiling with blue and white Chinese porcelain from various Berlin collections. Concerts of chamber music are held in the intimate wood-paneled **Eichengalerie** (☎ *(030) 3005395*) or the **Schlosskapelle** (☎ *(030) 8173364*).

If the line of people waiting to visit the Neringbau is too daunting, head for the Neuer Flügel to wander through the glittering Rococo rooms designed by Knobelsdorff, on the upper floor (*Obergeschoss*). The **Goldene Galerie** is a 138ft (42m) Rococo ballroom overlooking the garden, with pale green walls encrusted with gilded stucco. A bold decision was taken to replace the Rococo ceiling in the *Weisser Saal* (White Hall), destroyed by fire in 1943, with a modern abstract painting in a vaguely Rococo style. Several smaller rooms contain delightful 18thC Rococo paintings, including works by Watteau from Frederick the Great's collection in SCHLOSS SANSSOUCI. Inspired by an 18thC play, Watteau's shimmering *Embarkation for Cythera* (1720) depicts young women in crisp silk dresses preparing to board a ship that will take them to the temple of love on the Greek island of Cythera. The frothy Rococo works are a far cry from Jacques Louis David's heroic painting of *Napoleon crossing the St Bernard Pass*.

An entire room of Frederick the Great's apartments is taken up with a scale model of the Stadtschloss (city palace). Demolished in 1950, the old Imperial palace occupied the space now known as Marx-Engels-Platz. The detailed model shows the former position of the statue of the Great Elector and the 19thC NEPTUNSBRUNNEN. An adjoining room contains a reconstruction of Kaiser Wilhelm's bedroom in the Stadtschloss.

Laid out in 1701 by Simon Godeau, the **Schlosspark** (*open dawn-dusk*) was the first geometrical Baroque garden in Germany. Sentimental 19thC taste turned it into a rambling English-style park landscaped by Lenné, but the formal garden behind the Schloss has been recently restored to its original design. The clipped hedges and gravel paths soon give way to meandering paths dappled with sunlight, and one leads to a *Spielplatz* where children can play.

Suffused with the warmth of Berlin Neoclassicism, the **Schinkel-Pavillon** (*open Tues-Sun 10am-5pm*) is a peaceful place to retreat from the crowds. Almost no one visits the Italianate villa built by Schinkel in 1825 for King Friedrich Wilhelm III, yet it is one of his most elegant interiors. The delicate pavilion, with its frail iron balconies and *trompe l'oeil* murals, took 10yrs to restore and now houses a superb collection

Schloss Friedrichsfelde

of early 19thC Berlin paintings and porcelain. There are numerous sketches and architectural plans for Schinkel to pore over, including some elaborate theater sets for a production of *The Magic Flute*.

One room with warm red walls contains the Romantic *Panorama of Berlin*, painted by Eduard Gaertner from the roof of the FRIEDRICHSWERDERSCHE KIRCHE in 1834. Gaertner was also enlisted to produce the *Panorama of Moscow*. Yet another panorama, painted from the Kreuzberg summit by Hintze, shows a rural landscape that is now totally buried by apartment blocks and railroad yards. There are also some KPM porcelain vases decorated with Potsdam and Havel landscapes.

Hidden in the trees near the Spree, the three-story **Belvedere** was designed in 1790 by Langhans. Originally a tea-house, the elegant green and white Rococo edifice was reconstructed after World War II to hold a collection of porcelain dinner-services from the palace.

A path lined with yew trees leads to the **Mausoleum**, built after the untimely death of Queen Luise in 1810. The original portico (now among the follies on PFAUENINSEL) was replaced by Schinkel, who executed a design suggested by the bereaved King Friedrich Wilhelm III. The temple contains a melancholy marble monument of the young queen, carved by Christian Rauch in 1811-14.

You will need to spend at least a day at Charlottenburg to visit the main sights. Pause for coffee in the elegant **Café Möhring** (*Luisenplatz*), or at the **Orangerie** in the palace grounds. For a plain German lunch, try **Luisen-Bräu** (see page 110).

SCHLOSS FRIEDRICHSFELDE
Am Tierpark 125, Friedrichsfelde ☎ (0372) 5100111. Map 7D7 ✗ June-Sept, Tues-Sun 11am, 1pm, 3pm; Oct-May Tues-Fri 3pm, Sat, Sun 11am, 1pm, 3pm. U-Bahn to Tierpark.

A 17thC country house built for a naval officer in Dutch Baroque style now stands in the grounds of TIERPARK FRIEDRICHSFELDE. Restored in 1981, the Schloss has 16 Neoclassical rooms furnished with tapestries and paintings, and provides a rare opportunity to glimpse the interior of a Prussian country retreat.

SCHLOSS KLEIN-GLIENICKE ★ 🏛
To the N of Königstrasse, Zehlendorf ☎ (030) 8053041. Map 5E1. Park open daily, dawn-dusk ≡ S-Bahn to Wannsee, then bus 116 to Glienicker Brücke, or Line 1 boat to Glienicker Brücke.

Set in a rolling landscape on the shores of the Jungfernsee, Schloss Klein-Glienicke is one of the most pleasant spots in Berlin to spend a summer day. Overlooking the old Berlin to Potsdam road, the country house is close to another Hohenzollern retreat, the JAGDSCHLOSS KLEIN-GLIENICKE.

An old villa on the site was bought in 1824 by Prince Carl von Preussen, the brother of the future Kaiser Wilhelm I. Infatuated with Italy, Prince Carl commissioned his friend Schinkel to rebuild **Schloss Klein-Glienicke** in the style of an Italian villa. The former coach house (*Remise*) has been converted into a restaurant with a large terrace (*open Tues-Sun 10am-6pm*). Schinkel also designed the Italianate **Casino** which commands a sweeping view of the reed-fringed lake. Flanked by pergolas, the ocher building is decorated with *trompe l'oeil* frescos evoking Pompeian art.

The park is dotted with elegant little buildings modeled on Classical architecture. The **Kleine Neugierde** (Little Curiosity) was built in 1825 as a tea-house standing beside the Potsdam road. Facing the Glienicker Brücke, Schinkel's **Grosse Neugierde** (Large Curiosity) is an eye-catching rotunda surmounted by a tall lantern modeled on an Athenian monument. The view from the platform takes in the Glienicker Brücke and Schloss Babelsberg (see POTSDAM on page 129). Until recently, the prospect was marred by the blazing floodlights and tall observation towers along the nearby Berlin Wall, but almost all traces of the frontier have now been efficiently removed.

Other Italianate buildings are clustered around the main entrance on Königstrasse. When it rains, you can take shelter in the **Stibadium**, a semicircular Neoclassical pavilion designed by Ludwig Persius in 1840. The **fountain** nearby was designed by Schinkel. Flanked by two gilded lions on pedestals, it is modeled on a fountain at the Villa Medici in Rome.

During his tour of Italy, Prince Carl amassed a considerable collection of Classical spoils. Capitals, torsos, mosaics, doorways and gravestones were incorporated into the walls of several buildings, to form a curious open-air museum of antiquities. An unexpected heap of broken Classical columns in the park is intended to suggest a ruined temple, but the most eccentric building is the **Klosterhof**, designed by Ferdinand von Arnim in 1850. Hidden in a clump of trees near the Casino, it was constructed using architectural fragments from northern Italian churches. The cloister came from a Carthusian monastery on an island near Venice, the lion on a pillar is Venetian, while the strange capital decorated with a chained ape once adorned the campanile at Pisa.

The Italian architecture is set in a romantic English park with spreading chestnut trees and rolling lawns. Laid out by Peter Lenné, the head gardener at Sanssouci, the park even has an area marked on maps in English as the "Pleasure Ground." Wandering through the woods to the E, you may stumble upon other buildings, including the *Machinenhaus* (pump house) and the *Matrosenhaus* (boatmen's house), common features of 19thC Potsdam summer residences.

Take the Uferweg along the Havel shore (following the little white stone signs to Moorlake) to reach the **Teufelsbrücke** (Devil's Bridge). Spanning a deep ravine, the bridge was built in 1838 in the form of a ruin. The effect was so convincing that the city authorities took it for a real ruin and rebuilt it entirely, much to the dismay of local folly-lovers.

Continue past the **Jägertor**, a gate built by Schinkel in English Gothic style, and follow the path down to **Moorlake**. The **Wirtshaus Moorlake** (*Pfaueninselchaussee 2* ☎ *(030) 8052509, closed Tues*) is an attractive inn occupying Prince Carl's 19thC hunting lodge. A beguiling *Biergarten* overlooks the Havel. A pleasant stroll along the shore brings you soon to NIKOLSKOE and PFAUENINSEL.

SCHLOSS KÖPENICK
See KUNSTGEWERBEMUSEUM SCHLOSS KÖPENICK.

SCHLOSS TEGEL
Adelheidallee 19-20, Reinickendorf ☎ *(030) 4343156. Map 5B3. U-Bahn to Tegel, then a 5min walk.*

Deep in the woods NW of Berlin, the Neoclassical Schloss Tegel was built in 1820-24 by Schinkel for Wilhelm von Humboldt, the

SIEGESSÄULE
Grosser Stern, Tiergarten ☎ (030) 3912961. Map 2C5. Open Apr-mid Oct Wed-Mon 9am-5.45pm, Tues 3-6pm 🚌 Bus 100, 106, 341 to Grosser Stern.

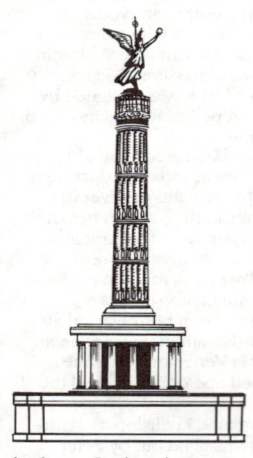

The Siegessäule (Victory Column) was originally erected on the square in front of the Reichstag in 1873 to commemorate a series of German victories over Denmark, Austria, and France. Designed by Heinrich Strade, the 220ft (67m) column surmounted by a gilded angel was decorated with reliefs showing scenes from the three wars.

The pompous column became a hated symbol of Prussian militarism after World War I, and in 1921 a group of local anarchists almost succeeded in blowing it up. The column stood in the way of Hitler's monumental avenue through the Tiergarten, and in 1939 it was rebuilt on the Grosser Stern — a broad traffic circle in the middle of the Tiergarten — where it now looks perfectly at home. Some 285 steps inside the column lead up to a cramped viewing platform with a dizzying view of the five avenues radiating through the Tiergarten.

SKULPTURENGALERIE
Arnimallee 23-27, Dahlem ☎ (030) 83011. Map 6E4. Open Tues-Fri 9am-5pm; Sat, Sun 10am-5pm ♿ 🚇 U-Bahn to Dahlem-Dorf.

The modern sculpture gallery at the Dahlem museum complex contains works from the former gallery of Christian art on the MUSEUMSINSEL. The collection was created in 1883 by Wilhelm von Bode, who fused Early Christian and Byzantine sculpture with German and Italian works. Some of the works were destroyed or stolen in World War II, while others (including statues charred in the firestorms of 1944-45) are now in the BODE-MUSEUM. But many of the finest works were shipped from the city during the war, and later returned to the Allied sector. The works are currently displayed in a museum built at Dahlem in 1966.

The **Early Christian and Byzantine Collection** is smaller than the corresponding department at the Bode-Museum, although it has some interesting Roman altars and Byzantine mosaics. The collection of **Medieval German Sculpture** contains melancholy oak statues of pious women. The exquisite Late Gothic craftsmanship of Tilman Riemenschneider is shown in the *Four Evangelists*, carved for a church altar in 1491.

The **Renaissance Collection** has two giant wooden figures from a church in the Bavarian town of Wasserburg. Carved by Martin Züm, they represent St Sebastian (invoked against plague) and St Florian (a protector against fire). The sculptures date from the Thirty Years' War (1618-48), when fire and plague were constant perils. The rather sad face of St Florian is apparently a likeness of Kaiser Ferdinand III, while the figure of St Sebastian was modeled on Elector Maximilian of Bavaria.

The **Italian rooms** contain some exceptional Renaissance busts, such as Desiderio da Settignano's 15thC bust of Marietta Strozzi, a Florentine girl. Notice also Francesco Laurana's impressive bust of Ferdinand II of Aragon, which stands on a Florentine pedestal carved at roughly the same time, imitating a display technique pioneered by Wilhelm von Bode.

The **Neoclassical collection** is dominated by Antonio Canova's overscaled *Dancer with Cymbals*, carved in 1809-12 for a Russian diplomat living in Vienna.

SPANDAU

w edge of Berlin. Map 5C2. U-Bahn to Altstadt-Spandau.

Situated at the confluence of the Spree and the Havel, the old town of Spandau was founded in 1232. Commanding an important river crossing, Spandau grew into a strategic military town. The imposing 16thC ZITADELLE SPANDAU still stands to the E of the old quarter. Although Spandau lost its independence when Greater Berlin was created in the 1920s, the district still retains something of the atmosphere of a small Prussian town.

Devastated in World War II both by Allied bombers and Russian tanks, the old streets of Spandau have been lovingly reconstructed with a mixture of old and new buildings painted in pastel tones. An attractive quarter surrounds the squat 15thC **St Nikolai-Kirche** (*off Carl-Schurz-Strasse*), dedicated to the popular 4thC St Nicholas of Myra, patron saint of merchants and children. The cobbled Ritterstrasse to the W contains old half-timbered houses and handsome Baroque buildings. Kinkelstrasse — known as the Judenstrasse (Jews' Street) until the Nazis renamed it in 1938 — leads N to the busy street Am Juliusturm. Cross the road to reach the pleasant old quarter around the Schleuse Spandau, a lock on the Havel river.

Spandau district includes a vast area of open fields and rustic summer houses to the S. Not widely known, the **Rieselfelder** is a quiet area of farmland crossed by straight footpaths (*bus 134 from Rathaus Spandau*).

Look out for information on the Spandauer Sommerfestspiele (*May-Sept*), a summer festival with classical and jazz concerts in an open-air theater at the citadel.

THE SPREE

Rising in the forests to the SE, the Spree meanders through Berlin from Köpenick to Spandau, where it enters the Havel under the shadow of Spandau's citadel. Gravel barges still occasionally negotiate the lock opposite the Märkisches Museum, but the main river traffic now consists of tour boats and motor cruisers.

Just beyond the lock, the river splits into the Spree and the Kupfergraben, forming the long island on which the 13thC settlement of Cölln grew up. The Spreeinsel (Spree Island) became the site of the DOM, MUSEUMSINSEL and the now destroyed royal palace.

There are attractive stretches of the river to the E of Köpenick, N of the Tiergarten and behind SCHLOSS CHARLOTTENBURG park. A series of elegant iron and stone bridges span the river in the Tiergarten and Mitte districts. See *Walk 1* on page 34 for a fuller description and for directions for a half-day stroll along its banks.

Tegel

TEGEL
In Reinickendorf, NW Berlin. Map 6B4 ✱ *U-Bahn to Tegel.*

Overlooking a sweeping bay at the N end of the Tegeler See, Tegel is one of Berlin's most attractive districts. Alt-Tegel is an attractive street with 19thC houses, cafés and restaurants, running from the U-Bahnhof to the waterfront. The old harbor to the N of Alt-Tegel is overlooked by elegant Post-Modern apartments built in the 1980s as part of the IBA plan to revitalize Berlin.

Alt-Tegel leads down to the **Greenwichpromenade**, an attractive lakeside promenade where steamers depart for Spandau and the Havel resorts. The meandering paths are lined with British red telephone booths and Victorian pillar (mail) boxes to evoke the jaunty atmosphere of an English seaside resort. A café even organises genteel Sunday tea-dances for elderly Berliners.

To the S of the old quarter are the giant Borsig engineering works, where steam locomotives were once built. Berlin's first skyscraper, constructed here in 1922-24, still dominates the neighborhood. The 11-floor edifice has a curious top tier that combines jagged German Expressionism with Gothic tracery.

The nearby **Russischer Friedhof** (*Wittestrasse 37, U-Bahn to Holzhauser Strasse*) is a cemetery with a richly carved wooden gatehouse leading to a 19thC Russian church with onion domes. The Russian composer Mikhail Glinka was buried here in 1857. The roaring autobahn traffic next to the wistful graves of Russian émigrés seems to sum up modern Berlin.

An idyllic wooded walk follows the shore of the Malchsee, an inlet N of the Greenwichpromenade reached by a handsome red iron bridge. Pause to admire the view from the promontory at the S end of the bay, then continue to the **Freizeitpark**, where children can romp in a big adventure playground while their parents fry *Bratwürste* on the park's open-air barbecues. A little wooden cabin signposted **Fahrrad und Spieleverleih** rents bikes and seats for children, footballs, croquet sets, giant chessmen, skipping ropes and a host of other toys. Energetic parents can rent rowboats at the **Tretbootverleih** (*open summer, daily 10am-7pm*).

Serious ramblers can strike off into the forest along the Mühlenweg, while swimmers should continue along the waterfront to the **Strandbad Tegel**, a quiet beach with old-fashioned wickerwork beach chairs (*Strandkörbe*) like those on the windy Baltic coast. The path ends at the **Tegelort-Seeterrassen** landing stage, where you can pick up a steamer to Tegel or Spandau. To pick up bus 222 back to Tegel, continue to the terminus at Tegelort.

Established in about 1724, **Alter Fritz** (*Karolienstrasse 12*) is Berlin's oldest surviving inn. Situated just N of Tegel, it was visited by Goethe and Frederick the Great. The restaurant serves traditional Berlin food, and there is a pleasant beer garden for idle summer days.

TIERGARTEN
Map 2C4 ✱ 🚇 *S-Bahn to Tiergarten or U-Bahn to Hansaplatz.*

"The real heart of Berlin is a small, damp black wood — the Tiergarten," ruminated Christopher Isherwood in 1932. Extending from the BRANDENBURGER TOR to the ZOOLOGISCHER GARTEN, the Tiergarten was originally a private hunting estate for Elector Friedrich III, situated outside the city walls.

Overlooking the river Spree, **Schloss Bellevue** was built in the

Tierpark Friedrichsfelde

18thC on the N edge of the Tiergarten. The Baroque palace is now the official Berlin residence of the German president.

In 1838, the Tiergarten became Berlin's first public park, with rambling paths and ponds laid out in romantic English style by the landscape gardener Peter Lenné. The park lost some of its quiet seclusion in 1936 when the Charlottenburger Chaussee (renamed the Strasse des 17. Juni to commemorate the 1953 East Berlin workers' uprising) was widened to provide a fast road from Mitte to the prosperous western suburbs. Another road-building scheme commissioned by Hitler in 1939 cut through the Tiergarten from N to S near the Reichstag.

The park was destroyed during the fighting at the end of World War II, and the elegant quarter of diplomatic residences on the Tiergartenstrasse to the S was left totally gutted. The former Japanese embassy now houses the **Japanisch-Deutsches Zentrum** (*Tiergartenstrasse 24-27*), which promotes cooperation between Japan and Germany. Several foreign governments are now toying with the idea of rebuilding their embassies at their prewar locations.

The few trees that remained after the fierce fighting were felled to provide fuel during the harsh winter of 1946, and the land was then used to grow potatoes. About one million trees were later replanted and many of the 19thC statues were restored, so that now you are hardly aware of the damage, except for the blackened statues around the Grossfürstenplatz, on the N edge of the park near the Kongresshalle.

Massive stone blocks from Hitler's Imperial Chancellery were used to build the **Sowjetisches Ehrenmal** (Soviet war memorial), at the point where the two main axes meet. The American-funded KONGRESSHALLE was built in the park, while the British contributed the **Englischer Garten**, to be found behind the statue of Bismarck at the SIEGESSÄULE.

The Tiergarten is a pleasant place to while away a sunny afternoon. You will find rhododendron (rosebay) beds S of the Grosser Stern, several children's playgrounds, and cafés hidden in the trees. Rowboats can be rented at the Neuer See. Remember to keep off the grass except at areas designated *Liegewiese*.

The park is dotted with picturesque 19thC statues representing mythological scenes as well as eminent Germans. The statues of Bismarck and Von Moltke, now on the Grosser Stern, were moved from the Platz der Republik in front of the Reichstag in 1939. The figures of Friedrich Wilhelm II, Queen Luise and Prinz Wilhelm are grouped together around an island to the S, while Goethe and Lessing lurk in the trees near the former site of the Berlin Wall.

TIERPARK FRIEDRICHSFELDE *(Zoo)*
Am Tierpark 125, Friedrichsfelde ☎ (0372) 5100111. Open daily 9am-dusk. Map 7D7 ▉ ✱ U-Bahn to Tierpark.

Founded in 1954 as East Berlin's answer to the ZOOLOGISCHER GARTEN, Friedrichsfelde zoo has rapidly built up a remarkable collection of 900 different species of animals. Rare antelopes, llamas and buffaloes roam contentedly in spacious enclosures, while special glass windows allow observation of the polar bears swimming at close quarters. There is a playground where children can imitate the antics of the monkeys, and two cafés with the added interest of tropical fish in tanks.

The zoo stands within an old country estate, landscaped in 1695 in the formal style of Dutch gardens then in vogue. The grounds to the N were later transformed by Peter Lenné into a

Topographie des Terrors

romantic 19thC English garden landscape. A spacious café terrace overlooks the formal Dutch gardens where deer graze and water fowl splash in the canals. The Baroque SCHLOSS FRIEDRICHSFELDE houses a small museum showing the Prussian country lifestyle.

TOPOGRAPHIE DES TERRORS
Stresemannstrasse 110, Kreuzberg ☎ (030) 25486703. Map 3D7. Open Tues-Sun 10am-6pm. U-Bahn to Kochstrasse; S-Bahn to Anhalter Bahnhof.

A bleak tract of wasteland known as the Prinz-Albrecht-Gelände marks the site of the Gestapo headquarters and other Nazi institutions. The old buildings were eventually razed to the ground, and the area remained a rubble-strewn wasteland for years. Recent excavations near the MARTIN-GROPIUS-BAU uncovered the cellars of the former School of Applied Arts, where the Gestapo tortured thousands of victims. A shed constructed on top of the cellars contains a moving exhibition of photographs and documents illustrating the Nazi terror and the destruction of the government quarter of Berlin.

Wooden steps lead to the top of a hillock constructed from the rubble of the art school. From here you can look across the eerie inner city wasteland where rabbits still run wild.

TREPTOWER PARK
Treptow. Map 7D6. S-Bahn to Treptower Park.

Laid out on the s bank of the Spree, Treptow's public park was landscaped in romantic English style in 1876. The park is now dominated by the **Sowjetisches Ehrenmal**, a colossal war memorial built to commemorate some 5,000 Russian soldiers who died fighting in the streets of Berlin at the end of World War II. Monumental gates and windswept flights of steps lead to a heroic 42ft-high (13m) statue of a Russian soldier rescuing a German child.

UNTER DEN LINDEN ★
Mitte. Maps 3-4C7-B8. U-Bahn to Französische Strasse; S-Bahn to Unter den Linden.

Berlin's famous avenue lined with linden or lime trees was a 17thC creation of the Great Elector to link the royal palace with the forests to the w (now the Tiergarten). The street was enhanced in the 18thC by Frederick the Great, who commissioned the Forum Fridericianum (now known as Bebelplatz), a square in the style of a Roman forum with the Staatsoper as the centerpiece. The w end of the street (between Friedrichstrasse and the BRANDENBURGER TOR) became the glittering hub of Imperial Germany at the end of the 19thC, and fashionable Berliners flocked to the famous Café Kranzler and the Hotel Adlon.

Unter den Linden lost its allure after World War II, when the East German government tore down anything that smacked of the Second or Third Reich, and put up bland modern office buildings in their place. The stretch to the w of Friedrichstrasse, once lined with ponderous Wilhelmine-style buildings, was wrecked by the Socialist planners, but many of the older Neoclassical and Baroque buildings E of Friedrichstrasse were judiciously rebuilt to their old splendor. Although Unter den Linden has lost its former allure, it is still a handsome and harmonious avenue, thanks to the East Germans' resolve to maintain the 19thC scale. Now that the old regime has shuffled off, the mile-long street is poised to become perhaps the most

Unter den Linden

elegant thoroughfare in Germany's capital.

It is no longer possible to stroll down the middle of the street, as rich Berliners did in the 19thC, but you can still wander along the broad sidewalks under the lime trees, which flower in early summer. Beginning at Friedrichstrasse (King Friedrich Wilhelm I's military road to the Tempelhofer Feld parade ground), head away from the Brandenburger Tor, keeping to the s side of the street. The curvaceous **Alte Königliche Bibliothek** (royal library), built in 1775, was modeled on the Hofburg in Vienna. But the voluptuous Baroque style did not impress Berliners, who dubbed it the *Kommode* (chest of drawers).

The library stands at the w end of Frederick the Great's Roman forum (formerly the Opernplatz, renamed Bebelplatz in honor of an East German socialist leader). The Enlightenment ideals symbolized by the square were brutally crushed when a gang of Nazi students gathered there in 1933 to set fire to a stack of books from the university library.

The elegant Neoclassical **Staatsoper** (State Opera House) stands in the middle of the square. Built by Knobelsdorff in 1742 for Frederick the Great, it burned down in 1843 but was rebuilt in its original style. It was hit by a bomb in 1941 and rebuilt immediately, only to be destroyed again in 1945. The East Germans carefully rebuilt it again, to provide East Berlin with a far more dazzling opera house than West Berlin could hope for.

The Catholic **St Hedwigs-Kathedrale** stands in the corner of the square. Modeled on the Pantheon in Rome, it was built in 1747, probably by Knobelsdorff, who perhaps followed sketches by Frederick the Great. The E side of the square is occupied by the **Prinzessinnenpalais** (Palace of the Princesses), now the Operncafé, and the **Palais Unter den Linden**, built by Langhans for the future Kaiser Wilhelm I.

Walk to the end of Unter den Linden and cross the Spree by the Marx-Engels-Brücke. Formerly the Schlossbrücke, it was built by Schinkel in 1822-24. The bridge leads to the windswept Marx-Engels-Platz, which marks the site of the Stadtschloss, the city palace of the Electors of Brandenburg. Rebuilt in Baroque style by Andreas Schlüter, the palace was devastated by bombs in World War II.

In 1950, the East Berlin mayor Walter Ulbricht ordered the palace to be demolished on the grounds that it symbolized Imperial Germany. All that now survives are some Baroque sculptures in the BODE-MUSEUM, and the palace balcony (where Karl Liebknecht proclaimed the German revolution in 1918), which has been piously incorporated into the facade of the **Staatsrat** (Council of State) building on the E side of the square. The modern building on the N side, the **Palast der Republik**, was once the seat of the East German parliament.

Cross the road and turn along the N side of Unter den Linden, past the MUSEUM FÜR DEUTSCHE GESCHICHTE, situated in the former arsenal. You come to the **Neue Wache**, a compact Neoclassical temple designed by Schinkel in 1816-18. Formerly a guard house, it was rebuilt after World War II as the *Mahnmal für die Opfer des Faschismus und Militarismus*, a memorial to the victims of fascism and militarism. Schinkel also designed the nearby **Maxim Gorki Theater**, originally a concert hall called the Sing Akademie, where performances were given by Brahms, Liszt and Paganini.

The dusty buildings of the **Humboldt-Universität** are farther along the avenue, located in the **Palais des Prinzen Heinrich**, a palace built in 1748 for Prince Heinrich, brother of Frederick the Great. The diplomat Wilhelm von Humboldt founded a school here in 1809 which later became Berlin University. Hegel and Einstein taught at the university, and Communist leaders such as Marx, Engels and Liebknecht were students there. Renamed after its founder in 1946, the Humboldt University lost its academic edge in 1948 when many disillusioned teachers left to found the Free University in Dahlem.

The nearby **Deutsche Staatsbibliothek** (National Library of Germany) was built in Neo-Baroque style by Ernst von Ihne in 1903-14. There are a few benches in the secluded courtyard, offering a moment's rest.

VIKTORIAPARK
Kreuzbergstrasse, Kreuzberg. Map 3E7-F7 ◊€ ▰ U-Bahn to Möckernbrücke.

The Viktoriapark is a romantic, landscaped park with ponds, a children's playground and a small zoo, but its most alluring feature is an artificial waterfall constructed on the N slope. Some 13,000 liters (2,860 gallons) of water tumble down the rocky clefts every minute, presenting an unusual sight as you approach the park along Grossbeerenstrasse.

The park was created in 1888-94 on the slopes of the Kreuzberg (Cross Hill), a natural hill named after a Neo-Gothic war memorial on the summit. Designed by Schinkel in 1818-21 to commemorate the Wars of Liberation, the memorial stands on a base modeled on the Iron Cross, a German military decoration first awarded during the Napoleonic Wars.

The park is a romantic place in which to wander, but you must, of course, remember as you toil up the steep paths, that here, as in all German parks, *bei Schnee und Glätte auf eigene Gefahr!* (use in snow and ice at own risk). If you reach the summit unscathed, you can enjoy the typical Berlin skyline of church spires mingled with chimneys. You'll find a beer garden named **Golgotha** on the S slope of the hill.

VOLKSPARK FRIEDRICHSHAIN
Am Friedrichshain. Map 7C6. Strassenbahn (tram) 24 or 28.

An attractive public park with a rose garden and a lake graces the former East Berlin district of Friedrichshain. The grand Neo-Baroque fountain near the main entrance was built in 1913. Known as the **Märchenbrunnen** (Fable Fountain), it is surrounded by statues of characters from traditional German fairy tales. The two artificial hills in the park reflect a darker side of German history; they were created from the rubble of flak bunkers destroyed after World War II.

WANNSEE
Zehlendorf. Map 5E2 ✱ S-Bahn to Nikolassee or Wannsee.

An inlet of the Havel river, the Wannsee became a fashionable resort in the 19thC, after Carl Conrad, a government official, built a villa here. Wealthy Berliners, including the artist Max Liebermann, built summer residences on the W side of the sea, while in recent years, yacht harbors have been squeezed into every available inlet.

The waterfront near Wannsee S-Bahn station is constantly bustling with cruise boats, including an old steamship, a Mississippi paddle steamer called the *Havel Queen*, and a bizarre vessel built to resemble a large black whale. Boats regularly sail from here to SPANDAU, SCHLOSS KLEIN-GLIENICKE, POTSDAM and PFAUENINSEL.

Zitadelle Spandau

For details of the various boat tour operators, see USEFUL ADDRESSES on page 15.

Berliners also flock to the Wannsee to bask on the longest inland beach in Europe, the **Strandbad Wannsee**, which stretches along the E shore of the lake (*bus 513 runs from S-Bahnhof Nikolassee to the beach on sunny days*).

To the N lies a tiny, wooded peninsula called the **Schwanenwerder** (Swan Island), dotted with elegant villas, including one (*Inselstrasse 10*) that was once owned by the Nazi propaganda chief Dr Goebbels. It was during a dinner party here in 1942 that prominent Nazis plotted the so-called "Final Solution," aimed at the total extermination of the Jews. The villa in the woods is now being turned into a permanent museum of the Holocaust.

A string of narrow lakes runs S from the Wannsee to enter the Havel at the Glienicker Brücke. A silent wooded park on the shore of the Kleiner Wannsee contains the **Kleistgrab** (follow the wooden sign on Bismarckstrasse marked *Zum Kleistgrab*). The grave marks the spot where the dramatist Heinrich von Kleist shot himself in 1811. "Now, Immortality, you are entirely mine," proclaims the inscription.

The Griebnitzsee used to be forbidden territory between East and West Berlin, but cruise boats now ply regularly between Wannsee and the Glienicker Brücke.

ZEUGHAUS   See MUSEUM FÜR DEUTSCHE GESCHICHTE

ZILLE-MUSEUM
At U-Bahnhof Nollendorfplatz, Schöneberg ☎ (030) 2167546. Map 2D5-6. Open Wed-Mon 11am-7pm. Closed Tues. U-Bahn to Nollendorfplatz.

A reconstructed apothecary's shop in the BERLINER FLOHMARKT provides an appropriately eccentric setting for a collection of etchings, drawings and paintings by Heinrich Zille (1858-1929). The cluttered interior is full of humorous, compassionate portraits of impoverished Berliners at the turn of the century.

Zille's fame rests on works such as *Zur Mutter Erde* (To Mother Earth), with its brawny Berlin matrons, drunken husbands and grubby children (including one dragging along a dead mouse on a string). When swimming became fashionable in 1907, Zille immediately captured the ridiculous appearance of plump Berlin women in bathing costumes. He continued to delight Berliners during World War I with strip cartoon tales of Vadding, a soldier in the trenches.

ZITADELLE SPANDAU
Am Juliusturm, Spandau ☎ (030) 3391297. Map 5C3. Open Tues-Fri 9am-5pm; Sat, Sun 10am-5pm ◂€ ᴸ (☎ in advance) ⇒ U-Bahn to Zitadelle, then a 5min walk.

A giant reproduction of Cranach's painting of Joachim II greets you upon arrival at Zitadelle U-Bahnhof, a modern subway station near Zitadelle Spandau built in the style of the old fortress, with handsome red brick pillars and doors painted with black and white diagonal lines. It is rather useful to study the enlarged 16thC Renaissance plans and maps in the station before visiting the citadel.

Standing at the confluence of the Spree and Havel rivers, Spandau citadel was built in the 14thC on an important trade route from Western Europe to Poland. The fortress was rebuilt in 1560-83 in a mighty Renaissance style, with acute-angled bastions projecting into the moat like arrow heads. The building was

Zoologischer Garten

completed by the military architect Graf Rochus von Lynar, whose bust glowers down at you from the U-Bahn entrance.

A small museum with scale models, paintings, tin soldiers and old guns occupies the restored **Torhaus** (gatehouse). A passage leads from there to the **Juliusturm**, a round brick tower dating from the 14thC. A sturdy wooden stair winds up to the battlements, which once offered a sweeping view of the medieval river and land routes. The prospect now takes in Spandau old town, the Grunewald and clusters of industrial chimneys.

A few old cannon are left in the citadel courtyard, along with a 19thC statue of a rather demonic-looking Albrecht the Bear of the House of Askanier, who drove the Slavs out of Brandenburg in the 12thC. The statue, and others now in the LAPIDARIUM, stood on the Siegesallee in the Tiergarten until World War II.

A restaurant within the fortress walls has a heavy medieval atmosphere, with food to match. After visiting the citadel, you can stroll into a rambling nature reserve created on a neck of land that is overgrown with wild flowers.

ZOOLOGISCHER GARTEN ★
Entrances at Hardenbergplatz or Budapester Strasse 26, Tiergarten ☎ (030) 254010. Map 2D4 ✱ ▣ Open daily 9am-6.30pm. U-Bahn or S-Bahn to Zoologischer Garten.

Berlin boasts one of the world's biggest and best-kept zoos, situated next to the main railroad station in the very heart of the metropolis. Its animal population increases every year, and at the last count there were 14,600 animals, representing 1,700 different species.

The zoo has been expertly designed to create habitats that are remarkably close to the natural environment. Monkeys perform wild acrobatics on the **Affen Insel** (monkey island), which is surrounded by water to prevent escapes, while the biggest collection of crocodiles in Europe bask in the sultry heat of the **reptile house**.

You can eavesdrop on the nocturnal activities of bats, owls and other creatures of the night in the eerie **Nachttierhaus**, which is artificially darkened by day and lit by night. Rare antelopes roam in unfenced enclosures near the Landwehrkanal, while beautiful Przewalski's horses from the Russian steppes are among the animals inhabiting an enclave on the other side of the canal. Finally, children can pet donkeys, sheep and chickens at the **Tierkinderzoo**.

The Zoologischer Garten dates back to 1841, when King Friedrich Wilhelm IV presented the city with his menagerie of beasts from Pfaueninsel to form Germany's first zoo. Built on the site of the royal pheasantry on the edge of the Tiergarten, the zoo was beautifully landscaped by Lenné with lakes and winding paths, and stocked with an impressive variety of rare species.

The zoo animals suffered alongside the Berliners during World War II. Martin Middlebrook's *The Berlin Raids* recounts a young Berlin woman's sadness on visiting the zoo after a devastating air raid in November 1943. "A terrible smell lingered above the total destruction of my beloved zoo. There were blasted and dead animals everywhere. The only living thing, in his big pond, was a big bull hippopotamus called Knautschke, still swimming while above him his shelter burned down."

The famous Knautschke was one of only 91 animals to survive the war, from a collection that numbered 4,000 mammals and birds and 8,000 fish.

HOTELS

Where to stay

Few Old Berlin hotels survived World War II, and most visitors will now find themselves staying in low-rise modern hotels in the Charlottenburg district. Some, such as the **Kempinski**, have tried to re-create an Old Berlin atmosphere, but many are simply functional. A welcome hint of the Post-Modern style has recently crept into the design of hotels such as the **Curator** and **Sorat**, and recently built hotels in Tegel and other Berlin districts offer visitors a greater choice as to location.

The reunification of Berlin means that visitors can now stay in hotels in Mitte and Potsdam, although standards of service and comfort are still sometimes disappointing, while prices have rapidly risen to Charlottenburg levels.

Although it may appeal to some travelers to stay on Unter den Linden or Alexanderplatz, others may prefer to wait until the dilapidated telephone system has been improved and the restaurants are rather less bleak.

In the following selection, addresses, telephone and public transportation details are given. Symbols show price categories, charge/credit cards and other noteworthy points. See page 5 for the full list of symbols.

It hardly needs saying that Berlin has boomed as a tourist and business destination since 1989, and it is now often impossible to find a hotel room on short notice. If you have difficulties, call **First Hotel Reservierung** (*Kurfürstendamm 180* ☎ *(030) 8811515* ✆ *(030) 8826644*), a free service that will try to find a room in one of several modern and well-situated hotels in Berlin and Potsdam.

Hotels classified by location

CENTER WEST
Bristol Kempinski Berlin ∎∎∎ to ∎∎∎∎
Curator ∎∎ to ∎∎∎
Inter-Continental Berlin ∎∎∎∎
Meineke ∎ to ∎∎
Mondial ∎∎ to ∎∎∎
Sorat ∎∎
Steigenberger Berlin ∎∎∎∎
CENTER EAST
Grand Hotel Berlin ∎∎∎∎

CHARLOTTENBURG
Kronprinz ∎∎
Seehof ∎∎∎
KREUZBERG
Riehmers Hofgarten ∎ to ∎∎
TEGEL
Sorat Humboldt-Mühle ∎∎∎
GRUNEWALD
Forsthaus Paulsborn
   ∎ to ∎∎

BRISTOL KEMPINSKI BERLIN
*Kurfürstendamm 27,
Charlottenburg, Berlin 15
☎ (030) 884340 ✆ (030) 8836075.
Map 2D4* ∎∎∎ to ∎∎∎∎ *325 rms* 🍴
AE ◉ ◉ VISA *U-Bahn to
Kurfürstendamm.*
The rounded modern facade of the Kempinski is one of the landmarks on Kurfürstendamm. Built in 1952, the hotel was named after the prewar Kempinski Haus Vaterland on Potsdamer Platz, a legendary establishment, run by Berthold Kempinski and his wife, which contained a ballroom, numerous restaurants and two hotels. The interior of the Haus Vaterland's successor is tastefully decorated with antique furniture, and guests have the run of three restaurants, a hairdresser, an indoor pool, sauna and gym.

CURATOR
*Grolmanstrasse 41-43,
Charlottenburg, Berlin 12
☎ (030) 884260 ✆ (030) 88426500. Map 2D4* ∎∎ to ∎∎∎
100 rms AE ◉ ◉ VISA *U-Bahn to
Uhlandstrasse, S-Bahn to
Savignyplatz.*
A well-designed modern hotel situated in a leafy street off Kurfürstendamm. You can breakfast outdoors in the summer, or bask on the roof terrace seven floors above the street. There is also a sauna where you can lose some of the pounds put on in the local German

101

Hotels

restaurants. The Curator is in the heart of an increasingly attractive neighborhood of stylish boutiques and cosmopolitan cafés, while the nearby Savignyplatz S-Bahn station is convenient for getting to the ICC and Mitte.

FORSTHAUS PAULSBORN
Am Grunewaldsee, Zehlendorf, Berlin 33 ☎ *(030) 8138010. Map 5D3 ▢ to ▢ 11 rms AE ⊙ ◎ VISA Taxi, or bus 115 to Pücklerstrasse, then a 10min walk through the woods.*
An attractive hotel in the depths of the Grunewald, not far from the Renaissance Jagdschloss Grunewald. Ideally situated for long rambles in the forest, but rather far from the main sights. The hotel has a rustic restaurant, closed on Mon.

GRAND HOTEL BERLIN
Friedrichstrasse 158-164, Mitte, 1080 Berlin. ☎ *(0372) 20923253 ⓕ (0372) 2294094. Map 4C8 ▧ 350 rms AE ⊙ ◎ VISA U-Bahn to Stadtmitte, S-Bahn to Friedrichstrasse.*
Dominating the corner of Unter den Linden and Friedrichstrasse, the Grand Hotel was built by the East Germans in 1987. With its airy fern-filled lobby and sweeping staircase, the hotel attempts to evoke a sense of prewar comfort and *Jugendstil* grandeur, although the service tends to be rather dour. Rooms are tastefully furnished in Old Berlin style, and there are several theme suites for those who would like to imagine themselves in the role of Frederick the Great or Wilhelm von Humboldt. The hotel has a bright, spacious swimming pool, a gym and three restaurants. Although ideally located for getting to the Museumsinsel, the hotel is in a neighborhood that does not swarm with activity after dark. But in a few years, Unter den Linden may well be *the* place to stay.

INTER-CONTINENTAL BERLIN
Budapester Strasse 2, Charlottenburg, Berlin 30 ☎ *(030) 26020 ⓕ (030) 260280760. Map 2D5 ▧ 582 rms ⊟ AE ⊙ ◎ VISA Bus 109 to Budapester Strasse; U-Bahn to Wittenbergplatz.*
A large modern hotel on the edge of the Zoologischer Garten, with airy and comfortable rooms (some with a view of the captive zebras). The hotel has a gym, a sauna and a large, bright swimming pool overlooking a garden. You can jog and rent boats in the Tiergarten, a 5min walk away.

The **Brasserie** offers Berlin specialties, while the old-style restaurant **Zum Hugenotten** sets the right tone for a serious business lunch. You can meet for drinks in the mock wood-paneled country inn, or sit by an open fire in the rooftop bar, watching the neon lights winking on Breitscheidplatz.

A good base for a serious business trip, the Inter-Continental Hotel boasts a Business Center (*open Mon-Fri 9am-5.30pm*) equipped with state-of-the-art Philips personal computers, desktop publishing facilities, laser printers, portable telephones and photocopiers. You can even hire an in-house secretary by the hour. Several new executive rooms are equipped with two telephone numbers, four outside lines and a fax, while the hotel has a conference capacity of up to 1,250. The airport bus stops at the hotel door, but the U-Bahn is a good 10min walk away.

KRONPRINZ
Kronprinzendamm 1, Wilmersdorf, Berlin 31 ☎ *(030) 896030 ⓕ (030) 8931215. Map 1D1 ▨ 53 rms AE ⊙ ◎ VISA Bus 104, 105, 110, 119, 129, 219 to Henriettenplatz.*
An attractive, family-run hotel in a large Old Berlin mansion dating from 1894, with a small garden sometimes used for sculpture exhibitions. Rooms are comfortable, and some have balconies where you can sit out on summer evenings. The hotel stands in a quiet street off the w end of Kurfürstendamm, not far from Schloss Charlottenburg and the ICC conference center.

MEINEKE
Meinekestrasse 10, Berlin 15 ☎ *(030) 882811 or 8834063. Map 2D4 ▢ to ▢ 68 rms AE ⊙ ◎ VISA U-Bahn to Kurfürstendamm.*
A small family-run hotel occupying an Old Berlin house in a quiet street off Kurfürstendamm. Rooms are spacious and elegantly furnished.

MONDIAL
Kurfürstendamm 47, Berlin 15 ☎ *(030) 884110 ⓕ (030) 88411150. Map 1D3 ▨ to ▧ 75 rms ⊟ ♿ AE ⊙ ◎ VISA U-Bahn to Uhlandstrasse; S-Bahn to Savignyplatz.*
A friendly hotel on Kurfürstendamm where you can recover totally from the city's hectic pace. Rooms are comfortably furnished, and there is

RESTAURANTS

a small swimming pool with a gym and medicinal baths. Conference facilities are also available. This is one of very few hotels equipped to accommodate disabled visitors.

RIEHMERS HOFGARTEN
Yorckstrasse 83, Kreuzberg, Berlin 61 ☎ *(030) 781011* ⓕ *(030) 7866059. Map 4E8 ▢ to ▣ 21 rms* 🄰🄴 ⓞ ⓒⓓ 🆅🅸🆂🅰 *U-Bahn or bus 119 to Mehringdamm.*

Situated in a handsome Old Berlin mansion overlooking a leafy avenue near the Viktoriapark, this small hotel is part of a residential complex designed in 1881-1900 by Wilhelm Riehmer. The rooms have a spacious elegance, together with useful gadgets such as a trouser-press. An excellent base for exploring Kreuzberg and Mitte.

SEEHOF
Lietzensee Ufer, Charlottenburg, Berlin 19 ☎ *(030) 320020* ⓕ *(030) 32002251. Map 1C2* ▥ *78 rms* 🍽 🄰🄴 ⓞ ⓒⓓ 🆅🅸🆂🅰 *U-Bahn to Sophie-Charlotte-Platz, or bus 110.*

This comfortable and quiet modern hotel on the shores of the Lietzensee is popular with musicians performing in Berlin. Bedrooms are furnished with elegance, and most have a view of the lake. The well-designed swimming pool is generous in size, with large windows looking out onto the park. The hotel is a 10min walk from the ICC conference center, and Savigny-platz is easily reached by bus.

SORAT
Joachimstaler Strasse 28-29, Charlottenburg, Berlin 15 ☎ *(030) 884470* ⓕ *(030) 88447700. Map 2D4* ▢ 🄰🄴 ⓞ 🆅🅸🆂🅰 *U-Bahn to Kurfürstendamm.*

A modern hotel off Kurfürstendamm decorated with artful flair. Rooms are furnished with quirky, modern furniture and striking lithographs by the German artist Wolf Vostell (who designed the discus-thrower on the roof). The buffet breakfast offers a tempting range of breads, German cold meats, and even Japanese dishes.

SORAT HUMBOLDT-MÜHLE
An der Mühle, Tegel, Berlin 27 ☎ *(030) (sister hotel) 884470* ⓕ *(030) (sister hotel) 88447700. Map 5B3* ▥ *107 rms* 🄰🄴 ⓞ ⓒⓓ 🆅🅸🆂🅰 *U-Bahn to Tegel.*

An attractive contemporary hotel overlooking the old harbor at Tegel. This is a medium-sized hotel (part of the Sorat group) and is ideal for travelers who prefer quiet suburbs and woodland walks to cinemas and restaurants. Parents can keep children amused for hours at the nearby lakeside park and beach, or take the steamer from Greenwich-promenade to Wannsee. The hotel has a fitness center and sauna, and you can look forward to a good breakfast at the end of an early morning run in the Tegel woods. A 5min taxi ride gets you to Tegel airport, while Kurfürstendamm is about 30 mins away by U-Bahn. The hotel opened in 1991, and telephone and fax numbers were not yet available. Details from the more central sister hotel **Sorat**.

STEIGENBERGER BERLIN
Los-Angeles-Platz 1, Charlottenburg, Berlin 30 ☎ *(030) 21080* ⓕ *(030) 2108117. Map 2D4* ▥ *397 rms* 🍽 🄰🄴 ⓞ ⓒⓓ 🆅🅸🆂🅰 *U-Bahn to Kurfürstendamm.*

A low-rise, modern hotel with a grand reception lobby and elegant rooms, facing a small park near Kurfürstendamm. The hotel has a sauna and an attractive circular swimming pool overlooking a leafy courtyard. The wood-paneled **Berliner Stube** serves local specialties, while the elegant **Park-Restaurant** offers well-prepared modern cuisine. Guests can borrow Siemens portable computers and software to use in their rooms.

Eating in Berlin

You can look forward to eating Berlin specialties such as *Eisbein* (boiled knuckle of pork) served with sauerkraut, or *Boulette* (cold hamburger). *Schweinefleisch* (pork) is the main meat served in German restaurants, but you might balance your diet by ordering the occasional Havel trout or North Sea fish. Dishes labeled *Berliner Art* should be treated cautiously, as Berliners sometimes have a rather strange art with cooking. When a

Restaurants

restaurant advertises *burgerliche Küche*, it should be taken as a warning not to expect anything refined. Many of the country inns on the shores of the Havel or the Grunewald lakes fall into this category; you go there to appreciate the rural setting or the amiable atmosphere rather than the cuisine.

Breakfast (*Frühstück*) is the meal that Berliners take most seriously. You can expect a generous buffet breakfast if you are staying in a large hotel, with various types of German bread and rolls, *croissants*, cold hams, spicy salamis, cereals, muesli and sometimes even German pastries and cakes. Many hotels will offer British-style bacon and scrambled egg as well, while the **Sorat** Hotel even provides Japanese specialties. It helps to be aware of the difference between *Vollmelch* (unskimmed milk) and the *Karnemelk* (buttermilk) that many tourists innocently add to their muesli.

Many cafés in Berlin offer excellent breakfasts during the day. **Café Möhring** (*at the corner of Kurfürstendamm and Uhlandstrasse*) is open for early risers at 7am, but many fashionable cafés don't begin serving until 10am or later, while **Café Nolle** continues serving breakfast until 6pm. Although most hotels include breakfast in the price of the room, you can still indulge in the Berlin custom of *Zweite Frühstück* (second breakfast) at a café.

You might revisit your favorite café in the afternoon for *Kaffee und Kuchen* (coffee and cake). This admirable German tradition is faithfully followed by young and old Berliners alike, and the chocolate cake in austere Kreuzberg artists' cafés can sometimes prove superior to the *Kuchen* eaten by elderly ladies at the **KaDeWe** department store or **Café Möhring**.

With so much eating going on throughout the morning and afternoon, Berliners tend to take lunch and dinner less seriously than in other countries. The business lunch is not a Berlin tradition, and most good restaurants, including those in major hotels, open only for dinner. Exceptions are **Rockendorfs**, **Zum Hugenotten** at the **Inter-Continental Hotel**, **Anselmo** (close to the ICC) and **Mario**.

Berliners are too restless to spend much time on lunch, and many prefer to snatch a *Bratwurst* (fried sausage) at a stand-up *Imbiss* counter. Even when eating gourmet food at the **KaDeWe**, Berliners eat at a remarkable tempo. If you find yourself hit by a sudden craving, you can pick up a sandwich or cheese cake at the **Mini Bistro** (*in the ticket-hall at Wittenbergplatz U-Bahnhof*) before rushing off to catch the U-Bahn.

You can eat well in the evening, but you should reserve ahead, as good restaurants often have only a few tables. When reserving a table, you should ask whether payment by charge or credit card is accepted. Much of the best cooking in Berlin currently goes on in the kitchens of Italian restaurants. Some of them offer old-fashioned Italian pasta dishes, while others prepare the more refined meat and sauce inventions of the northern cities. Young, sophisticated Berliners adore Italian food, and many modern café menus will feature pasta dishes rather than lumpen German food.

Restaurants in East Berlin are currently in a state of flux as they try to raise the standard of their cooking and service to West Berlin levels. The cynicism fostered by the old regime lingers on in many places, and eating out east of the Brandenburg Gate is still as hazardous as before reunification. You will, of course, occasionally have to dine somewhere in Mitte, in which case you might try the **Ermelerhaus**.

Restaurants

The following selection of restaurants uses symbols to show price categories, charge/credit cards and other noteworthy points. See page 5 for the full list of symbols. Times are specified when restaurants are **closed**.

Restaurants classified by type of cuisine

AUSTRIAN
Bamberger Reiter ////
FRENCH
Paris Bar //□
Zum Hugenotten //// to ////
GERMAN (SOPHISTICATED)
Alt Luxemburg //// to ////
Rockendorfs Restaurant ////
GERMAN (TRADITIONAL)
Blockhaus Nikolskoe □
Ermelerhaus □
KaDeWe Feinschmeckeretage □ to //□
Lutter & Wegner □

Meineke 10 □ to //□
Spreegarten □
GREEK
Fofis Estiatorio //□
ITALIAN
Alfons //□
Anselmo //□ to ///□
Mario //□
Ponte Vecchio ///□
Savonia //□
Tavola Calda //□
Trio //□ to ///□
Tucci //□ to ///□
THAI
Mahachai //□

ALFONS
Wilmersdorfer Strasse 79, Charlottenburg ☎ (030) 3242282. Map 1D3 //□ Closed Mon; lunch ▨ ◉ ◯ ᵥₛₐ U-Bahn to Adenauerplatz.
A spacious, modern Italian restaurant decked with chrome and mirrors. Chef Alfons Brosius offers a varied menu with both traditional regional cooking and modern Italian dishes.

ALT LUXEMBURG
Pestalozzistrasse 70, Charlottenburg ☎ (030) 3238730. Map 1C3 //// to //// No cards. Closed Sun; Mon; lunch. U-Bahn to Wilmersdorfer Strasse.
A comfortable, old-fashioned restaurant, with mirrors, chandeliers and paintings to lend an air of elegance. The chef fastidiously prepares daring dishes such as catfish in curry sauce or breast of guinea-fowl. Reservations advisable.

ANSELMO
Damaschkestrasse 17, Wilmersdorf ☎ (030) 3233094. Map 1D2 //□ to ///□ Closed Mon. Bus 110 or 204 to Holtzendorffplatz; S-Bahn to Charlottenburg.
Anselmo Bufacchi's modern Italian restaurant is one of the few in Berlin where you can eat throughout the day. The cooking is classical Italian, with dishes such as quail with olives, or breast of duck simmered in dark, sweet Marsala wine. There's a wide choice of fish dishes, including sole with salmon in white wine.

BAMBERGER REITER
Regensburgerstrasse 7, Schöneberg ☎ (030) 244282. Map 2E5 //// No cards. Closed Sun, Mon, lunch, first 2wks Jan and first 2wks Aug. U-Bahn to Viktoria-Luise-Platz.
Franz Raneburger's sophisticated cuisine combines traditional recipes from his native Tirol with the best elements of *nouvelle cuisine*. Whether the dish is goose liver served in pastry, or almond soufflé with fruits, Raneburger prepares the finest ingredients with consistency and flair. The handsome rustic interior is decorated with antiques, and you can linger over brandies until long after midnight. Reservations a must.

BLOCKHAUS NIKOLSKOE
Nikolskoer Weg, Wannsee ☎ (030) 8052914. Map 5E2 □ No cards. Closed Thurs. Bus 216 from S-Bahnhof Wannsee.
The Blockhaus Nikolskoe is just the sort of eating place that Berliners hope to find after a brisk walk through the forest. Perched on a hill above the Havel, the restaurant occupies an imitation Russian log cabin in the Düppel woods. This curious edifice was built by the sentimental Friedrich Wilhelm III for his daughter, Charlotte, who married Czar Nicholas I. With its ornate balconies laden with geraniums, it still has a hint of old Russia, although the red and white cloths could be Bavarian.

The solid, North German style of cooking is better than in many

Restaurants

restaurants dotted along the Havel shore. Try the homemade *Eisbein-sülze* (pork in jelly), washed down with a glass of Charlottenburger Pilsner. For those who have seen enough pork in Berlin, there is trout or *Matjes* (Dutch cured herring) on the menu. The waiters are polite, if rather solemn. Should the weather be mild, you can sit out on a terrace for a superb view of the Havel.

ERMELERHAUS
Märkisches Ufer 10-12, Mitte ☎ *(0372) 2755103. Map 4C9* ❒ *No cards. U-Bahn to Spittelmarkt.*

When hunger strikes on a stroll through Mitte, you might try one of the restaurants in the Ermelerhaus, a pale yellow Neoclassical mansion on the Spree waterfront. Built by a Berlin coffee merchant in 1808, it is decorated with friezes illustrating the owner's trade. The **Raabediele** restaurant in the cellar is decorated in German farmhouse style, with pine walls and painted chairs. Friendly and relaxed, it offers warming north German winter cooking, such as *Berliner Kohlroulade mit Speckwickel* (pork wrapped in cabbage with bacon), or unwieldy hunks of *Eisbein*. The building also houses an elegant *Weinrestaurant* (☎ *(0372) 2755103* ❒) at the top of a grand Baroque staircase, and a café on the ground floor.

FOFIS ESTIATORIO
Fasanenstrasse 70, Charlottenburg ☎ *(030) 8818785. Map 2D4* ❒ *No cards. Closed lunch. U-Bahn to Uhlandstrasse.*

A bustling, informal Greek restaurant with polished wooden floors, and white walls hung with vibrant abstract paintings. It is perhaps the Mediterranean atmosphere, rather than the plain Greek-style cooking, that draws Berlin artists and businessmen here. It is certainly fascinating to watch as the waiters dash around recklessly with tureens of cream of scampi soup or plates of bubbling moussaka. Fofis attracts a fashionable crowd all year, especially on summer evenings, when the terrace is always full.

KADEWE FEINSCHMECKER-ETAGE
Tauentzienstrasse 21-24 (6th floor). Map 2D5 ❒ *to* ❒ *Open Mon-Fri 9am-6.30pm, Sat 9am-2pm. Closed Sun. U-Bahn to Wittenbergplatz.*

Even the most sophisticated Berliners love to perch at the crowded counters in KaDeWe's huge delicatessen department to sample the *Feinschmecker* (gourmet) dishes. A rather noisy crowd gathers around the beer pump, while smart executives congregate after work at the champagne bar. The atmosphere is informal, like a good beer garden, but the food far superior. One stand (**Le Nôtre**) offers coffee, croissant and brioche for breakfast (*9am-11am*) or rich *Heidelbeeretorte* (bilberry tart) to bolster your strength mid-afternoon. A sausage counter sells plump *Münchener Weisswurst* to expatriate Bavarians requiring their traditional mid-morning snack. Those wanting to try a genuine Berlin food can start at the soup counter with a bowl of *Erbsensuppe* (thick pea soup) or *Kartoffelsuppe* (potato soup), then wander across to the **Zum Hackepeter** kitchen, which doles out *Eisbein mit Sauerkraut*, *Bouletten* (cold hamburgers), *Kartoffelsalat* (potato salad) and *Lübars Landschinken* (Lübars country ham), which you can wash down with a glass of *Berliner Weisse*. To complete the Berlin eating experience, try a *Kartoffelpuffer mit Apfelmus* (potato pancake with apple sauce) at the **Kartoffelacker** counter.

Sitting at the fish counter (which has a view of the Gedächtniskirche), you can sample *Rotbarschfilet* (fillet of red perch), served with a glass of 1987 Riesling Kabinett. Or order half a dozen Sylt oysters with a glass of 1984 Riesling at the elegant **Austernbar** (oyster bar). Other counters offer Dutch raw herring served with a glass of Bremen-brewed Beck's beer, Normandy *crêpes* accompanied by French cider, or a selection of ice creams. The only drawback of this wonderful Berlin institution is that it all shuts down at 6.30pm sharp.

LUTTER & WEGNER
Schlüterstrasse 55, Charlottenburg ☎ *(030) 8813440. Map 1D3* ❒ *Closed lunch* 🆎 ◉ ◉ 🚌 *Bus 109 to Bleibtreustrasse or S-Bahn to Savignyplatz.*

A convivial Berlin *Weinstube* where the candles flicker until 3am. The wine bar was founded in 1811, although the wood-paneling and mottos in Old German Gothic script are not original. The cooking here has become more refined in recent

Restaurants

years, while the portions have dwindled somewhat. A convivial place to drop into for a light supper or a glass of wine.

MAHACHAI
Schlüterstrasse 60, Charlottenburg ☎ (030) 310879. Map 1D3 ▯ No cards. S-Bahn to Savignyplatz or bus 149 to Schlüterstrasse.
A well-run Thai restaurant that is always crowded. The bamboo hut style of decor may not be to everyone's taste, but the cooking is excellent, with specialties such as crispy fried duck served with bamboo shoots and almonds. The service is efficient and friendly, and it is worth reserving ahead unless you are prepared to perch on a bamboo bar stool.

MARIO
Leibnitzstrasse 43, Charlottenburg ☎ (030) 3243516. Map 1D3 ▯ No cards. Closed Sat. S-Bahn to Savignyplatz, or U-Bahn to Wilmersdorfer Strasse.
An intimate Italian restaurant off Savignyplatz, where stars such as Wim Wenders and Bruno Ganz occasionally eat. Creative Italian cooking served with flair.
Reservations advised.

MEINEKE 10
Meinekestrasse 10, Charlottenburg ☎ (030) 8823158. Map 2D4 ▯ U-Bahn to Kurfürstendamm.
A friendly, crowded Berlin restaurant just off Kurfürstendamm, with a sidewalk terrace, and attractively decorated with dark wooden furnishings, antique clocks, and flickering candles. It offers solid, reliable German dishes daily from noon until 1am. Try *Leber "Berliner Art"* (liver garnished with sliced onion and apple).

PARIS BAR
Kantstrasse 152, Charlottenburg ☎ (030) 3138052. Map 2D4 ▯ No cards. Closed Sun. Bus 149 to Uhlandstrasse.
An attractive restaurant off Savignyplatz that emulates a Paris Left Bank brasserie. Plain French cooking is served from noon until after midnight by waiters dressed in traditional long aprons. The straight rows of tables are covered with starched white cloths, while the yellowing walls are hung with Surreal art, including a bizarre painting with an overflowing ashtray and a dusty wine bottle glued to it. Paris Bar attracts an unusually broad range of customers, from radical artists dressed entirely in black to prim folk up from Bavaria. Solitary diners can come to eat here armed with a novel. Charge and credit cards are frowned upon.

PONTE VECCHIO
Spielhagenstrasse 3, Charlottenburg ☎ (030) 3421999. Map 1C2 ▧ Closed lunch ▯ U-Bahn to Bismarckstrasse.
Careful and creative Italian cooking based on the regional specialties of Tuscany. The decor is plain and old-fashioned by Berlin standards, but dishes such as skewered fillet of lamb or ricotta in zucchini flower provide more than enough visual excitement.

ROCKENDORFS RESTAURANT
Düsterhauptstrasse 1, Reinickendorf ☎ (030) 4023099 ▥ Closed Sun, Mon AE ▯ ▯ ▯ VISA S-Bahn to Waidmannslust, or bus 222 from U-Bahnhof Tegel.
Siegfried Rockendorf's restaurant is situated in an elegant villa in a quiet N Berlin suburb. Combining French style with the best German ingredients available, Rockendorf creates exquisite dishes such as quail mousse with artichoke and truffle salad, or breast of wild duck with grated apple. Despite the remote location, the small restaurant is constantly full; reservations essential.

SAVONIA
Windscheidstrasse 31, Charlottenburg ☎ (030) 3241807. Map 1C2 ▯ Closed Sun; lunch AE ▯ ▯ VISA U-Bahn to Sophie-Charlotte-Platz; bus 149 to Kaiser-Friedrichstrasse.
A small old-fashioned Italian restaurant offering traditional regional cooking. Italian fish dishes with lobster or tuna are stylishly prepared.

SPREEGARTEN
Uhlandstrasse 173, Charlottenburg ☎ (030) 8826867. Map 2D4 ▯ U-Bahn to Uhlandstrasse.
This bustling, friendly restaurant is crammed with enormous wooden cupboards, heavy gilt mirrors, and chandeliers. The kitchen produces plain, well-prepared dishes such as *Kohlroulade mit Specksauce* (pork *roulade* wrapped in cabbage with bacon sauce), and the service is efficient and friendly.

CAFÉS

TAVOLA CALDA
*Leibnitzstrasse 45,
Charlottenburg* ☎ *(030) 3241048.
Map 1D3* ◫ *No cards. S-Bahn to Savignyplatz.*
An intimate Italian restaurant off Savignyplatz, offering traditional Italian dishes with pasta and *scaloppine* (scallops). Decorated in a tasteful modern style, this is one of the few good restaurants in Berlin where you can meet for lunch.

TRIO
*Klausenerplatz 14,
Charlottenburg* ☎ *(030) 3217782.
Map 1B2* ◫ *to* ▥ *No cards.
Closed Wed; Thurs; lunch. Bus 145 or 204 to Klausenerplatz.*
Situated on a leafy square near Schloss Charlottenburg, Trio is an elegant restaurant, decorated with modern paintings hung on white walls. The handwritten menu — fiendishly difficult to read — features modern Italian dishes such as veal cutlets in mustard sauce.

TUCCI
*Grolmanstrasse 52,
Charlottenburg* ☎ *(030) 3139335.
Map 2C4* ◫ *to* ▥ *S-Bahn or bus 149 to Savignyplatz.*
A fashionable café-restaurant off Savignyplatz, with bare wooden floors, wiry black chairs and artificially aged walls. Run by friendly young Berliners, it offers simple, well-prepared Italian regional cooking, such as *Pappardelle con Ragù*. Tucci appeals especially to Berliners in their thirties, reminding them perhaps of lingering summers in Tuscany.

ZUM HUGENOTTEN
*Hotel Inter-Continental,
Budapesterstrasse 2,
Charlottenburg* ☎ *(030) 26020.
Map 2D5* ▥ *to* ▥ AE ◉ ◉ VISA
Last orders 11pm.
With its wood-paneled walls and old paintings, the Inter-Continental Hotel's elegant restaurant is an ideal location for a business lunch or a lingering dinner. Taking its name from the Huguenots who settled in Berlin in the 17thC, Zum Hugenotten offers fastidiously prepared French *nouvelle cuisine* dishes, together with a few specialties of the German kitchen. Some rare vintages have gathered dust in the hotel's extensive wine cellar.

Cafés

Expressionist artists of the 1920s depicted Berlin cafés such as the Romanische (destroyed in 1943) as chaotic, somewhat seedy venues frequented by artists, prostitutes and businessmen. Almost all the legendary cafés were destroyed during World War II, but you may still find a hint of *fin-de-siècle* Berlin at **Café Möhring** (*Kurfürstendamm 213, map 2D4*). Today's most exciting meeting places tend to be modern, cosmopolitan cafés off Savignyplatz or in Kreuzberg. Most of the cafés in Mitte and other former East Berlin districts have rather dreary imitation 19thC interiors, with wooden furnishings and a few wilting ferns. Those looking for fashionable, buzzing cafés should head to Prenzlauer Berg, to places such as **Kaffeestube** (*Husemannstrasse 6*). Ice cream bars in East Berlin — if they continue to exist — are a touching last reminder of the innocent optimism of the Socialism of the 1950s. Try the decadent ice cream sundaes at **Mocca-Milch-Eis-Bar** (*Karl-Marx-Allee 35, Mitte*), a spacious modern milk bar painted in pastel tints and filled with plants.

AEDES
*Stadtbahnbogen 599, off
Savignyplatz, Charlottenburg.
Map 2D4.*
Situated in one of the brick arches under Savignyplatz S-Bahnhof, this modern café is popular with young bohemians. The café forms part of the Aedes architecture gallery (see GUIDE TO BERLIN'S GALLERIES on page 27) and the walls are crammed with Utopian projects. Aedes is a good spot for quiet conversation in the evening, although the entire building shudders every time a train passes overhead. Open for breakfast.

BEER HALLS AND BEER GARDENS

EINSTEIN STADTCAFÉ
Kurfürstenstrasse 58, Tiergarten. Map 3D6. U-Bahn to Nollendorfplatz.
A vast café situated in an Old Berlin villa, Einstein has the faded elegance of a Viennese coffee house, with its huge mirrors, plump sofas and marble-topped tables. Serious, fashionable Berliners wearing the maximum of black clothing come here to drink coffee, read the newspapers and feast on the moist, delicious *Apfelstrudel*. The geranium-filled garden at the back is the perfect place to while away a summer afternoon in the city, and the restaurant (☎ *(030) 2615096* 🗐 AE 🔲 🔘 VISA) stays open until 2am.

LEYSIEFFER
Kurfürstendamm 218, Charlottenburg. Map 2D4.
A delicatessen and café situated in an 1897 building that once housed the Chinese embassy. With its stucco ceilings and ornate wood-paneling, the first-floor café is one of the few relics of Old Berlin still standing on Kurfürstendamm. Order a breakfast of croissants with honey and jam, or a pastry and coffee, and you can perch at the bay window table to watch the teeming Berlin street life as it circulates below.

MOCCA-MILCH-EIS-BAR
Karl-Marx-Allee 35, Mitte. Map 6C6.
Situated on a spectacular Socialist boulevard, this coffee bar and ice cream shop is a marvelous relic of the 1950s. The huge glass walls and curving mezzanine floor symbolize the mood of confidence in East Berlin society before the Soviet tanks rolled in. Painted pink and filled with plants, coffee bars such as this one were where young East Berliners once came to have some innocent fun.

MÖHRING
Kurfürstendamm 234, Charlottenburg. Map 2D4.
Situated near the Gedächtniskirche, Möhring evokes the atmosphere of Old Berlin with its spacious Neoclassical interior decorated with nostalgic photographs of Kurfürstendamm in the 1930s. The first Café Möhring — opened on the Kurfürstendamm in 1898 — was destroyed in World War II, and there are now four successors to choose from, although this branch is the most authentic. An elegant spot for breakfast *(from 9am)* or *Kaffee und Kuchen* (coffee and cake).

MÖHRING
Kurfürstendamm 213, (at Uhlandstrasse) Charlottenburg. Map 2D4.
Rebuilt on the site of the famous Berlin café frequented by Maxim Gorki, Möhring (*open 7am-10pm*) serves five different types of breakfast. The *kleines Frühstück* is enough to sustain most people, while the *Berliner Frühstück* is best left to Berliners — unless you seriously want to begin the day with *Solei* (pickled egg).

SHELL
Knesebeckstrasse 22, Charlottenburg. Map 2D4. S-Bahn or bus 149 to Savignyplatz.
This airy modern café situated in an old gas-station on Savignyplatz attracts a lively evening crowd of young, cosmopolitan Berliners. The café menu features well-prepared, sustaining northern German dishes, such as fillet of pork wrapped in cabbage and served with homemade noodles. The spacious terrace, on what was once the garage forecourt, is particularly pleasant on hot summer evenings when the excited buzz of voices seems to conjure up a mood reminiscent of 1920s Berlin.

Beer halls and beer gardens

Berlin beer halls are generally less boisterous than their Bavarian counterparts, perhaps because the beer is normally served in modest 20cl. glasses rather than the 1-liter *Mass* jugs common in Southern Germany. A waitress serves you at the table; pay for what you have consumed at the end.

The list of dishes is chalked up on a blackboard, and you order at the counter. Expect to be served hearty German specialties throughout the year, such as knuckle of pork (*Eisbein*), meatballs (*Bouletten*), eel in herb sauce (*Aal grün*),

NIGHTLIFE & THE PERFORMING ARTS

mashed peas (*Erbspüree*), and potato pancake dusted with sugar (*Kartoffelpuffer*). Beer halls are normally open noon-midnight.

The beer in Berlin, and throughout Germany, is of excellent quality, due to the 1516 *Reinheitsgebot* (Pure Beer Law), which forbids the use of chemicals in the brewing process. *Schultheiss* and *Kindl* are the largest Berlin brewers, but a few small independents have recently launched new brands of beer brewed by traditional Berlin methods.

Berliner Weisse (Berlin white beer) is the local drink for hot summer days. A light wheat beer, it comes in a chalice-shaped glass, and is served with a slice of lemon and a straw. Berliners, never timid in their tastes, traditionally order it *mit Schuss* — a dash of red or green syrup. A *Rode Weisse*, laced with *Himbeere* (raspberry syrup), has a sparkling, fruity character. The *Grüne* version, served with a squirt of *Waldmeister* (the herb woodruff), is a peculiar taste unique to Berlin. A *Weizenbiere* (not to be confused with *Berliner Weisse*) is a Bavarian wheat beer, which often features on lists of beers in Berlin cafés. You may be offered the choice of *Hefe* (yeasty) or *Kristall* (clear).

Aschinger (*Kurfürstendamm 26, map 2D4*) makes a pleasant, light-brown house brew, which can be sampled in an elegant tiled basement beer hall filled with gleaming copper brewing equipment. The cooking is of the plain, North German style, and the Bavarian background music is almost unobtrusive, making this a pleasant place for quiet conversation.

Founded in 1987, **Luisen-Brau** brewery (*Luisenplatz 1 at Schloss Charlottenburg*) has a beer hall with a Neoclassical interior and long wooden benches. One of Berlin's most alluring brews, Luisen-Brau is produced on the premises, using Bavarian hops and soft Brandenburg water. The kitchen prepares plain German specialties such as *Lamm Haxe* (knuckle of lamb) or *Spiessbraten* (roast pork stuffed with chopped ham).

Loretta in der City (*Lietzenburgerstrasse 87, map 2D4*) is a spacious beer garden not far from Kurfürstendamm, with a fairground Ferris wheel, and strings of lights dangling from the trees. The food is simple, but the festive mood is appealing, especially to children. After a cruise on the Havel, you might try **Loretta am Wannsee** (*Kronprinzessinnenweg 260, near S-Bahnhof Wannsee*), a rambling beer garden shaded by trees. **Luise** (*Königin-Luise-Strasse 40*) is a popular beer garden near the Dahlem museums, where you can sip a *Berliner Weisse* after a long day looking at paintings. Children are welcome to rollick around in the small playground. **Alter Krug** (*Königin-Luise-Strasse 52*) has a rambling garden that is popular with everyone from elderly professors' wives to local students.

Nightlife & the performing arts

From the impeccable acoustics of the Philharmonie concert hall to radical plays set in abandoned factories, reunited Berlin can now claim to be one of the world's most exciting cities after dark. Music fills the air every night in Berlin, and the city currently boasts three opera houses and a host of symphony and chamber orchestras. Nights in Berlin can be as wild as you want, and many of the bars stay open until dawn. Browse through the daily listings in *Zitty* (thick and radical) or *Tip* (glossy and mainstream) to find out what's happening in Berlin's theaters, concert halls, cinemas and cabarets, or just stroll down Kurfürstendamm to join in the fun.

Performing arts

Tickets
Reserve well in advance for classical concerts, plays, cabarets and dance events. This can conveniently be done at one of the *Theaterkassen* in the city.

Berlin Ticket Theaterkassen have branches in major department stores, including **KaDeWe** (*Tauentzienstrasse* ☎ *(030) 241028*), **Wertheim** (*Kurfürstendamm 24* ☎ *(030) 8825254*), **Hertie** (*Wilmersdorfer Strasse* ☎ *(030) 3129497*), **Europa-Center**, (*Tauentzienstrasse 9* ☎ *(030) 2617051*) and **Karten-Service** (*Hardenbergstrasse 6* ☎ *(030) 3137007*). **Theaterkasse Zehlendorf** (*Am Rathaus, Zehlendorf* ☎ *(030) 8011652*) also handles concerts in Potsdam, Dresden and Vienna.

The performing arts

Alternative centers
Germany's radicals, alternative thinkers, pacifists, dissidents and environmentalists have flocked to Berlin since 1945, setting up various alternative cultural centers that challenge mainstream society.

UFA-Fabrik (*Viktoriastrasse 10-18, Tempelhof* ☎ *(030) 7528085, U-Bahn to Ullsteinstrasse*) offers circus acts, radical theater, children's shows and offbeat movies (original-language versions) in a converted former UFA film studio.

Cinema
Berlin played a short but illustrious role in the development of film in the 1920s, and although the last surviving studios at Potsdam are now in dire financial straits, the city still hosts one of the world's foremost film festivals each February. Berlin's biggest movie theaters are clustered around **Bahnhof Zoo** and along **Kurfürstendamm**, while more daring films are screened by independent film theaters located **Off-Ku'damm** or in **Kreuzberg**.

Sadly for non-German-speaking cinemagoers, Berlin cinemas tend to show foreign films dubbed into German. Those rare cases in which a cinema shows a film in the original language are listed as **OF** (*Originalfassung*) if they are in the original language, and **OmU** (*Originalfassung mit Untertiteln*) if German subtitles are used.

Arsenal Welserstrasse 25 ☎(030) 246848. Map **2**D5. U-Bahn to Wittenbergplatz. Undubbed films.
Schlüter Schlüterstrasse 17, Charlottenburg ☎(030) 3138580. Map **1**D3. Bus 249 to Schlüterstrasse. Intimate Art Deco cinema run by an affable bearded Berliner who occasionally delivers a brief talk before the film.
Studio Kurfürstendamm 71 ☎(030) 3245003. Map **1**D3. U-Bahn to Adenauerplatz. Original-language films.
Waldbühne Glockenturmstrasse, Charlottenburg ☎(030) 8827011. Bus 249 to Scholzplatz. Open-air amphitheater built in the forest for the 1936 Olympics, now used in the summer for films and concerts.

Circus
Berliners, otherwise an urbane crowd, still seem to retain a naive affection for circus acts.
Tempodrom In den Zelten, Tiergarten ☎(030) 3944045. Map **3**B6. Bus 100 to Kongresshalle. Closed winter. A unique mix of traditional circus acts, alternative cabaret and live bands, in a tent pitched next to the Kongresshalle.

Performing arts

Classical and popular concerts

Berlin offers a vast choice of concerts, from the grandest operas to intimate chamber music. The city's orchestras and rock groups perform throughout the year in grand concert halls, restored churches, libraries, palaces, art schools and open-air theaters. Watch out for occasional concerts of Baroque chamber music held in the old palaces of BRITZ, FRIEDRICHSFELDE and SANSSOUCI, or in the scintillating **Eichengalerie** at SCHLOSS CHARLOTTENBURG. The monthly *Berlin Programm*, available at most German tourist offices, has all the details.

Eissporthalle Jafféstrasse   Charlottenburg ☎(030) 30384387. S-Bahn to Westkreuz or (better) bus 219 to Messedamm. Concerts by famous rock bands.

Hochschule der Künste   Hardenbergstrasse 33, Charlottenburg ☎(030) 31852374. Map **2**C4. U-Bahn to Zoologischer Garten. Classical concerts and jazz performances.

Kammermusiksaal   ☎ (030) 254880. Map **3**C7. M-Bahn to Kemperplatz or bus 148 to Philharmonie. Concert hall for classical and modern chamber music, built in the 1980s next to the Philharmonie.

Loft   Nollendorfplatz 5, Kreuzberg ☎(030) 2161020. Map **2**D6. U-Bahn to Nollendorfplatz. Innovative rock groups.

Philharmonie   Matthäikirchstrasse 1, Tiergarten ☎(030) 254880. Map **3**C7. M-Bahn to Kemperplatz or bus 148 to Philharmonie. Extraordinary in-the-round concert hall built in the 1960s by Hans Scharoun to house the renowned Berlin Philharmonic Orchestra. Advance sales begin 2-3 weeks before the concert, and tickets sell out almost at once.

Cultural institutions

Several national centers actively promote the film, theater and literature of their respective countries.

Amerika-Haus   Hardenbergstrasse 22, Charlottenburg ☎(030) 3900070. Map **2**C4. U-Bahn to Zoologischer Garten. Classic US movies and theater.

British Centre   Hardenbergstrasse 20, Charlottenburg ☎(030) 3110990. Map **2**C4. U-Bahn to Zoologischer Garten. Classical music and films from the UK.

Deutschlandhaus   Stresemannstrasse 90, Kreuzberg ☎(030) 2611046. Map **3**D7. S-Bahn to Anhalter Bahnhof. German music and talks.

Haus der Kulturen der Welt   Kongresshalle, John-Foster-Dulles-Allee 10 ☎(030) 394031. Map **3**B6. Bus 100 to Kongresshalle. Non-European culture in a futuristic 1950s building.

Institut Français de Berlin   Kurfürstendamm 211, Charlottenburg ☎(030) 8818702. Map **2**D4. U-Bahn to Uhlandstrasse. French films and plays.

Jüdisches Gemeindehaus   Fasanenstrasse 79-80, Charlottenburg ☎(030) 88420333. Map **2**D4. U-Bahn to Uhlandstrasse. Jewish plays and concerts.

Jazz

Big, friendly international jazz festivals are held in June and late Oct to early Nov (see CALENDAR OF EVENTS on page 33), but folk and blues sounds can be heard throughout the year in dimly-lit cafés. Concerts usually begin as late as 10-11pm. In the summer, jazz bands can be heard at the **Naturtheater Hasenheide** and other open-air venues.

Blues Café   Körnerstrasse 11, Tiergarten ☎(030) 2613698.

Nightlife

Map **3**D6. U-Bahn to Kurfürstenstrasse. Classic blues.
Flöz Nassauische Strasse 37 ☎(030) 8611000. Map **2**E4. U-Bahn to Hohenzollernplatz. Berlin bands improvising jazz and salsa.
Go In Bleibtreustrasse 17, Charlottenburg ☎(030) 8817218. Map **1**D3. S-Bahn or bus 149, 249 to Savignyplatz. Folk groups from every continent.
Quasimodo Kantstrasse 12a, Charlottenburg ☎(030) 3128086. Map **2**D4. U-Bahn to Zoologischer Garten. Top international musicians playing all styles of jazz.

Opera and ballet

Opera-lovers in Berlin have an enviable choice of classical and modern performances in three opera houses.
Deutsche Oper Berlin Bismarckstrasse 35, Charlottenburg ☎(030) 3410249. Map **1**C3. U-Bahn to Deutsche Oper. Austere postwar concert hall for opera and modern ballet.
Deutsche Staatsoper Unter den Linden 7, Mitte ☎(0372) 2004762. Map **4**C8. U-Bahn to Französische Strasse. Bombed 18thC opera house, recently restored by the East German government, provides a glittering Baroque setting for classical opera and ballet.
Komische Oper Behrenstrasse 55-57, Mitte ☎(0372) 2292555. Map **4**C8. U-Bahn to Französische Strasse. Operettas and ballet in a concert hall modeled on the Paris Opéra Comique.

Theater

Classical and modern German theater flourishes in Neoclassical buildings, art schools, cellars, former cinemas, converted factories and open-air amphitheaters. The heyday of Berlin theater was in the 1920s, when innovative playwrights such as Erwin Piscator and Max Reinhardt engaged in daring social criticism, but this radical tradition was crushed by the Nazis. A revival began with Bertolt Brecht's return to East Berlin in 1949, and the city now hosts numerous groups performing mainly experimental works.
Berliner Ensemble Bertolt-Brecht-Platz, Mitte ☎(0372) 2888155. Map **4**B8. U-Bahn or S-Bahn to Friedrichstrasse. Classic performances of Brecht's plays in one of the last bastions of Socialist theater in East Berlin.
Deutsches Theater Schumannstrasse 13a, Mitte ☎(0372) 2871225. Map **3**B7. U-Bahn or S-Bahn to Friedrichstrasse. Theater run by Max Reinhardt from 1905-33, where Pola Negri, Ernst Lubitsch and Marlene Dietrich performed.
Schaubühne am Lehniner Platz Kurfürstendamm 153, Charlottenburg ☎(030) 890023. Map **1**D2. Bus 119 to Lehniner Platz. Restored 1920s cinema designed by Erich Mendelsohn, now home to one of Germany's most innovative theater companies.
Theater des Westens Kantstrasse 12, Charlottenburg ☎(030) 31903193. Map **2**D4. U-Bahn to Zoologischer Garten. Broadway-style musicals in a flamboyant 19thC theater.

Nightlife

The flashing neon around the spotlit spire of the Gedächtniskirche marks the hub of Berlin's nightlife. Stroll down the broad tree-lined Kurfürstendamm to savor the irresistible allure of Berlin after dark, then explore the streets radiating from

Nightlife

Savignyplatz to find the *Off-Kinos* (independent cinemas) and sleek cafés where fashionable Berliners gather in the evening. For a glimpse of radical Berlin, wander along Oranienstrasse in search of *die Szene* (as Berliners dub the "in" places), or join the *Wessis* (West Berliners) currently sniffing out the fashionable cafés of Prenzlauer Berg.

Bars

Licensing legislation is unexpectedly lax in Berlin, and bars can opt to stay open up to 23hrs per day (with 1hr off to clean up). Most places keep fairly normal hours, but you can, if you have enough stamina, while away the night in the bustling bars at Savignyplatz, Nollendorfplatz or Kreuzberg. Here are just a few places to try.

Filmbühne Steinplatz, Charlottenburg. Map **2**C4. U-Bahn to Zoologischer Garten. Friendly bar attached to cinema screening innovative films. Overcrowded during Berlin Film Festival.

Kaffeestube Husemannstrasse 6, Prenzlauer Berg. U-Bahn to Dimitroffstrasse. Handsome bar in a restored East Berlin street.

Kaminbar Hotel Inter-Continental, Budapesterstrasse 2, Tiergarten. Map **2**D5. Bus 109. Elegant penthouse bar with a blazing winter fire.

Leydicke Mansteinstrasse 4, Schöneberg. Map **3**E6. U-Bahn to Kleistpark. Ancient bar crammed with nostalgic Berliners sipping liqueurs and fruit wines.

Sperlingsgasse Lietzenburgerstrasse 82-84. Map **2**D4. U-Bahn to Uhlandstrasse. Arcade off Kurfürstendamm crammed with 13 bars that you'll either love or loathe.

Cabarets and revues

Until recently, cabarets and variety shows in postwar Berlin tended to be a pale reflection of the acts that flourished in the 1920s. Transvestite acts in which men dress up in feathers and frocks are all the rage in Berlin, but a sharper humor now infects several variety shows in the city, as reunification problems begin to bite. You need to speak fluent German to get the gags.

Chez Nous Marburgerstrasse 14 ☎(030) 2131810. Map **2**D4. U-Bahn to Augsburgerstrasse. Transvestite show.

Die Distel Friedrichstrasse 101, Mitte ☎(0372) 2004704. Map **4**B8. U-Bahn or S-Bahn to Friedrichstrasse. Classic Berlin cabaret now casting a sardonic eye on 40yrs of Socialism.

Friedrichstadtpalast Friedrichstrasse 107, Mitte ☎(0372) 2836474. Map **4**B8. U-Bahn or S-Bahn to Friedrichstrasse. Released from the straitjacket of state control, this once-drab theater now stages spicy satirical reviews playing on the preoccupations of *Ossis* and *Wessis* (East and West Berliners).

Quartier Potsdamer Strasse 96, Tiergarten ☎(030) 2629016. Map **3**D6. U-Bahn to Kurfürstenstrasse. Berliners are wild about this revamp of a 1920s variety show launched in 1990, complete with troupes of magicians, jugglers and dance bands. The most talked-about period detail is the telephone at each table, which you can use (if bold enough) to call up a stranger across the hall.

Casino

For those with Deutschmarks to burn, the **Spielbank Berlin** (*Europa-Center, map* **2** *D5, open daily 3pm-3am*) runs roulette, poker and baccarat games.

Discos

Young Berliners dance to the latest sounds in cramped clubs in

SHOPPING

Kreuzberg, though mainstream revelers prefer to boogie and bop the night away in the big discos near Bahnhof Zoo. Discos in Berlin, as in every city, are often choosy about whom they admit. The unofficial rule in Kreuzberg is to dress totally in black. Most discos come to life after 11pm. The pick of the bunch:

Dschungel   Nürnbergerstrasse 53, Charlottenburg ☎(030) 246698. Map **2**D5. U-Bahn to Augsburgerstrasse. U-Bahn to Augsburgerstrasse. Fashionable and fun.

Metropol   Nollendorfplatz 5, Schöneberg ☎(030) 2164122. Map **2**D6. Open Fri, Sat 10pm-4am. U-Bahn to Nollendorfplatz. Dancing to chart hits in a spectacularly-lit former Art Deco theater.

Shopping in Berlin

When it comes to shopping, Berlin is still very much a divided city. While West Berliners feasted on the products of the Federal Republic's economic miracle, those in the Soviet sector had to make do with drab clothes and Trabant cars powered by two-stroke engines. Although the Wall dividing the city has now vanished, there still exists an invisible division between the poor East and the rich West, and although a few smart stores have now opened on Friedrichstrasse, it will be some years before East Berlin is a place for serious shopping.

West Berlin's best stores proudly display their merchandise along Kurfürstendamm, a leafy avenue with broad sidewalks stretching W from the broken spire of the Gedächtniskirche. You can satisfy every whim and desire in the countless stylish shops specializing in clothes, shoes, porcelain, art books or kitchen accessories. Original fashion stores are found in the streets that intersect Kurfürstendamm — they tend to become more unconventional as you travel west. **Fasanenstrasse**, **Uhlandstrasse** and **Uhlandpassage** stock dresses and shoes for flaunting at the theater or opera house, while **Bleibtreustrasse** boutiques offer a more raw chic for wild parties. As if that were not enough, there are elegant shopping streets in many West Berlin suburbs, such as **Schlossstrasse** in Steglitz, where you will find major department stores and stylish fashion shops.

For reading matter, browse in the **bookstores** clustered around Savignyplatz. **Kiepert** (*Hardenbergstrasse 4-5, Charlottenburg* ☎ *(030) 3110090, map* **2** *C4* AE ◎ VISA) has a vast stock of German books on all subjects. Glance in the travel department for early 20thC copies of *Cook's Traveller's Handbook to the Rhine* or old maps of Prussia, or head down the street to **Antiquariat Kiepert** (*Knesebeckstrasse 20-21, Charlottenburg* ☎ *(030) 3135000, map* **2** *D4*) for classic editions of pre-1914 Baedeker guides. For books on Berlin architecture or the movies of Marlene Dietrich, visit **Bücherbogen** (*Stadtbahnbogen 593, off Savignyplatz, Charlottenburg* ☎ *(030) 3121932, map* **2** *D4*), a striking, modern bookstore located in one of the brick arches below S-Bahnhof Savignyplatz, specializing in art, architecture, cinema and photography. Luxury art books for the collector are sold at **Wasmuth** (*Hardenbergstrasse 9a, Charlottenburg* ☎ *(030) 316920, map* **2** *C4*).

The attractive Neoclassical kiosk on Kurfürstendamm (*at Uhlandstrasse*) sells a wide variety of **international newspapers and magazines**, but the biggest selections are at the **Europa Presse Center** (*Europa Center, Charlottenburg* ☎ *(030) 2613003, map* **2** *D5, open daily until 10.45pm*) and

Shopping

Internationale Presse (*Joachimstalerstrasse 1, Charlottenburg* ☎ *(030) 8817256, map 2 D4, open daily until 10pm*).

The department store **KaDeWe** (**Ka**ufhaus **de**s **We**stens) (*Tauentzienstrasse 21, Schöneberg* ☎ *(030) 21210, map 2 D5*), ranks second in the world in size (after Harrods of London) with a quarter of a million items spread over six vast floors. Take the elevator to the delicatessen (*Feinschmeckeretage*) on the 6th floor (see also RESTAURANTS), where 25,000 different types of food are irresistibly displayed, including 1,500 cheeses and 400 types of bread. There are rare Japanese delicacies, Alois Dallmayr coffees, Twining teas, Lübeck marzipan and Beluga caviar. Join the Berliners perched on stools at the Lenôtre cake counter before submerging yourself in KaDeWe's other floors.

Berlin's other department stores are eclipsed by KaDeWe, although they can be useful for basic needs such as toothpaste or tights. The main department stores are **Wertheim** (*Kurfürstendamm 231, Charlottenburg* ☎ *(030) 882061, map 2 D4*), good for stylish clothes, **Karstadt** (*Wilmersdorfer Strasse 109, Charlottenburg* ☎ *(030) 31891, map 1 D3 and locations in Tegel, Steglitz, Tempelhof, Neukölln and Wedding*) and **Hertie** (*Wilmersdorferstrasse 118, Charlottenburg* ☎ *(030) 310311, map 1 D3*).

While many sleek Paris fashion designers have shops in Berlin, the city also offers a good opportunity to check out German designers, many of whom have established a loyal following abroad. **Jil Sander** of Hamburg is Germany's top fashion designer (*Kurfürstendamm 48* ☎ *(030) 8833730, map 1 D3*), creating crisp, sober clothes for working women. **Soft** (*Bleibtreustrasse 6, Charlottenburg* ☎ *(030) 3121403, map 1 D3*) sells Cologne designer Caren Pfleger's luxurious clothes, plus many major French designers.

Selbach (*Kurfürstendamm 195* ☎ *(030) 8832526, map 1 D3*) stocks adventurous contemporary fashions for women by major German designers, while **Lange** (*Fasanenstrasse 29, Charlottenburg* ☎ *(030) 8826208, map 2 D4*) has seductive black frocks styled by Renate Günthert. **Horn** (*Kurfürstendamm 213, Charlottenburg* ☎ *(030) 8814055, map 2 D4*) is the place to go for colorful, sporty sweaters by Uta Raasch of Düsseldorf or chic menswear by Wolfgang Joop.

Although Munich, Hamburg and Düsseldorf are the main centers of German fashion, Berlin is beginning to establish a reputation for innovative design. **Fifty Fifty** (*Pariser Strasse 20, Charlottenburg* ☎ *(030) 8839615, map 1 D3*) exhibits extravagant fashions by seven Berlin designers, while **Molotow** (*Gneisenaustrasse 112, Kreuzberg* ☎ *(030) 6930818, map 4 E8*) sells clothes for men and women styled by more than 70 Berliners. **Maren Grebe** (*Kurfürstendamm 190-192* ☎ *(030) 8818864, map 1 D3*) sells her crisp creations in a striking Neoclassical interior, while women's gowns modeled on the styles of a century ago are sold at **Simone** (*Uhlandstrasse 170, Charlottenburg* ☎ *(030) 8838662, map 2 D4*).

Serious Berlin men shop at **Sør** (*Bleibtreustrasse, Charlottenburg, map 1 D3* AE ◉ VISA), a comfortable, traditional store selling classic suits and pullovers. **Schrill** (*Bleibtreustrasse 46, Charlottenburg* ☎ *(030) 8824048, map 1 D3*) caters to daring German males who do not recoil at the thought of wearing ties decorated with reproductions of Van Gogh or Picasso paintings. **Man Store** (*Uhlandpassage, Charlottenburg, map 2 D4* AE ◉ ◎ VISA) sells bizarre underwear for the boldest of Berlin men.

Shopping

For **children's clothes** in styles that have not changed since the age of the Kaisers, go to **Boom** (*Ublandpassage, Charlottenburg, map 2 D4* [AE] [O] [VISA]), or browse in **Pusteblume** (*Europa-Center, Charlottenburg* ☎ *(030) 2622810, map 2 D5*) for attractive clothes for under-12s. Finally, it's fun to rummage in the vast stock of second-hand clothes sold by the kilo at **Garage** (*Ahornstrasse 2, Schöneberg* ☎ *(030) 2112760, map 2 D5*), where less affluent Berliners find the stuff they need to be stylish paupers. **Highlights** (*Hohenzollerndamm 111, Wilmersdorf* ☎ *(030) 8265935*) sells second-hand clothes by Jil Sander and Lange, plus major Italian labels.

Berlin has several **flea markets** packed with evocative souvenirs of the past. For postcards, old banknotes, tin toys or dolls, go to the bizarre BERLINER FLOHMARKT, which has taken over a disused overground station at Nollendorfplatz (*map 2 D6*). The **Zille-Hof** (*under the arches of the S-Bahn at Fasanenstrasse, Charlottenburg, map 2 D4*) is named after the Berlin artist Heinrich Zille and sells a suitably bizarre assortment of dusty dolls, old metal signs, rusty baby carriages (prams), and faded photographs from the era of the Kaisers.

Of the open-air markets, the **Grosser Berliner Trodelmarkt** (*Strasse des 17 Juni, at S-Bahnhof Tiergarten, map 2 C4, open Sat, Sun 10am-5pm*) has the biggest choice of old objects, but the **Kreuzberger Krempelmarkt** (*Reichpietschufer, at Linkstrasse, map 3 D7, open Sat, Sun 8am-3.30pm*) is a better place to pick up a bargain. For local atmosphere, explore the market held around the ruined 19thC brick church on **Winterfeldtplatz** (*Schöneberg, map 2 E5, open Wed, Sat 8am-1pm*), where genial young Berliners sell organic vegetables, pottery, jaunty suspenders (braces), books, and pickled herring rolls to munch. The square is surrounded by attractive local cafés, although the curious **Café die Ruine**, which once flourished in a bombed-out apartment, seems to have become a ruin itself. An eccentric market garden nearby, however, continues to thrive in the shell of a prewar building.

For **food and drink**, the biggest choice is KaDeWe's 6th-floor delicatessen. Take home some Lübeck marzipan or a loaf of German bread, but note that UK and US regulations forbid the import of meats. **King's Teagarden** (*Kurfürstendamm 217* ☎ *(030) 8837059, map 2 D4*) stocks more than 170 varieties of tea, all of which can be sampled in an upstairs room overlooking Kurfürstendamm.

The streets around Savignyplatz abound in small shops selling exclusive **jewelry**. **Covarrubias** (*Bleibtreustrasse 50, Charlottenburg* ☎ *(030) 7845712, map 1 D3* [AE] [O] [VISA]) has rare and unusual metal or stone objects ranging from Balinese stone deities to African necklaces. **Galerie Lalique** (*Bleibtreustrasse 47, Charlottenburg, map 1 D3*) stocks jewelry made by hand in Berlin *ateliers*, while **Beate Brinkmann** (*Knesebeckstrasse 29, Charlottenburg* ☎ *(030) 8836740, map 2 D4* [AE] [O] [VISA]) fashions necklaces in elegant and eccentric styles. Finally, the irresistible **Maria Makkaroni** (*Bleibtreustrasse 49, Charlottenburg, map 1 D3* ☎ *(030) 3128584*) sells a bizarre assortment of jewelry, costumes, and accessories which prove just right for Berlin parties.

Gleaming German **kitchen equipment** is sold at **Zwilling J.A. Henckels** (*Kurfürstendamm 33, map 2 D4*), including scissors, kitchen knives and cutlery. **Bad + Baden** (*Ublandpassage, Charlottenburg, map 2 D4, no cards*) has everything for the bath, including luxurious towels, joke

Shopping

sponges, and perhaps Berlin's best selection of clockwork bath toys. They also sell a perfume called Berlin West, packaged like a fragment of the Berlin Wall.

Not far from Schloss Charlottenburg, the **Gipsformerei** (plaster-cast workshop) of the **Staatliche Museen Preussischer Kulturbesitz** (*Sophie-Charlotten-Strasse 17-18* ☎ *(030) 3217011, map 1 C2, open Mon-Fri 9am-4pm, Wed 9am-6pm*) is crammed with **plaster-cast models** of selected exhibits from the Prussian state museums (see page 45), including buddhas, Greek gods and hauntingly beautiful busts of Nefertiti that you may be tempted to ship back home.

For witty or arty **postcards** to send from Berlin, try **Ararat** (*Schlüterstrasse 22, Charlottenburg* ☎ *(030) 3124445, map 1 D3* and *Bergmannstrasse 99a, Kreuzberg* ☎ *(030) 6935080, map 4 E8*), whose vast range of cards is carefully classified by category. You can search the files for everything from cats to curios. Look through the Berlin collection for nostalgic prewar views of the Gedächtniskirche or scenes at the Wall in November 1989. For **stationery**, go to **Schaberow** (*Hardenbergstrasse 1, map 2 D4* ⬥ ⬥ ⬥) where they have notebooks, elegant pens, artists' paints and wrapping paper.

PosterGalerie 200 (*Kurfürstendamm 200* ☎ *(030) 8821959, map 2 D4*) sells unusual **posters**, including a gloriously bawdy cartoon titled *Berlinplanzen*(Urinals of Berlin). **Nielsen Design** (*Kantstrasse 41, Charlottenburg* ☎ *(030) 3134564, map 1 D3*) is the place to pick up artistic German calendars or striking posters, including a wondrous view of Berlin by night.

Collectors should note that the Berlin **porcelain** factory founded in the 18thC by Frederick the Great continues to produce high-quality ware in traditional or modern designs. **Staatliche Porzellan Manufaktur** (*Kurfürstendamm 26a* ☎ *(030) 8811802, map 2 D4*) is filled with Rococo-style statuettes and imitation Art Deco vases manufactured in the state-owned KPM factory in the Tiergarten district, while **Yokohama Haus** (*Kurfürstendamm 214, map 2 D4* ☎ *(030) 8819158*) sells rival Meissen ware. **Galerie Lietzow** (*Knesebeckstrasse 76* ☎ *(030) 8817574, map 2 D4*) sells unusual modern ceramics, and **Rosenthal Studio** (*Kurfürstendamm 226* ☎ *(030) 8817051, map 2 D4*) stocks porcelain and glass by some of the world's most creative designers.

For stylish **shoes**, try **Moos Grund** (*Bleibtreustrasse 40, Charlottenburg* ☎ *(030) 8837962, map 1 D3*) or **Schuhtick** (*Savignyplatz 11, Charlottenburg* ☎ *(030) 3124955, map 2 D4*). **Budapester Schuhe** (*Kurfürstendamm 199* ☎ *(030) 8811707, map 1 D3* ⬥ ⬥ ⬥) has sturdy men's shoes for tramping in the Grunewald, hand-made by Ludwig Reiter of Vienna or Alden of New England, plus chic women's shoes by Pink Flamingo of Zurich. **Sack & Pack** (*Kantstrasse 48* ☎ *(030) 3121513, map 1 D3* ⬥ ⬥ ⬥ ⬥) is crammed with leather satchels, briefcases, handbags and wallets.

For **toys**, investigate **Heidi's Spielzeugladen** (*Kantstrasse 61, Charlottenburg* ☎ *(030) 3237556, map 1 D3*), which is packed with traditional German puppets, wooden train sets and books, or go to **Vogel** (*Uhlandstrasse 137, Charlottenburg* ☎ *(030) 872377, map 2 E4*) for a wide choice of children's toys and games. It is worth a detour to **Berliner Zinnfiguren** (*Knesebeckstrasse 88, Charlottenburg* ☎ *(030) 310802, map 2 C4*) to take a look at the vast stock of hand-made miniature tin soldiers, including regiments of Prussian soldiers marching in formation.

Potsdam

30km (19 miles) SW of Berlin. Population: 140,000. Tourist information: Friedrich-Ebert-Strasse 5 ☎ Potsdam 21100. The area code for Potsdam is 03733 if calling from West Berlin, and 003733 from elsewhere in Germany.

Reunified Berlin contains such a wealth of sights that most visitors will have little need to venture farther afield. But if time permits, it is well worth heading out to the old Baroque town of Potsdam in Brandenburg state, to wander among the summer palaces of Frederick the Great and other Prussian kings. On the following 14 pages, all the sights are listed in detail and several walking itineraries are suggested. You will find recommendations about hotels (✎), restaurants (☱), cafés (☕) and shopping, as well as basic information on getting around.

Surrounded by lakes and forests, Potsdam was, and will be again, one of Germany's finest Baroque towns. The atmosphere of neglect lingers on, in the streets where crumbling 19thC apartments with cavernous doorways, and many other buildings, still bear the marks of the 1945 shelling. But they may now soon be restored, and this could make Potsdam into one of the most scintillating Baroque towns of Europe.

History

Older than Berlin, Potsdam originated as a 10thC Slavic settlement on the banks of the River Havel. The attractive setting appealed to the Great Elector, who built a royal palace, the Stadtschloss, near the river in 1664. It was here that he issued the Edict of Potsdam in 1685, which guaranteed religious freedom to Huguenots expelled from France. Encouraged by this enlightened attitude, some hundreds of Protestants settled in Potsdam, bringing new skills and generating a cosmopolitan air that survives to this day.

His grandson, Friedrich Wilhelm I, the Soldier King, drastically altered the character of Potsdam by erecting several enormous garrisons to house his rapidly multiplying Prussian regiments. At the same time, Friedrich Wilhelm laid out the Baroque Neustadt to the N of the old town, reflecting the Prussian king's strict character in its regimented grid pattern of streets.

Everything about Potsdam smacks of the Great little Frederick, but nothing is more striking than the superabundance of statues. They swarm! *— there is a whole garrison turned into marble, or stone, good, bad, and indifferent. They are as numerous in the gardens as the promenaders...The effect, to my taste, is execrable or ridiculous. Solitude and stillness seem the proper attributes of a statue. We have no notion of marbles mobbing.*

Letter from Thomas Hood, 1836

Potsdam's military role continued under his son, Frederick the Great, who built the **Kleine Kaserne** (*Wilhelm-Pieck-Strasse 67*), the **Infanteriekaserne** (*Hegelallee 33*) and the **Grosses Militärwaisenhaus** (Great Military Orphanage) (*Otto-Nuschke-Strasse 34*). But Frederick the Great's main contribution to Potsdam was the creation of fanciful Rococo palaces (some of which he designed) and vast formal gardens at his French-style summer retreat of Sanssouci.

Elegant Neoclassical buildings were added at Sanssouci by Friedrich Wilhelm IV in the 19thC. While still Crown Prince, he commissioned Schinkel to design SCHLOSS CHARLOTTENHOF and

Potsdam

the RÖMISCHE BÄDER (Roman Baths). Later, as king of Prussia, he followed in his great-grandfather's footsteps by designing several Italianate buildings, including the FRIEDENSKIRCHE and the monumental NEUE ORANGERIE.

Thus Potsdam is surrounded by all manner of palaces, gardens, pumping houses and follies. Energetic visitors can track down **Schloss Lindstedt**, built on a hill to the NW for Friedrich Wilhelm IV, the **Marmorpalais** in the NEUER GARTEN, built for Friedrich Wilhelm II, SCHLOSS BABELSBERG to the E, built for the Crown Prince, later Kaiser Wilhelm I, and SCHLOSS CECILIENHOF to the N, built for Kaiser Wilhelm II.

During the 19thC, Potsdam became an increasingly important center of science and technology. An institute of astronomy was built on the Telegraphenberg in Teltower Vorstadt, a suburb to the S. On the same hill stands the inaccessible Einsteinturm, an extraordinary Expressionist tower designed by Erich Mendelsohn in 1920-21 and used by Einstein to test the theory of relativity.

On a rainy day in March 1933, uniformed Nazis marched through the streets of Potsdam to the Garrison Church, for the first meeting of the Fascist parliament following the burning of the Reichstag. The military town — dubbed the "birthplace of the Third Reich" — became an obvious attack for Allied bombers, and much of the old quarter was destroyed in 1945, including the Stadtschloss (Royal Palace).

The Potsdam Agreement, signed in SCHLOSS CECILIENHOF in 1945, established the postwar division of Germany, and brought Potsdam within the Soviet-run sector. The frontier between Potsdam and West Berlin (the Berlin Wall) ran down the middle of the Havel and along the bank of the Griebnitzsee, and the favorite residence of the Hohenzollern became a dreary, dilapidated town dominated by a large Soviet military base.

With the end of the Cold War, Potsdam recovered its cosmopolitan bustle, and its link with Frederick the Great (who fell from favor under the Communists) was symbolically restored in 1991 when the king's bones were brought back from Schloss Hechingen, where they had been been taken for safety during World War II, and buried in the royal crypt at Sanssouci.

Getting there

Once a bureaucratic and logistic nightmare for visitors from West Berlin, the town now makes an easy day excursion by S-Bahn, bus or boat. The **S-Bahn** runs hourly from Wannsee to Potsdam Stadt station, a 10min walk from town; **bus 113** runs the 45min journey from S-Bahnhof Wannsee to Bassinplatz in the town center, along an interesting, although bumpy route; **bus 116** runs from S-Bahnhof Wannsee to the Glienicke Brücke, where you can walk across the bridge to pick up Potsdam **tram 93**.

Tickets issued by the Berlin transportation authority (BVG) are valid on buses from Berlin to Potsdam, and on the S-Bahn from Wannsee to Potsdam, but not on Potsdam local transportation.

Getting around

Potsdam's public transportation network of trams and buses is run by **ViP** (☎ *Potsdam 22966*). You can buy a multiple ticket (valid for up to 8 rides) at the ViP office near the Glienicke Brücke, or at the Weisse Flotte office near the Lange Brücke. Ask for a *Liniennetzplan* (network map).

Push the button marked *Türöffner* to open the tram or bus doors, then insert the ticket carefully into the *Entwerter* and push the button to obliterate one section.

Walks around Potsdam

With its palaces, parks, lakes and eccentricities, Potsdam is a marvelous town to explore on foot. For those with time to spare, the three itineraries described below take in the main sights, as well as some elusive delights.

WALK 1: THE TOWN
Map page 122-123. Tram 91, 93, 95, 96, 98 to Alter Markt. Allow 2hrs.

Potsdam's 18thC **Neustadt** (New Town) survived the bombs of World War II, and is now one of the finest examples of Baroque town planning in Germany.

Beginning at S-Bahnhof Potsdam Stadt, cross the Havel by the Lange Brücke. The island on the right, **Freundschaftsinsel**, has peaceful gardens, fountains and an open-air theater. Turn right to reach Am Alten Markt. The Neoclassical **Nikolaikirche** (*open Mon-Sat 10am-noon, 2-5pm, Sun 11.30am-5pm*) on the square was designed by Karl Friedrich Schinkel and built in 1830-37 by Ludwig Persius. Its lofty dome was added in 1842-50. Bombed in 1945, the church has since been meticulously restored. An information folder is available in many languages.

Two bombed buildings on the square were restored in the 1960s to form a cultural center, the **Haus Marchwitza**, with several restaurants and a café. The former **Rathaus** (town hall) on the left was built in 1753 by Johann Boumann and Carl Hildebrant. Modeled on a Palladian villa, it has a curious cupola surmounted by a gilded figure of Atlas. The statues symbolizing civic virtues were carved by Johann Heymüller. To the right, the **Knobelsdorff-Haus** is a handsome, pale green Rococo mansion built by Georg Wenzeslaus von Knobelsdorff in 1750. The two caryatides supporting the balcony have the air of typical Prussian *Landsknechte* (mercenaries), with their lank moustaches and ragged costumes.

The bombed Stadtschloss, which formerly stood on the S side of the square, was not saved by the East Germans. The ruins of the royal palace were demolished in 1961, leaving just the solitary Corinthian colonnade designed in 1745 by Knobelsdorff. Known as the Havelkolonnaden, it now stands near the steamer landing-stage on the Havel.

The former **Marstall** (royal stables) still stand on the opposite side. The long red ocher building was originally built by Johann Nering in 1685 as an orangery overlooking the long-vanished Lustgarten (pleasure garden). Converted to stables in 1714, the edifice was greatly extended by Knobelsdorff in 1746. The architrave is crowned with symbolic statues of rearing horses, carved by Friedrich Christian Glume.

Walk along the front of the Marstall, now the FILMMUSEUM, and turn right at the end to reach Schlossstrasse. **Am Neuen Markt** — a deserted, leafy square overshadowed by moldering Baroque mansions — is hidden behind the Marstall. The Neoclassical building in the middle of the square is the **Ratswaage** (weighhouse), constructed in 1836. To the left is the former **Kutschstall**, a decayed Baroque coach house built in 1787-91 by Andreas Krüger. The gate is festooned with military trophies and surmounted by a *quadriga* (4-horse chariot).

Leave the square on the N side and cross Yorckstrasse, one of Potsdam's filled-in canals, then head down Wilhelm-Staab-Strasse, a well-preserved Baroque street. Continue along Jägerstrasse, then turn right into Brandenburger Strasse, an

Potsdam/Walks

attractive pedestrianized street lined with modest 18thC houses that now contain shops and cafés. It leads to Bassinplatz, a large square overlooked by dusty gable houses built in the 18thC by Frederick the Great to tempt skilled Dutch craftsmen to Potsdam. The basin that gave the square its name was dug in 1739 to create the air of a Dutch town canal, but, later, repeated silting problems caused it to be filled in.

A whimsical Dutch quarter known as the HOLLÄNDISCHES VIERTEL was laid out N of Bassinplatz in 1742. To reach it, leave the square on the N side by Benkertstrasse, then turn left into Mittelstrasse, the main street of the 18thC model quarter. Designed by Johann Boumann, the houses here are rather less grand

KEY TO NUMBERED BUILDINGS

1. Historische Windmühle
2. Friedenskirche
3. Brandenburger Tor
4. Dampfmaschinenhaus
5. Chinesisches Teehaus
6. Potsdam Museum
7. Marstall
8. Jagdschloss Gleini
9. Nikolaikirche
10. Haus Marchwitza

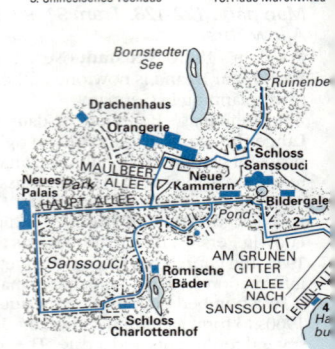

Walk 2

than those on Bassinplatz, suggesting provincial Holland rather than urbane Amsterdam. With their broad facades and green and white shutters, they are very much a German version of Holland. The East German authorities, quite unlike the Dutch, let the houses fall into ruin, but the quarter is now slowly being rebuilt.

Now turn right up Friedrich-Ebert-Strasse to reach the **Nauener Tor**, a city gate built in 1755. Frederick the Great commissioned this curious English mock-Gothic-style edifice, which launched the Neo-Gothic movement on the mainland of Europe.

The street leads to the **Nauener Vorstadt**, a 19thC suburb filled with villas that are grand, if rather dilapidated. Turn left along Reiterweg and right up Jägerallee. A lane to the right takes you into the RUSSISCHE KOLONIE ALEXANDROWKA, a settlement built in 1826 to house Russian soldiers. At the end of the street, turn left up Puschkinallee, and take the path left through the woods to discover the secluded **Russian Orthodox Church**.

You can follow Puschkinallee farther to reach the old Jewish cemetery, then turn right up **Pfingstberg**, a hill landscaped by Peter Lenné in 1849. Standing on the summit are the ruins of a summer palace built by Persius in the 1840s for Friedrich Wilhelm IV, and the derelict **Pomonatempel**, built in 1801 by Schinkel as his first commission. Return down Puschkinallee to pick up route 95, or continue along Pfingstberg to reach SCHLOSS CECILIENHOF.

WALK 2: PARK SANSSOUCI
Tram 94, 96 or bus 695 to Platz der Nationen. Allow 2hrs.
The palaces and gardens at Sanssouci cover an extensive area to the W of the old town. The 18thC and 19thC landscaped grounds are dotted with an extraordinary variety of palaces, temples,

122

Walks/Potsdam

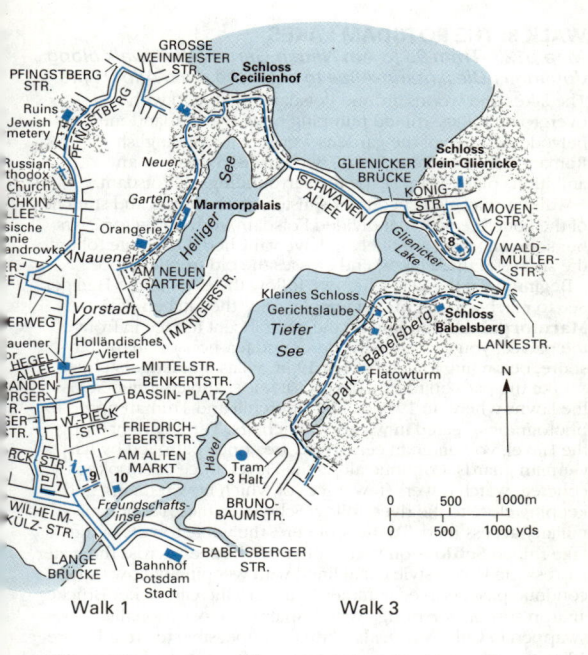

Walk 1   Walk 3

belvederes, statues, fountains, vineyards and grottos. Frederick the Great gave Sanssouci its Baroque grandeur, commissioning SCHLOSS SANSSOUCI, the NEUES PALAIS and the CHINESISCHES TEEHAUS. In the 19thC, buildings in a more restrained Neoclassical style were added by Friedrich Wilhelm IV. These included SCHLOSS CHARLOTTENHOF, the RÖMISCHE BÄDER and the FRIEDENSKIRCHE.

Schloss Sanssouci can be frustrating to visit, as the compulsory guided tours are frequently oversubscribed; the Neues Palais and Schloss Charlottenhof, although just as interesting architecturally, are far less crowded, and the Orangerie and Römische Bäder frequently remain almost deserted.

The main entrance to the park is near the Brandenburger Tor, built in 1770. Walk down the **Allee nach Sanssouci**, an almost rural lane which suddenly turns sharp right to give visitors a thrilling first view of the Baroque *Schloss*. Head toward the palace, then turn left at the pond and follow the **Hauptallee** (main avenue). If you turn left into the woods, you should come upon the bizarre CHINESISCHES TEEHAUS.

From here, follow the meandering path to the right, past the **Meierei** (dairy) to reach the **Römische Bäder**. Continue to **Schloss Charlottenhof** and follow the straight path beyond, then turn right along the avenue leading to the NEUES PALAIS. Now turn right along the Hauptallee, then left at the circle of statues. Climb up to the ORANGERIE for a panorama over the gardens, and, if you feel fit, continue up the hill to the RUINENBERG, for a closer look at its curious group of mock-ruins. From the summit, you get a good view of **Schloss Sanssouci** to the S. Descend there to bring an end to the walk.

123

Potsdam/Walks

WALK 3: THE POTSDAM LAKES
Map p123. Tram 95 to Am Neuen Garten, then walk along Johannes-Dieckmann-Allee to enter the park. Allow 3hrs.

The lakes and woods around Potsdam are dotted with overgrown follies, ruined pumping houses and abandoned belvederes. Most of the gardens were created in English Romantic style by Peter Lenné, who in 1833 drew up an ambitious plan to landscape the surroundings of Potsdam.

Walkers may also encounter sinister watch towers and stretches of the concrete wall that divided Potsdam from Berlin for 29yrs, but soon all traces are likely to have vanished. Our route follows the shores of three lakes, and crosses the old frontier twice.

Beginning at the NEUER GARTEN, follow the edge of the Heiliger See to reach a mock ruined temple, once the kitchen of the **Marmorpalais**. Standing on the magnificent terrace in front of the palace, you can see belvederes and tea-houses on the far shore, belonging to flamboyant 19thC villas on Mangerstrasse.

Take the path on to SCHLOSS CECILIENHOF, and continue across the lawns where, in 1945, Stalin, Churchill and Truman posed for photographs, seated in wickerwork chairs. Turning right along the Havel, you enter an eerie, wild area once patrolled by East German guards. Continue along the Havel, once overlooked by concrete watch towers (few traces of which now remain), and, keeping close to the river, follow Schwanenallee, formerly a military access road. To the N of here, the white towers of the fake ruined **Schloss** on PFAUENINSEL can be seen across the water.

Cross the Dutch-style canal lined with weeping willows, and continue past decayed summer-houses to the Glienicker Brücke, an iron suspension bridge where spies were occasionally swapped in Cold War deals. Virtually impossible to cross before 1990, the bridge is now jammed with traffic. On the far side, you come to the entrance to SCHLOSS KLEIN-GLIENICKE. Cross the road here to enter a small 19thC park landscaped by Lenné. Following the edge of the Glienicker Lake, you come to a little promontory with a good view of two Schinkel buildings: the Nikolaikirche to the SW in Potsdam and SCHLOSS BABELSBERG on the wooded hill to the S. Continue past JAGDSCHLOSS GLIENICKE, a former hunting lodge, then turn left to leave the park.

On Königstrasse turn right, then right again down Mövenstrasse and continue along Waldmüllerstrasse. The villas on the right once had the Berlin Wall running through their back gardens. Now turn right down Lankestrasse, an old cobbled lane leading to Park Babelsberg across an old bridge that was once heavily guarded. Turn right along the edge of Glienicker Lake to reach the abandoned 19thC pumping house of SCHLOSS BABELSBERG. Built in the style of a Gothic castle, it later served a genuine defensive role when the East Germans blocked up the windows to prevent escapes during the Cold War. Farther on, you come upon a building, in English Neo-Gothic style, the **Kleines Schloss**, that once housed the ladies-in-waiting employed at Schloss Babelsberg. Make a short detour up a path behind the building to discover a genuine medieval relic, the **Gerichtslaube** (pavilion of the law courts), a folly assembled from fragments of Berlin's old town hall. Continue along the shore of the Tiefer See to **Strandbad Babelsberg** *(open 9am-7pm)*, a lakeside beach with *Strandkörbe* (wickerwork chairs with high, basket-shaped backs to keep off the wind). Follow the path straight ahead, turn left on the paved road and right at a white building. A path ascends to the tram 94 halt at Bruno-Baum-Strasse; use the *Zentrum* platform to get back to the town center.

Sights and places of interest

It would be impossible to see all Potsdam's sights in a single visit. The palaces and gardens at Sanssouci alone require at least a day, while another day is necessary to do justice to the old town.

BILDERGALERIE *(Picture Gallery)*
In the E wing of Schloss Sanssouci ☎ Potsdam 22655. Open mid-May to mid-Oct 9am-noon, 12.45-5pm. Closed every 4th Wed of month. Tram 94, 96 to Platz der Nationen, or bus 695 to Schloss Sanssouci.

The Bildergalerie is Germany's oldest museum, built in 1755-63 by Johann Gottfried Büring to house Frederick the Great's ever-growing collection of Baroque art. The long facade is lined with figures symbolizing the Arts and the Sciences (Painting is shown with brushes in her hand; Geometry supports a globe), while the keystones above the windows are decorated with busts of such artists as Dürer and Cranach.

The care taken to protect the gallery floor (visitors must put on felt slippers) has not been extended to the Baroque paintings, which are in urgent need of repair. But a few appealing works of local interest have survived, such as Julius Schoppe's *Kaiser's Pine in Klein-Glienicke Park*, and Karl Blechens's *Interior of the Palm House on Pfaueninsel*, which invests the iron and glass structure with a hint of Oriental mystery. A view of the *Spittelmarkt in 1833* by Eduard Gaertner provides a sad glimpse of what is forever lost.

CHINESISCHES TEEHAUS
s of Sanssouci park ☎ Potsdam 93628. Open mid-May to mid-Oct 9am-noon, 12.45-5pm. Closed every 2nd Mon of month. Tram 91, 94, 96 to Schloss Charlottenhof.

Deep in the woods of Sanssouci, Frederick the Great's round Chinese tea-house was built to rival the extravagant Rococo buildings of Bavaria. Designed in 1754-56 by Johann Gottfried Büring, the rotunda is a riot of Frederician Chinoiserie, with gilt tassels hanging from the roof and ornate columns shaped like palm trees.

Encircling the tea-house is a terrace dotted with bizarre gilt statues carved by Johann Peter Benckert and Johann Heymüller. A solitary Chinese philosopher is perched on the roof, while whiskered old Chinamen sit with demure European ladies drinking tea or nibbling exotic fruit. The inside, recently restored, contains a profusion of gilt stucco and twisted candlesticks, while the domed ceiling is decorated with pale *trompe l'oeil* frescoes showing Oriental men flirting with Western women amid a torrid landscape of palms, monkeys and parrots.

DAMPFMASCHINENHAUS
s of Wilhelm-Külz-Strasse at Leninallee ☎ Potsdam 24106. Open mid-May to mid-Oct 9am-noon, 1-5pm; closed Mon, Tues ✗ Tram 91, 94, 96 to Auf dem Kiewitt.

One of Potsdam's most endearing eccentricities is a steam pumping house disguised as an Oriental Mosque, which stands amid postwar apartment blocks on an inlet of the Havel. Built by Ludwig Persius for Friedrich Wilhelm IV in 1842, its steam-driven pumps (made at the Borsig factory in Berlin) once filled the reservoir on RUINENBERG from which Sanssouci's fountains were supplied. The chimney is disguised as a minaret, and the giant pumps are housed in a domed hall whose Moorish arches and arabesques were based on the mosque in Córdoba. The guided tour (in German) includes a demonstration of the restored steam pump, which is controlled by a regulator crowned with a Prussian eagle.

FILMMUSEUM
Karl-Liebknecht-Forum 1 ☎ Potsdam 23675. Open Tues-Sun 10am-5pm. Tram 91, 93, 95, 96, 98 to Alter Markt.

The Potsdam suburb of Babelsberg was the home of Germany's first German movie studio. Established in 1911, it grew into the giant UFA studios, where many famous German movies — such as *The Blue Angel* and Fritz Lang's *Metropolis* — were shot. These featured costly sets inspired by Expressionist architecture and painting. A cinema museum was established in Potsdam as early as 1922, but the archives were destroyed in a bombing raid.

Replaced in 1977-80, the collection is now housed in the former Prussian royal stables (*Marstall*) (see *Walk 1* on page 121). Four different movies are screened daily in a luxurious theater. The selection is international, although foreign movies are normally dubbed into German. The museum café (*open Wed-Sun 11am-6pm*) serves coffee and beer, but not much else, in a pleasant Biedermeier interior decorated with potted plants.

FRIEDENSKIRCHE
Am Grünen Gitter. Tram 94, 96 or bus 695 to Platz der Nationen.

Inspired by the Romanesque churches of Rome, King Friedrich Wilhelm IV sketched the plans for the Friedenskirche, built in 1844-54 on the edge of a small lake. The church may be a copy, but, if you can get inside, you will see a genuine Byzantine mosaic in the apse. Bought for the Prussian monarch in 1834, it comes from a demolished church on the Venetian island of Murano.

NEUE KAMMERN
W of Schloss Sanssouci ☎ Potsdam 22823. Open Apr-Sept 9am-5pm; Feb, Mar, Oct 9am-4pm; Nov-Jan 9am-3pm. Closed Fri; daily noon-12.30pm. Tram 91, 94, 96 to Platz der Nationen, or bus 695 to Schloss Sanssouci.

Built by Knobelsdorff in 1747 as an orangery, the Neue Kammern was turned into guest quarters by King Friedrich I. The rooms are richly decorated with Rococo reliefs.

NEUE ORANGERIE
N of Schloss Sanssouci ☎ Potsdam 26189. Open May-Oct 9am-noon, 1-5pm. Closed every 4th Thurs of month. Bus 695 to Orangerie.

Dominating the slopes above Sanssouci, the Neue Orangerie was designed by Friedrich Wilhelm IV as an overscaled version of an Italian Renaissance villa. The building was meant to stand on a grand Roman avenue leading to Schloss Lindstedt, but the plan was never realized.

The Orangery once contained guest quarters occupied by Czar Nicholas I and his wife Charlotte, the daughter of Friedrich Wilhelm III, but it has suffered from years of neglect, and the long glazed galleries, where tropical palms once flourished, are now dilapidated.

Summer concerts of chamber music are given in the courtyard, and the view of Schloss Sanssouci from the tower (*Turm*) is worth the climb.

NEUER GARTEN
Am Neuen Gartenstrasse. Tram 95 to Am Neuen Garten, then a 5min walk along Johannes-Dieckmann-Allee.

Bounded by two lakes, the Neuer Garten was created in 1787-91 as a summer residence for King Friedrich Wilhelm II. With its winding lakeside paths, sweeping lawns and secret follies, it is perhaps Potsdam's most romantic park, yet it remains far less crowded than Sanssouci in the summer.

Idyllically sited on the edge of the Heiliger See, the **Marmorpalais** was designed by Karl von Gontard in 1787 as an Italianate villa, and aggrandized a few years later by Carl Langhans. An army museum once located here was quickly closed following the political upheavals of 1989, leaving uncertain the future role of the summer palace. Linked to the palace by an underground passage, the lakeside kitchen (*Küche*) was designed by Karl von Gontard to evoke a ruined Classical temple sinking into the sand. Fragments of columns dotted among the pine trees enhance the melancholy effect. To the N of the palace, an ice store was built in the shape of a miniature Egyptian pyramid.

Situated on the main avenue, the **Holländisches Etablissement** is another Prussian whimsy: a row of red-brick houses with Dutch gables, built as servants' quarters. Like the Dutch quarter in Potsdam, the houses here have rather Germanic proportions. An orangery — concealed behind the gable houses — was designed in Egyptian style, with mock hieroglyphics and brooding sphinxes. And as if that were not variety enough, SCHLOSS CECILIENHOF, near the Jungfernsee, is modeled on an English Tudor manor.

NEUES PALAIS
w end of Park Sanssouci ☎ Potsdam 93143. Open Apr-Sept, 9am-5pm; Feb, Mar, Oct 9am-4pm; Nov-Jan 9am-3pm. Closed daily 12.45-1.15pm; every 2nd and 4th Mon in month ✗ ▣ Bus 695 to Neues Palais, or S-Bahn to Wildpark.

A stiff walk down the Hauptallee brings you to the Neues Palais, built in 1763-69 by Büring, the architect of the Chinese tea-house. Frederick the Great apparently commissioned the palace to prove that the Seven Years' War had not bled Prussia dry. He seldom visited the building, however, preferring the more intimate charms of Schloss Sanssouci, and its 200 rooms served merely as guest quarters. An extraordinary collection of 428 statues were carved for the balustrades. Several colossal figures, located on the forecourt and once supporting ornate lamps, revealed cleverly concealed old gas pipes following damage suffered during World War II.

Not content with one extravagant gesture, Frederick commissioned Karl von Gontard to build the palatial servants' quarters to the W, known as the *Communs* after a similar building at Versailles. Two giant wings are linked by a triumphal arch decorated with a sculptural group commemorating the Seven Years' War of 1756-63.

The Neues Palais is far less crowded than Schloss Sanssouci, although its ballrooms and concert halls are just as splendid. The guided tour is not compulsory, but you do have to wear protective footwear — after a long walk down the dusty main avenue it is actually rather pleasant to glide across the parquet ballroom floors in enormous felt slippers.

The rooms are hung with Flemish and Dutch Baroque works, but perhaps the most interesting paintings are historical studies such as Franz Krüger's *Parade on Unter den Linden*, showing the confident swagger of the Prussian army after the victory at Waterloo, and Adolph Menzel's *Coronation of King Wilhelm I at Königsberg in 1861*, depicting jewel-laden princesses, Prussian aristocrats and pompous generals.

The palace boasts a bizarre grotto festooned with elaborate fountains, and sea monsters fashioned from glinting minerals and shells. Elsewhere, there's a theater, and a 19thC bathroom equipped with bells for summoning various servants including the dressmaker (*Schneiderin*).

Frederick the Great sketched the designs for the two Classical temples near the palace, built by Karl von Gontard in 1768. The *Antikentempel* (s of the Hauptallee) was built for the royal collection of antiquities, while the *Freundschaftstempel* (Temple of Friendship) to the N was erected as a memorial to Countess Wilhelmine von Bayreuth.

POTSDAM MUSEUM
Wilhelm-Külz-Strasse 8-12 and 13 ☎ Potsdam 21865. Open Tues-Sun 10am-5pm. Tram 91, 93, 95, 96, 98 to Alter Markt.

A deserted aquarium, faded photographs of the German royal family at Sanssouci, and a cabinet of *Schuttpflanzen* (plants that thrive amid the rubble of bombed cities) are among the curiosities at Potsdam's excellent local history museum. The extensive collection is housed in two handsome buildings in the old town: the period up to 1900 in a Baroque mansion constructed by Johann Boumann, while 20thC history occupies a corner of the imposing Hiller-Brandtsche Häuser, an 18thC apartment block modeled on Inigo Jones's Banqueting Hall in London.

The older museum explains the formation of the watery Havel landscape, and the distinctive ecology of postwar bomb sites. Fascinating sections cover Slavonic settlements, local parks, Prussian soldiers' blue and red uniforms, Potsdam porcelain, the 19thC Russian colony, and local shops that supplied the imperial court.

The 20thC museum has a superb map of Potsdam in 1912, showing features that have disappeared, like the Stadtschloss, bombed in World War II, the Dutch canal in Dortustrasse, the numerous *Kaserne* (barracks), the *Kriegsschule* (military academy) in Teltower Vorstadt where World War I officers were trained, and the *Naturtheater für die Heimatspiele* (an open-air amphitheater for staging native German theater).

Old photographs show the Zeppelin base in the Brandenburger Vorstadt, the bizarre Expressionist tower in Teltower Vorstadt, and the notorious Nazi rally in Potsdam's Garnison-Kirche on a wet March day in 1933. Prussian *Pickelhaube* helmets, postage stamps overprinted with Nazi slogans, a cash register overflowing with worthless one-million-Mark notes, and a mock-up of a bombed street are reminders of Potsdam's troubled history.

RÖMISCHE BÄDER
s end of Park Sanssouci ☎ Potsdam 93211. Open mid-May to mid-Oct. 9am-noon and 12.30-5pm. Closed every 3rd Mon of month. Tram 94, 96 to Schloss Charlottenhof.

Overlooking a little lake, the mock Roman Baths are a delightful Neoclassical curiosity designed by Schinkel in 1829. Grouped around an atrium, the intimate rooms are decorated with imitation Pompeian frescos and Classical landscapes. An attractive colonnade overlooks a canal in which a gondola prow has been placed to evoke Venice. The Neoclassical pavilion on the water's edge to the S of the baths was once an elegant tea-house.

RUINENBERG
Bus 695 to Schloss Sanssouci, then a 5min climb.
A curious cluster of mock Classical ruins was built for Frederick the Great in 1748 on the aptly-named Ruinenberg hill that overlooks Sanssouci. Its architect was the prolific Knobelsdorff. With its crumbling temple and toppled column, this Frederician folly strangely resembles the ruins of Berlin and Potsdam in 1945. A pool built as a reservoir to supply Sanssouci's fountains is now eerily stagnant, and the Cyrillic names of Soviet soldiers carved on Classical columns add to the melancholy romance of the spot.

RUSSISCHE KOLONIE ALEXANDROWKA
W of Puschkinallee in Nauener Vorstadt. Tram 95 to Kapellenberg.
The story of Potsdam's Russian colony has the air of an old folk tale. In 1812 a group of Russian soldiers from the Singers' Corps was captured and brought to Potsdam. When Russia later became an ally of Prussia, the Czar presented the singers to a Potsdam regiment. Friedrich Wilhelm III then had the delightful idea of creating a mock Russian village for the musicians, and in 1826 he commissioned Peter Lenné to design 13 identical wooden houses. Surrounded by rambling apple orchards, the habitations, each one bearing the name of a Russian singer, have steep roofs and ornate carved balconies. As at NIKOLSKOE, they reflect Friedrich Wilhelm III's fondness for Russian peasant life, which was sparked off by the marriage of his daughter, Charlotte, to the future Czar Nicholas I. The colony was named Alexandrowka after the Prussian Czarina.

The fantasy is completed by a **Russian Orthodox Church** hidden in the Kapellenberg woods (walk up Puschkinallee from the tram terminus, then take the footpath to the left through the trees). Dedicated to St Alexander Newski, the exotic church with pink walls and onion-shaped domes was designed by Schinkel following a plan sent from St Petersburg. A little graveyard contains the tombs of expatriate Russians who died in Potsdam. By a strange quirk of history, a large garrison of Soviet troops was, until recently, stationed nearby. As they gradually withdraw, Potsdam's links with Russia will sadly fade.

SCHLOSS BABELSBERG
E of Potsdam. Tram 94 to Bruno-Baum-Strasse, then a 20min walk, or tram 93 to Glienicker Brücke, then a 10min walk, or bus 691 to Babelsberg-Nord.
Situated in a wooded park above the Tiefer See, Schloss Babelsberg was built by Schinkel in 1833 as a summer residence for the Crown Prince, later Kaiser Wilhelm I. Princess Augusta, Wilhelm's consort, asked Schinkel to model the building on Windsor Castle, which was seen on a tour of Britain in 1826. The rambling Neo-Gothic palace now houses the **Museum für Ur- und Frühgeschichte**, a small museum of local prehistory.

The park was originally laid out by Peter Lenné in 1834 in the same style as Schloss Klein-Glienicke across the water, but it was later redesigned by Hermann Fürst Pückler-Muskau. The grounds are dotted with mock Gothic curiosities, including kitchens linked to the palace by an underground passage. The **Kleines Schloss** down by the water's edge was built in 1841 for Princess

Potsdam/Schloss Cecilienhof

Augusta's ladies-in-waiting, but perhaps the most curious building is the **Flatowturm**, a hilltop tower used for guests, modeled on the Frankfurt-am-Main Eschenheimer Tor, which is still standing.

Hidden by trees on a nearby summit, the **Gerichtslaube** is a romantic folly constructed from fragments of Berlin's old town hall on Alexanderplatz, which was demolished in 1871. Its 13thC Gothic arcade surmounted by a 15thC Renaissance gallery forms a bizarre architectural puzzle.

SCHLOSS CECILIENHOF
Neuer Garten ☎ Potsdam 22579. Open May-Oct, Tues-Sun 9am-5pm, and every 1st and 3rd Mon of month, 9am-4pm ✗ ≡ Bus 695 to Cecilienhof.

Built during World War I for the Crown Prince, Schloss Cecilienhof is a rambling country house designed in a typical English suburban style, with ivy-clad brick walls, half-timbered gables and leaded glass windows. The Allied Powers met in this comfortable old mansion in 1945 to discuss the terms of the Potsdam Agreement.

The guided tour takes in the wood-paneled room where the treaty on the postwar division of Germany was signed by Stalin, Churchill and Truman. Looking through the bay window, you can see the Havel river, which, until 1990, formed the boundary between East Germany and West Berlin.

SCHLOSS CHARLOTTENHOF
s end of Park Sanssouci ☎ Potsdam 92774. Open mid-May to mid-Oct 9am-12.30pm, 1-5pm. Closed every 4th Mon of month. Tram 94, 96 to Schloss Charlottenhof.

One of Germany's finest Neoclassical buildings, Schloss Charlottenhof was built by Schinkel in 1826-28 as a summer palace for the Crown Prince, the future Friedrich Wilhelm IV. The intimate rooms are inspired by English domestic interiors, with writing desks equipped with curious gadgets, and bay windows overlooking Peter Lenné's neat English lawns and picturesque ponds.

The walls are crammed with romantic paintings of the Rhine, Italy and the Alps, including Caspar David Friedrich's *Gartenterrasse*, which expresses the German romantic longing for the mountains.

Imitation Pompeian frescoes decorate the dining room, while the breakfast room is painted a deep red. But the most curious part of the villa is the bedroom, where a blue and white awning has been hung above the bed in imitation of a desert tent.

SCHLOSS SANSSOUCI
w of Potsdam ☎ Potsdam 23931. Open Apr-Sept 9am-5pm; Oct, Feb, Mar 9am-4pm; Nov-Jan 9am-3pm. Closed daily 12.30-1pm, and 1st and 3rd Mon of month ✗ (compulsory) lasts 40mins. Tram 94, 96 to Platz der Nationen, or bus 695 to Schloss Sanssouci.

Designed in 1744 by Georg Wenzeslaus von Knobelsdorff from a sketch by Frederick the Great, Schloss Sanssouci was the first summer palace to be built at Potsdam. The long, low Baroque building overlooks a terrace, where Frederick tried to give a French air to his country retreat by planting vines. The very name *sans souci* (carefree) suggests that Frederick was trying to escape from the stiff formality of the Prussian court to enjoy the sensual pleasures depicted by his favored artist, Watteau. But his duties

Visitor facilities/Potsdam

caught up with him, the vines withered, and life at Sanssouci became as dull as in Berlin.

The palace has just 13 rooms, including a circular library with lavish Rococo decoration, and a beautiful music room decorated with reliefs illustrating Ovid's *Metamorphoses*, where Frederick liked to play the flute.

The **Damenflügel** (*open mid-May to mid-Oct Wed-Sun 9-11.45am, 12.30-5pm; mid-Oct to mid-May Sat, Sun 9am-noon, 1-4pm*) was added to the w by Persius, to accommodate the queen's ladies-in-waiting. The rooms are furnished with Biedermeier cabinets and paintings.

After a visit to Sanssouci, you might be tempted to hike to the summit of the Klausberg hill to enjoy the view from the café terrace at the **Drachenhaus** (W of the Neue Orangerie). Modeled on the Chinese pagoda at London's Kew Gardens, the Drachenhaus (dragons' house) was built in 1770 by Karl von Gontard. The eccentric pagoda was once the home of a gardener employed by Frederick the Great to tend a vineyard planted on the slopes of the Klausberg.

The **Hotel Potsdam** (*Lange Brücke* ☎ *Potsdam 4631, 184 rms* AE ◉ ◯ VISA *Tram 91, 93, 95, 96, 98 to Alter Markt*) is a modern high-rise hotel built on the site of the royal pleasure gardens. Rooms are comfortable but bland, with extensive views of Potsdam and the Havel. Weisse Flotte cruise ships depart from the pier beside the hotel, and the main sights in Potsdam are within easy walking distance. **Schloss Cecilienhof** (*Am Neuen Garten* ☎ *Potsdam 23141, 36 rms* AE ◉ VISA *Bus 695 to Cecilienhof*) is a comfortable country house hotel situated in the wing of the palace where the Potsdam Accord was signed. The bedrooms are adequate, but the atmosphere of old East Germany still haunts the building. Only stay here if you have a car.

Most restaurants in Potsdam are still rather unfriendly, but **Bolgar** (*Brandenburger Strasse 35* ☎ *Potsdam 22505, closed Sun eve, Mon*) is a cheerful Bulgarian restaurant decked with festive green and red streamers. The menu features Central European specialties such as Bulgarian *Schopska-salat* (salad with sheep's-milk cheese, gherkins, tomatoes and onions) and Hungarian goulash. Try the Ukrainian *Soljanka mit Sauerrahm* (soup with bacon, onions and sour cream).

There are no places to eat in the grounds of Sanssouci, but several leafy beer gardens situated around the perimeter of the park may be worth tracking down on summer days. A lane leads off Zur historische Mühle (near the old windmill behind Schloss Sanssouci) to an extensive beer garden, where you can fill up on *Weissbier* and *Bratwurst*, or *Kaffee und Kuchen*, while chickens cluck around your feet. The establishment has several antiquated weighing machines for those who are beginning to worry about the effects of too much hearty German food.

While wandering in Potsdam, you might stop at the **Stadtcafé** (*Brandenburgerstrasse 16*), a pleasant café with a small terrace, or the **Café Heider** (*Friedrich-Ebert-Strasse 30*), which boasts a leafy terrace overlooking the Nauener Tor. The drab atmosphere fostered by East German state control lingers on in many Potsdam cafés, but those at the **Filmmuseum** and in the **Haus Marchwitza** on Am Alten Markt have brightened up considerably since unification.

Shopping Western stores are likely to transform the Brandenburger Strasse within a few years, but currently the choice is rather limited. **Buch und Bild** (*Brandenburger Strasse 57*) has a good selection of Potsdam guidebooks, art books and postcards, while **Das Internationale Buch** (*Friedrich-Ebert-Strasse 17*) has cleared out most of its Russian stock to make way for detailed maps and guide books. **Noten und Bücher** (*Friedrich-Ebert-Strasse 14*) has a range of classical music scores.

Boat trips **Weisse Flotte Potsdam** (☎ *Potsdam 21090*) runs regular cruises from the Langen Brücke pier to the Potsdam lakes and Wannsee.

SPECIAL INFORMATION/Excursions and children

Other excursions

If you are seriously overcome with *Wanderlust*, take the train from Berlin-Lichtenberg station to **Dresden** on the river Elbe (200km/125 miles s of Berlin, 2½hrs by train). Virtually obliterated in an air raid at the end of World War II, the capital of Saxony is being restored to its former Baroque splendor. The exquisite Zwinger palace of August the Strong has now been carefully reassembled, although the Frauenkirche still remains a heap of blackened rubble.

Leipzig (217km/136 miles sw of Berlin, 2hrs by train) was a major prewar book-publishing center. Businessmen still flock to trade fairs in Leipzig, but the center is now a rather jarring mixture of restored Baroque buildings and plain modern offices.

There are ample forests, lakes and fields to explore within the boundaries of Berlin, but you might be tempted to explore the **Spreewald**, a region of woods and canals about 1hr's drive to the SE, described by the 19thC poet Theodor Fontane as a "rural Venice." Or head for the pleasant town of **Lübbenau** on the Spree, where you can clamber aboard a flat-bottomed punt for a tranquil tour of the local waterways. See USEFUL ADDRESSES on page 16 for details of bus tours to the Spreewald.

Berlin and Potsdam for children

Beaches and swimming pools Berlin's numerous sandy beaches provide an unexpected treat for children. The main beach at WANNSEE often gets crowded, but there are countless secret sandy coves on the shores of the GRUNEWALD lakes that are easily reached by S-Bahn or U-Bahn.

Boat and bus trips Every child except the most seasickness-prone should be taken on at least one trip on the Havel. Berlin children particularly appreciate jaunts on the *Moby Dick*, a big boat in the shape of a whale that departs from Wannsee pier. A trip on a Berlin double-decker bus might also be fun. (See BERLIN BY BUS on page 42.)

Castles Berlin's Baroque palaces tend to display too much precious porcelain to be child-friendly, but older kids might enjoy a trip to the moated ZITADELLE SPANDAU.

Museums and workshops The MUSEUM FÜR VERKEHR UND TECHNIK is a good place to take older children on a rainy day. There are buttons to push, pulleys to yank, and computers programmed to compose music. The big locomotives can't be climbed on, but there is a marvelous overgrown railroad yard at the back for romping around.

Teenagers might enjoy the neck-breaking spectacle of film footage of modern Berlin to be viewed at PANORAMA. The giant dinosaur skeletons and precious minerals at the MUSEUM FÜR NATURKUNDE might appeal, and the MUSEUM FÜR VOR- UND FRÜH-GESCHICHTE has good dioramas of prehistoric settlements.

Parks and zoos *Mit Kind und Kegel 'raus nach Tegel* (Head out to Tegel with a child and a ball), a local preacher urged city dwellers back in 1793. Nowadays children can be kept amused all day at Tegel, and toys can be rented on the spot. There's miniature golf near the steamer pier on the Greenwich-promenade, while the **Freizeitpark** is a safe place to let off steam, with an adventure playground, trampolines, rowboats, and toys for hire. You can also rent bicycles for adults and children and pedal along the shore to Tegel beach.

Sports and activities/Special information

The ZOOLOGISCHER GARTEN and the TIERPARK FRIEDRICHSFELDE are well-run modern zoos, with an incredible array of animals kept in natural environments, and the AQUARIUM, with its reptiles and rare fish, may help to engage young imaginations. The TIERGARTEN has boats to rent, the VIKTORIAPARK has a waterfall and a small zoo, while **Freundschaftsinsel** at Potsdam has a small playground, and rowboats to rent.

Restaurants and cafés Restless children are free to romp around Berlin's beer gardens, some of which have playgrounds. **Loretta in der City** (see page 110) has a magical atmosphere in the evening, when it is lit by thousands of lamps and the Ferris wheel slowly turns. Farther out of town, the **Chalet Suisse** in the Grunewald (see *Walk 3* on page 39) has a rambling garden filled with gurgling fountains, and a large playground complete with a model tractor. Ice cream was one of the rare luxuries in East German life, and the many *Eis Cafés* in Mitte and Prenzlauer Berg are popular places for young families.

Views Many youngsters love the thrill of ascending to dizzying heights. The best views can be had from the FRANZÖSISCHER DOM, the FUNKTURM and the FERNSEHTURM, as well as from the SIEGESSÄULE column.

Other activities For details of puppet shows, circuses and other children's activities, take a look in *Zitty* magazine under *Kind & Kegel*.

Sports and activities

The woods and lakes near Berlin offer visitors ample opportunities for walking, cycling, jogging, swimming and boating, while sports centers, stadiums and clubs cater to a wide variety of other leisure activities. **Activities** are listed here alphabetically, with a section on **Spectator sports** at the end.

For details of all sporting events and sports associations, contact **Landessportbund Berlin** (*Jesse-Owens-Allee 1-2, Charlottenburg* ☎ *(030) 300020*). The office is situated in a street named after the black American athlete who enraged the Nazis by stealing the limelight at the 1936 Olympics.

Billiards The **Billard Centrum** (*Nollendorfplatz 3-4, Schöneberg* ☎ *(030) 2163361, map 2 D6*) is a favored haunt.

Boating Rowboats can be rented at the Strandbad on the WANNSEE, the Neuer See in the TIERGARTEN, the Schlachtensee in the Grunewald, and the Freizeitpark at TEGEL.

Bowling Berlin has numerous bowling alleys. The best-located for visitors are **Bowling am Kurfürstendamm** (*Kurfürstendamm 156, Wilmersdorf* ☎ *(030) 8825030, map 1 D2*) and **Bowling am Studio** (*Kaiserdamm 80, Charlottenburg* ☎ *(030) 3027094*).

Cycling Despite Berlin's flat terrain, cycling is not popular, but it is an ideal way to explore the Grunewald and other forests. There is an extensive network of cycle lanes (mainly running along the sidewalks), but it is generally wise to take cycles out to the suburbs by S-Bahn or U-Bahn. For other information, including details on using the S- and U-Bahns, see page 12.

Fitness facilities **City-Fitness** (*Uhlandstrasse 185, Charlottenburg* ☎ *(030) 8818688, map 2 D4*) is a friendly gym in the heart of the city.

Ice-skating There are rinks at the **Eissporthalle** (*Jafféstrasse, Charlottenburg* ☎ *(030) 30381*) and the **Eisstadion** (*Fritz-Wildung-Strasse, Wilmersdorf* ☎ *(030) 8234060*).

Special information/Sports and activities

During the winter months, some of the frozen lakes are safe for skating. Take your cue from the natives.

Riding Certain paths in the Grunewald are marked out for horseback riding. The main school is **Reitschule Onkel Toms Hütte** (*Onkel-Tom-Strasse 172, Zehlendorf* ☎ *(030) 8132081*).

Roller-skating The main rinks are the **Rollerskating-Center** (*Hasenheide 108, Kreuzberg* ☎ *(030) 6211028*) and, in summer only, the **Rollschuhbahn in Wilmersdorf** (*Fritz-Wildung-Strasse, Wilmersdorf* ☎ *(030) 8234060*).

Running The TIERGARTEN is the most central park for running, but you can also limber up before breakfast in the quiet park behind SCHLOSS CHARLOTTENBURG. The Grunewald route described in *Walk 3* on page 39 can be done as an energetic run, as can the Spree route as far as the REICHSTAG (see *Walk 1* on page 34). The 50km **Berlin Marathon** is held annually on the first Sun in Oct.

Skiing and tobogganing There are several artificial ski-slopes built on the rubble hills created after World War II. In winter, the Grunewald **Teufelsberg** becomes Alpine, with its ski slopes and long toboggan run.

Sports centers The East German government encouraged its promising athletes to win Olympic medals by building excellent sports centers, such as the **Sport- und Erholungszentrum** (*Leninallee 77, Friedrichshain* ☎ *(0372) 42283320, S-Bahn to Leninallee*), a well-equipped complex with a swimming pool, sauna, gym, roller-skating rink, bowling alley, table-tennis, mini-golf and sports for children. The leisure center **Meretva** (*Glockenturmstrasse, Charlottenburg* ☎ *(030) 3042255*) has tennis courts, a swimming pool, sauna and bowling alley.

Swimming Many Berlin districts have excellent swimming pools, but the most spectacular architecturally is the **Stadtbad Neukölln** (*Ganghoferstrasse 3-5* ☎ *(030) 68092653*), a monumental Neoclassical edifice completed in 1914, with marble and mosaics inspired by the Thermae at Pompeii. **Blub** (*Buschkrugallee 64, Neukölln* ☎ *(030) 6066060, map 7E6*) is a modern leisure pool, equipped with wave machines, a slide, whirlpools and a sauna. To escape the sweltering city, West Berliners take the S-Bahn to **Strandbad Wannsee** (*Wannsee-badweg* ☎ *(030) 8035450*), a popular open-air pool, while East Berliners head in the opposite direction to the **Strandbad Müggelsee** (*Fürstenwalder Damm, Rahnsdorf, S-Bahn to Rahnsdorf, then a 10min walk through the woods*). For a quieter dip, try the Strandbad at TEGEL.

Tennis and squash Playing facilities are often booked up way ahead, but you can try to get a court at **Tennis + Squash City** (*Brandenburgische Strasse 53, Wilmersdorf* ☎ *(030) 879097*), with 11 squash courts and seven tennis courts you can rent by the hour. The **Squash Center Alt-Lietzow** (*Alt-Lietzow 15-19, Charlottenburg* ☎ *(030) 3421844, map 1B3*) has 12 courts. For information on other clubs open to nonmembers, contact **Berliner Tennis-Verband** (☎ *(030) 8255311*).

Walking There are excellent forest and lakeside walks, particularly in the **Grunewald**, the **Tegeler Forst**, the **Spandauer Forst**, the **Düppel Forst** and along the **Havel shore**. The S-Bahn gets you to the Grunewald, while the U-Bahn stations at Tegel and Onkel-Toms-Hütte make good starting points for a ramble. Some half-day walks along the **Spree**, around **Kreuzberg** and in the **Grunewald** are given on pages 34-40, and others appear in the entries on TEGEL and GRUNEWALD. For walks around **Potsdam** see pages 121-124.

WORDS AND PHRASES

Spectator sports   Berlin offers many opportunities. The best soccer games can be seen at the **Friedrich-Ludwig-Jahn-Sportpark** (home to BFC Dynamo) and the **Stadion an der Wuhlheide** (FC Union Berlin's ground). Blau-Weiss 90 plays at the **Olympic Stadium**. For fixtures, contact **Berliner Fussball-verband** (Berlin soccer association) (☎ *(030) 8911047*). **Ice-hockey** matches often take place at the Eissporthalle.
   Rowing regattas take place at the **Hohenzollernkanal**, **Volkspark Jungfernheide** and the Regattastrecke in **Grünau**. **Sailing regattas** are held at the **Tegeler See**, **Gatow** and **Grünau**. Berlin also hosts international **swimming contests** and **tennis tournaments**. **Trotting races** are run some Suns at **Trabrennbahn Karlshorst** or **Trabrennbahn Mariendorf**.

German in a nutshell

German is not an easy language because of its complex sentence structure and compound words. Even Germans can be defeated by their unwieldy words: car (*Kraftfahrzeug*), for example, is almost always written *Kfz*, which adds to the confusion for visitors. In written German, nouns are always written with an initial capital letter. The old script form of ss (ß) can still be seen.

English is widely spoken in former West Berlin, but in some parts of East Berlin you are more likely to meet people whose second language, if any, is Russian.

BASIC COMMUNICATION

Yes/no   ja/nein
Please   bitte (informal) bitte schön (formal)
Thank you   danke
Thank you very much   danke schön
You're welcome   bitte sehr
Excuse me   entschuldigen Sie
Sorry   tut mir leid
Hello   guten Tag
Good morning/evening/night   guten Morgen/Abend/Nacht
Goodbye   auf Wiedersehn (formal), auf Wiederhören (on the telephone)
Mr/Mrs   Herr/Frau
Miss   Fraülein
Ladies   Damen
Gentlemen   Herren
This one/that one   dieses/jenes
Big/small   gross/klein
With/without   mit/ohne
Hot/cold   heiss/kalt

Cheap   billig
Expensive   teuer
Good/bad   gut/schlecht
Rest room/toilet   Toiletten/WC
I speak English   ich spreche Englisch
Do you speak English?   sprechen Sie Englisch?
I don't speak German   ich spreche kein Deutsch
I don't understand   ich verstehe nicht
I don't know   ich weisse nicht
I am American/British   ich bin Amerikaner/Engländer (female: Amerikanerin/Engländerin)
Where is ...?   Wo ist ...?
Do you have ...?   bitte, haben Sie ...?
I'd like ...   ich möchte ...
How much does it cost?   wieviel kostet das?

NUMBERS: 0 null, 1 eins, 2 zwei, 3 drei, 4 vier, 5 fünf, 6 sechs, 7 sieben, 8 acht, 9 neun, 10 zehn, 11 elf, 12 zwölf, 13 dreizehn, 14 vierzehn, 15 fünfzehn, 16 sechzehn, 17 siebzehn, 18 achtzehn, 19 neunzehn, 20 zwanzig, 21 einundzwanzig, 22 zweiundzwanzig, 30 dreissig, 40 vierzig, 50 fünfzig, 60 sechzig, 70 siebzig, 80 achtzig, 90 neunzig, 100 hundert.
1992/93/94 neunzehn hundert zwei/drei/vier und neunzig

THE CALENDAR: Day Tag, Month Monat, Year Jahr, Today Heute, Yesterday Gestern, Tomorrow Morgen.
   Monday Montag, Tuesday Dienstag, Wednesday Mittwoch, Thursday Donnerstag, Friday Freitag, Saturday Samstag or Sonnabend, Sunday Sonntag.

Words and phrases

January Januar, February Februar, March März, April April, May Mai, June Juni, July Juli, August August, September September, October Oktober, November November, December Dezember.

TIME: ... o' clock ... Uhr, quarter past ... viertel nach ...,
half-past five halb sechs (i.e. half of six), quarter to ... viertel vor ...
What time is it? wie spät ist es?

SIGN DECODER

Achtung beware
Anmeldung reception
Aufzug elevator
Ausgang exit
Auskunft information
Ausverkauf clearance sale
Baden verboten no swimming
Besetzt full/occupied
Betreten verboten no trespassing
Betriebsferien closed for vacation
Bitte nicht stören do not disturb
Dom cathedral
Dorf village
Drücken push
Eingang entrance
Eintritt frei admission free
Einwurf insert
Erdgeschoss/Parterre ground floor
Etage floor
Erste hilfe first aid
Feiertags geschlossen closed on holidays
Fernsprecher telephone
Feuermelder fire alarm
Flughafen airport
Frei vacant
Freibad open-air swimming pool
Friedhof cemetery
Fussgängerzone pedestrian mall

Gasse lane
Gefahr danger
Geöffnet/offen open
Geschlossen closed
Gesperrt out of order
Hof courtyard
Insel island
Kirche church
Krankenhaus hospital
Lebensgefahr danger
Nicht berühren do not touch
Notausgang emergency exit
Polizei police
Privatgrundstück private property
Rathaus town hall
Rauchen verboten no smoking
Rolltreppe escalator
Ruhetag closed all day
Selbstbedienung self-service
Sonderangebot special offer
Tor gate
Turm tower
Verkehrsamt/Verkehrsverein tourist office
Viertel district/quarter
Wald forest
Wechsel currency exchange
Ziehen pull
Zutritt verboten no admission

PUBLIC TRANSPORTATION

Abfahrt departures
Ankunft arrivals
Bahnsteig track/platform
Bushaltestelle bus stop
Einsteig vorn/hinten enter at front/rear
Entwerter ticket-stamping machine
Fahrkarten ticket office
Gepäckaufbewahrung checked luggage

Gleis track/platform
Hauptbahnhof (Hbf) main railroad station
Liegewagen couchette
Nichtraucher nonsmoking car
Raucher smoking car
Reserviert reserved
Schlafwagen sleeper
Speisewagen restaurant car

SHOPPING

Laden shop
Apotheke dispensing pharmacy
Buchhandlung bookstore
Drogerie pharmacist/chemist
Friseur hairdresser
Geschenkartikel gifts

Kaufhaus department store
Konditorei pastry store
Kunstgewerbe craft store
Postamt post office
Reisebüro travel agency
Schuhgeschäft shoe store

FOOD AND DRINK

Waiter/waitress Herr Ober/Fräulein
Snacks Erfrischungen
Breakfast Frühstück
Lunch Mittagessen
Dinner Abendessen
The bill, please die Rechnung, bitte

Menu Speisekarte
Snack bar Schnellimbiss
Draft beer Bier vom Fass
Light ale Helles Bier
Brown ale Dunkles Bier
Lager/bitter Pilsener/Altbier
Red wine Rotwein

136

STREET NAMES

White wine Weisswein
Dry/sweet trocken/süss
Mineral water Mineralwasser
Orange juice Orangensaft
Apple juice Apfelsaft
Milk Milch
Salt Salz
Pepper Pfeffer
Mustard/oil Senf/Öl

Vinegar Essig
Bread/roll Brot/Brötchen
Butter Butter
Cheese Käse
Fruit Obst
Coffee Kaffee
Tea Tee
Chocolate Schokolade
Sugar Zucker

MENU DECODER

Auflauf soufflé
Aufschnitt sliced cold meats
Bauernbrot coarse rye bread
Bauernomelett omelet + bacon + onions
Bismarckhering pickled herring
Blau steamed, + butter
Blutig rare
Bockwurst giant boiled sausage
Boulette cold hamburger
Bratkartoffeln fried potatoes
Bratwurst fried sausage
Durchgebraten well done
(Gekochtes) Ei (boiled) egg
Ente duck
Erbsensuppe thick pea soup
Fasan pheasant
Fleisch meat
Forelle trout
Frühlingssuppe vegetable soup
Gänseleberpastete goose liver pâté
Gebacken baked
Gedämpft steamed
Gefrorene ice cream
Gefüllt stuffed
Gegrillt grilled
Gekocht boiled
Gemüse vegetables
Gepökelt pickled
Geräuchert smoked
Geschmort stewed, braised
Halbdurch medium
Hausfrauenart with apple, onions + sour cream

Hausgemacht homemade
Holländisch with mayonnaise
Jägerart in a red wine sauce + mushrooms
Kartoffelsalat potato salad
Klösse/Knödel dumplings
Kräuter herbs
Lachs salmon
Leberwurst liver pâté
Linsensuppe lentil soup
Matjeshering small, cured herring
Ochsenschwanzsuppe oxtail soup
Pfannkuchen pancake
Rahm cream
Räucheraal smoked eel
Rauchwurst smoked sausage
Roh raw
Röst fried
Rotkraut red cabbage
Sahne cream
Schinken ham
Schweinshaxe knuckle of pork
Schnitzel veal escalope
Sosse sauce
Spargel asparagus
Speck bacon
Spiess skewered
Sülze jellied pressed meat
Topf stew
Truthahn turkey
Überbacken au gratin
Zwiebel onion

List of street names

All streets and bridges mentioned in the book that fall within the area covered by our maps are listed here. Map numbers are printed in **bold type**. Some smaller streets are not actually named on the maps, but the map reference given should be enough for you to find your way.

Adenauerplatz, **1**D3
Ahornstr., **2**D5
Akademie, Platz der, **4**C8
Alexanderplatz, **4**B9
Almstadtstr., **4**B9
Altonaer Str., **2**C5
Alt-Lietzow, **1**B3
Am Berlin Museum, **4**D8
Am Köllnischen Park, **4**C9
Am Kupfergraben, **4**B8
Am Rathaus, **2**F5

Am Weidendamm, **4**B8
Askanischer Platz, **3**D7
Augsburgerstr., **2**D4-5

Bebelplatz, **4**C8
Bellevue Ufer, **3**B5
Bergmannstr., **4**E8-9
Bernburger Str., **3**C7-D7
Bertolt-Brecht-Platz, **4**B8
Bismarckstr., **1**C2-3
Bleibtreustr., **1**D3

Blücherplatz, **4**E8
Bodestr., **4**B8-9
Breitscheidplatz, **2**D4
Buckower Damm, **6**E5
Budapester Str., **2**D5
Buschkrugallee, **7**E6

Chamissoplatz, **4**E8
Chausseestr., **3**-**4**A7-8
Clara-Zetkin-Str., **3**-**4**B7-8
Clayallee, **5**E3

137

Street names

Damaschkestr., 1D2
Dimitroffstr., 7C6
Dudenstr., 3F7

Eiserne Brücke, 4B8
Ernst-Reuter-Platz, 2C4

Fasanenstr., 2C4-D4
Französischer Str., 4C8
Franz-Klühs-Str., 4D8
Friedrichs Brücke, 4B9
Friedrichstr., 4B8-D8

Gertrauden Brücke, 4C9
Gleisdreieck, 3D7
Gneisenaustr., 4E8-9
Grolmanstr., 1-2C3-D4
Grossbeerenstr., 3E7
Grosse Hamburger Str., 4A8-B8
Grossfürstenplatz, 3C6
Grossgörschenstr., 3E6
Grosser Stern, 2C5

Hagelbergerstr., 3E7
Hallesches Ufer, 3-4D7-8
Hansabrücke, 2B5
Hansaplatz, 2B5
Hardenbergplatz, 2D4
Hardenbergstr., 2C4-D4
Hasenheide, 4E9-F10
Hauptstr., 3E6-F6
Hausvogteiplatz, 4C8
Haydnstr., 2B5
Henriettenplatz, 1E2
Hirtenstr., 4B9
Hohenzollerndamm, 1-2F2-E4
Hohenzollernplatz, 2E4
Holsteiner Ufer, 2B5
Holtzendorffplatz, 1D2
Holzhauser Str., 6B4
Hütten Weg, 5E3

In den Zelten, 3B6
Insel Brücke, 4C9
Invalidenstr., 3B6-A7

Jannowitzbrücke, 4C10
Joachimstalerstr., 2D4
Jungfernbrücke, 4C9
John-Foster-Dulles-Allee, 3C6-B7

Kantstr., 1-2D3-4
Kaiser-Friedrichstr., 1B2-D2
Karl-Liebknecht-Str., 4B9
Karl-Marx-Allee, 4B10
Kemperplatz, 3C7
Klausener Platz, 1B2
Kleine Alexanderstr., 4B9
Klingelhöferstr., 3D6
Klopstockstr., 2C5
Knesebeckstr., 2D4
Kochstr., 4D8
Koenigs Allee, 5D3
Königstr., 5E1-2

Körnerstr., 3D6
Königin-Luise-Str., 5-6E3-4
Krausnickstr., 4B8
Kreuzbergstr., 3E7
Kronprinzendamm, 1D1
Kronprinzen Ufer, 3B7
Kurfürstendamm, 1-2E1-D4
Kurfürstenstr., 2-3D5-6

Lehniner Platz, 1D2
Leibnitzstr., 1C3-D3
Leipziger Platz, 3C7
Leipzigerstr., 3-4C7-8
Lessingbrücke, 2B5
Lietzenburgerstr., 1-2D3-5
Lietzensee Ufer, 1C2
Lindenstr., 4C8-D8
Linkstr., 3C7-D7
Los-Angeles-Platz, 2D4
Luftbrücke, Platz der, 4F8
Luisenplatz, 1B2
Lustgarten, 4B8
Luther Brücke, 2B5
Lützowplatz, 3D5

Mansteinstr., 3E6
Marburgerstr., 2D4
Märkisches Ufer, 4C9
Marschallbrücke, 3B7
Marx-Engels-Brücke, 4B9
Marx-Engels-Platz, 4B9
Matthäikirchstr., 3C7
Mauerstr., 3-4C7-8
Mehringdamm, 4E8
Mehringplatz, 4D8
Meinekestr., 2D4
Methfesselstr., 3F7
Moabiter Brücke, 2B6
Möckernbrücke, 3D7
Moltke Brücke, 3B7
Monbijou Brücke, 4B8
Monbijoustr., 4B8
Münzstr., 4B9

Nassauische Str., 2E4
Neue Schönhauser Str., 4B9
Nikolaikirchplatz, 4C9
Nollendorfplatz, 2D6
Nürnbergerstr., 2D5

Oberwasserstr., 4C9
Oranienburger Str., 4B8
Oranienplatz, 4D9
Oranienstr., 4D9
Otto-Grotewohl-Str., 3C7

Pariser Platz, 3C7
Pariser Str., 1D3
Pestalozzistr., 1C2-3
Platz der Akademie, 4C8
Platz der Luftbrücke, 3C8
Pohlstr., 3D6-7
Poststr., 4C9
Potsdamer Platz, 3C7

Potsdamer Str., 3E6-D6

Rathausbrücke, 4C9
Rathausstr., 4B9
Rathenauplatz, 1E1
Regensburgerstr., 2E4-5
Reichpietschufer, 3D7
Reichstagufer, 3B7
Richard-Wagner-Platz, 1C3
Rolandufer, 4C9

Sächsische Str., 1D3-E3
Savignyplatz, 2D4
Schaperstr., 2D4
Schiffbauerdamm, 3-4B7-8
Schillstr., 2C5
Schleswiger Ufer, 2B5
Schleusenbrücke, 4C9
Schlossbrücke, 1B2
Schlosstr., 1B2
Schlüterstr., 1C3-D3
Schönebergerstr., 3D7
Schumannstr., 3B7
Siegesallee, 3C6
Siegmunds Hof, 2B5
Sophienstr., 4B8-9
Sophie-Charlotten-Str./Platz, 1C2
Spandauer Damm, 1B2
Spielhagenstr., 1C2
Spreeufer, 4C9
Spreeweg, 3C5-6
Stauffenbergstr., 3C6
Steinplatz, 2C4
Str. des 17. Juni, 2-3C4-7
Stresemannstr., 3-4C7-D8

Tauentzienstr., 2D5
Tegeler Weg, 1A2-B2
Tempelhofer Ufer, 3D7
Tiergartenstr., 3C6
Trebbiner Str., 3D7

Uhlandpassage, 2D4
Uhlandstr., 2C4-F4
Universitätsstr., 4B8
Unter den Linden, 3-4C7-B8

Viktoria-Luise-Platz, 2E5

Weidendammer Brücke, 4B8
Welserstr., 2D5-E5
Werderstr., 4C8-9
Wilhelmstr., 4C8
Wilmersdorfer Str., 1C3-D3
Windscheidstr., 1C2-D2
Winterfeldplatz, 2E5
Wittenbergplatz, 2D5

Yorckstr., 3E7

Zimmerstr., 4C8

138

Index

Bold page numbers refer to main entries. *Italic page numbers* refer to illustrations and maps. See also the LIST OF BERLIN STREET NAMES on pages 137-8.

Accidents, 17
Addresses and telephone numbers, **15-17**
Ägyptisches Museum, 43, **45**, 50, 82, 89
Air Ministry, 37
Air travel/airports, 9, 10, 16
Albrecht the Bear, 7, 100
Alexander I, Czar, 45
Alexanderplatz, 41, **45-6**
Altdorfer, 58
Alte Königliche Bibliothek, 23, **97**
Alternative centers, **111**
Altes Museum, *24*, 36, **46**, 57, 73, 78-9, *78*, 80
Ambulances, 17
American Express, 8-9, 10, 17
Amerika-Gedenkbibliothek, 38
Anhalter Bahnhof, 7, 37
Antikenmuseum, 43, 45, **46-7**, 89
Aquarium, 42, **47**, 133
Architecture, **22-5**
Arnim, Ferdinand von, 91
Arnolfini, Giovanni, 59
Art, **26-8**
Art Deco, 53, 68
Art Nouveau, 24, 30, 35, 53, 68
Augustus the Strong, 30, 132
Avus, 61

Ballet, **113**
Baluschek, Hans, 72
Banks, 13
Baroque architecture, **22-3**
Bars, **114**
Bauhaus, **24-5**, 30, 53, 72
Bauhaus-Archiv, 25, 42, **47**
Beaches, 44, **132**
Beckmann, Max, 48, 81
Bedford, Sybille, 70
Beer halls and beer gardens, **109-10**
Begas, Reinhold, 81
Behrens, Peter, 24
Benckengraff, Johann, 30
Benckert, Johann Peter, 125
Benz, Karl, 76
Berger, Ines, 73
Bergman, Ingmar, 29
Berlin Airlift, 39
"Berlin painter," 46

Berlin-Museum, 38, 43, **47-8**, 49, 65
Berlin-Pavillon, 35, **48-9**
Berlin Wall, 6, 7, 21, 27, 29, 42, 43, **49**, 52, 62, 66-7, 70, 74, 86, 87, 91, 120, 124
Berliner Ensemble, 36, 52, **113**
Berliner Flohmarkt, **48**, 99, 117
Berliner Secession, 26
Beuys, Joseph, 46
Bicycles, 12, **133**
Bildergalerie, **125**
Biller family, 69
Billiards, **133**
Bismarck, Otto von, 19, 69, 95
Bladelin, Pieter, 59
Blechen, Karl, 125
Blockhaus Nikolskoe, **82-3**, 105
Boat trips, 15-16, **42-3**, 98, **131**, **132**
Boating, **133**
Böcklin, Arnold, 81
Bode, Wilhelm von, 50, 84, 92, 93
Bode-Museum, 36, 41, 43, 46, **49-51**, 58, 77, *78*, 79, 81, 92, 97
Bookstores, 115
Borsig, August, 55, 76
Botanischer Garten, 41, **51**
Böttger, Johannes, 30
Botticelli, Sandro, 58
Boumann, Johann, 23, 121, 122, 128
Bowling, **133**
Brandenburg, 18, 62
Brandenburger Tor, 23, 42, **51-2**, *51*, 71, 94, 96
Breakfast, 104
Brecht, Bertolt, 20, 36, 52, 55, 64, 113
Brecht-Weigel-Haus, **52**
Breitscheidplatz, **52**
Brendel, Johann, 85
Britz, **52-3**, 112
Britzer Garten, **53**
Bröhan, Karl, 53
Bröhan-Museum, **53**, 89
Die Brücke, 26, 53-4
Brücke-Museum, **53-4**
Bruegel, Pieter the Elder, 60, 69
Bundestag, 21
Bureaux de change, 13
Büring, Johann Gottfried, 23, 125, 127
Buses, 10, 11, 16, **42**, 120, 132

Cabaret, **114**
Cafés, **108-9**, **131**, 133
Calendar of events, **33-4**
Canova, Antonio, 93
Carl von Preussen, Prince, 83, 90-1
Carove, Giovanni, 69
Cars:
  accidents, 17
  breakdowns, 17
  documents, 8
  driving in Berlin, 12
  renting, 12
Casino, **114**
Castles, 44, **132**
Cézanne, Paul, 79
Chagall, Marc, 79
Charge cards, 9, 17
Charlotte, Princess (Czarina Alexandra), 82-3, 105, 127, 129
Charlottenburg, 22, **32**, 41, **54**, 101
  see also Schloss Charlottenburg
Checkpoint Charlie, 37, **62**
Chemists, 24-hour, 17
Children, **132-3**
Chinesisches Teehaus, 23, 123, **125**
Christus, Petrus, 59
Churches, 16, 44
Cinema, **28-9**, **111**
Circus, **111**
Citny, Kiddy, 48
Climate, 10
Clothes, 10
  shopping, **116-17**
Cobra group, 46
Cold War, 21, 25, 52, 62, 124
Conrad, Carl, 98
Consulates, 16
Cook, Captain James, 77
Courbet, Gustave, 81
Cranach, Lucas the Elder, 59, 63, 69, 99, 125
Credit cards, 9, 17
Cultural institutions, **112**
Currency, 8
Currency exchange, 13
Customs and excise, 9
Cycling, 12, **133**

Dada, 26
Dahlem, **32**, 45, **54-5**, 79

139

Index

Dahme river, 66
Daimler, Gottlieb, 76
Daimler-Benz, 25, 66
Dalí, Salvador, 27
Dampfmaschinenhaus, **125-6**
Darnton, Robert, 31
David, Jacques Louis, 89
Deighton, Len, 29, **31**
Dentists, 17
Department stores, **116**
Derossi, Pietro, 37
Desiderio da Settignano, 93
Deutsche Staatsbibliothek, 98
Deutscher Dom, 23, 86
Deutsches Rundfunk-Museum, **55**
Dietrich, Marlene, 28, 48, 55, 113
Disabled visitors, 15
Discos, **114-15**
Dix, Otto, 7, 26, 69, 83
Döblin, Alfred **31**, 46
Doctors, 17
Documents required, 8
Doesburg, Theo van, 24
Dom, 34, 36, 42, 46, **55**, 93
Donatello, 51
Dorotheenstadt, 22
Dorotheenstädtischer Friedhof, 52, **55**
Drachenhaus, **131**
Dresden, 132
Driver's licenses, 8
Dubuffet, Jean, 27
Düppel Forst, 135
Duquesnoy, François, 51
Dürer, Albrecht, 58-9, 69, 125
Duris, 46
Dutch East India Company, 37
Duty-free allowances, 9

Edel, Ulrich, 29
Egyptian Museum *see* Ägyptisches Museum
Eiserne Brücke, 36
Eiswerder, 43
Electric current, 14
Emergency information, **17**
Englischer Garten, 95
Engravings Collection *see* Kupferstichkabinett
Ephraim, Veitel Heine, 55-6
Ephraimpalais, **55-6**, 82
Ermelerhaus, 36
Ernst, Max, 27
Ethnography, Museum of *see* Museum für Völkerkunde
Etiquette, 14
Eurocheques, 8
Europa-Center, **52**

Expressionism, 26, 27, 48, 53
Eyck, Jan van, 59

Fassbinder, Rainer Werner, 29, 83
Fax services, 14
Feininger, Lyonel, 48
Felixmüller, Conrad, 72
Fernsehturm, 41, 42, **56**, 76, 133
Ferries, 9-10, **11**
Fetting, Rainer, 48
Fichte, Johann Gottlieb, 55
Film industry, **28-9**, **111**
Filmmuseum, 121, **126**
Fire services, 17
First aid, 17
Fischerinsel, 36
Fitness facilities, **134**
Flea markets, **47-8**, **117**
Folklore Museum *see* Museum für Volkskunde
Food and drink:
 bars, **114**
 beer halls and beer gardens, **109-10**
 cafés, **108-9**
 restaurants, **103-8**
 shopping, **117**
Football, **135**
Foreign exchange, 13
Forests, 44
Fosse, Bob, 29
Französischer Dom, 23, **56**, 86, 133
Französischer Friedhof, **55**
Frederick the Great, 19, 22, 23, 30, 51, 56, 65, 69, 79, 88, 89, 94, 96-7, 118, 119, 120, 122, 123, 125, 127-8, 129, 130-1
Freie Universität, **54-5**
Freizeitpark, 94, 132-3
French Cathedral *see* Französischer Dom
Freundschaftsinsel, 121, 133
Freybrücke, 43
Friedenskirche, 120, 123, **126**
Friedländer, Max, 59
Friedrich, Caspar David, 57, 130
Friedrich, Prince, 68
Friedrich I, King, 18, 86, 126
Friedrich III, Elector, 18, 69, 94
Friedrich III, King, 22
Friedrich Karl, Prince, 63
Friedrich Wilhelm, Great Elector, 18, 22, 23, 36, 63, 69, 77, 89, 96, 119
Friedrich Wilhelm I, King, 18-19, 23, 47, 69, 97, 119

Friedrich Wilhelm II, King, 19, 85, 95, 120, 127
Friedrich Wilhelm III, King, 43, 46, 82-3, 85-6, 89, 90, 105, 126, 129
Friedrich Wilhelm IV, King, 19, 50, 65, 78, 82, 100, 119-20, 122, 123, 125, 126, 130
Friedrichs Brücke, 36
Friedrichsfelde, 112
Friedrichshagen, 66
Friedrichstadt, 22, 47
Friedrichswerder, 22
Friedrichswerdersche Kirche, 24, **56-7**, 73, 80, 90
Friseurmuseum, **87**
Fuller, Sam, 29
Funcke, Cornelius, 30
Funkturm, 55, **57**, 133

Gaertner, Eduard, 48, 57, 72, 90, 125
Galerie der Romantik, **57**, 80, 88
Galleries, **27-8**, 44
Gatow, 63
Gauguin, Paul, 53
Gay, Peter, 31
Gedenkstätte Deutscher Widerstand, **57-8**
Gedenkstätte Plötzensee, **58**
Gemäldegalerie, 50, 54, **58-60**, 67
General delivery, 10
Georg-Kolbe-Museum, **60**
George IV, King of England, 86
Gerichtslaube, 124
Gericksteg, 43
German Broadcasting Museum, **55**
German Folklore, Museum of *see* Museum für Deutsche Volkskunde
German History, Museum of *see* Museum für Deutsche Geschichte
German Resistance Memorial *see* Gedenkstätte Deutscher Widerstand
Gertrauden Brücke, 36-7
Gestapo, 96
Gilly, Friedrich, 23
Gleisdreieck, 37, 66
Glienicker Brücke, 43, 62, 124
Glinka, Mikhail, 94
Glockenturm, 83
Glume, Friedrich Christian, 121
Godeau, Simon, 89

Index

Goebbels, Dr, 20, 85, 99
Goes, Hugo van der, 59-60
Goethe, Eosander von, 88
Goethe, Johann Wolfgang von, 94, 95
Gontard, Karl von, 23, 56, 64, 65, 86, 126, 127, 128, 131
Gotzkowsky, Johann Ernst, 30
Goya, Francisco José de, 79
Goyen, Jan van, 60
Griebnitzsee, 43
Gropius, Martin, 72
Gropius, Walter, 24-5, 42, 47, 53, 72
Grosser Müggelsee, **66**
Grosz, George, 26
Grunewald, **32**, **39-40**, *40*, 41, 42, 43, 54, **60-1**, 62, 69, 101, 132, 133, 134, 135
Grünewald, Matthias, 69
Grunewaldsee, 39
Grunewaldturm, 43, **61**

Haarlem School, 63
Hagemeister, Karl, 53
Hamburger Bahnhof, **61**, 75
Hansabrücke, 35
Hansaviertel, 25, 41, 49, **61-2**
Haus am Checkpoint Charlie, 37, **62**
Haus der Kulturen der Welt, **66**
Haus Marchwitza, 121
Havel river, 42-3, 61, **62-3**, 98, 99, 119, 124, 130, 132, 135
Heartfield, John, 26, 55, 83
Heckel, Erich, 53, 81
Hegel, Georg Wilhelm Friedrich, 55
Henselmann, Hermann, 64
Herrmann, Curt, 48
Herzog, Werner, 29
Heymüller, Johann, 121, 125
Hildebrant, Carl, 121
Hintze, 90
History, **18-21**
Hitchcock, Alfred, 29
Hitler, Adolf, 7, 20-1, 25, 26-7, 55, 58, 74, 83, 88, 92, 95
Hoffmann, Friedrich, 55
Hohenzollern family, 6, 77, 78, 79
Holbein, Hans the Younger, 59
Holidays, public, 12
Holländisches Etablissement, **127**
Holländisches Viertel, 122
Holocaust, 8, 99
Hood, Thomas, 119
Hoogh, Pieter de, 60
Hotels, **101-3**, **131**
Huelsenbeck, Richard, 26
Humann, Carl, 84
Humboldt, Wilhelm von, 24, 91-2, 98
Humboldt-Universität, 36, 42, **97-8**
Hummel, Johann, 57, 80
Hundekehlefenn nature reserve, 39
Hundekehlesee, 39

IBA architecture, **25**, 38, 65-6, 94
Ice-skating, **134**
Ihne, Ernst von, 50, 98
Impressionism, 26
Insel Brücke, 36
Insurance, 8
Isherwood, Christopher, 6, 29, **31**, 60, 94
Islamisches Museum, **84**
Isozaki, Arata, 38

Jacobi, Johann, 89
Jaeckel, Willy, 53
Jagdschloss Glienicke, **63**, 90, 124
Jagdschloss Grunewald, 22, 39, 54, 61, **63**
Jannings, Emil, 28
Jannowitzbrücke, 36, 41
Japanisch-Deutsches Zentrum, 95
Jazz, **112-13**
Jewelry shops, **117**
Jews, 20-21, 73, 81, 87, 112
Joachim II, Elector, 22, 51, 61, 63, 66
Jüdische Abteilung des Berlin Museums, **73**
Jugendstil *see* Art Nouveau
Jungfernbrücke, 37

KaDeWe, 8, 13, 104, 106, **116**, 117
Kaiser-Wilhelm-Gedächtniskirche, 7, 42, 52, 61, **63-4**, *64*, 69-70
Kammergericht, 47, **65**
Kammermusiksaal, 67
Kandinsky, Wassily, 20, 24, 47, 69
Karl-Marx-Allee, 62, **64**
Käthe-Kollwitz-Museum, **64-5**
Kirche St Peter und Paul, **83**
Kirchner, Ernst Ludwig, 26, 48, 53, 54
Kladow, 43, 63
Klee, Paul, 24, 47
Klein, César, 26
Kleines Schloss, 124
Kleist, Heinrich von, 65, 99
Kleistgrab, **99**
Kleistpark, 41, 51, **65**
Knobelsdorff, Georg Wenzeslaus von, 22, 23, 88, 89, 97, 121, 126, 129, 130
Knobelsdorff-Haus, 121
Knoblauch, Eduard, 65, 81
Knoblauchhaus, **65**, 82
Kokoschka, Oscar, 80
Kolbe, Georg, 60
Kollwitz, Käthe, 64-5, 83, 87
Kongresshalle, 35, 42, **65-6**, 95
Köpenick, **32**, **66**, 68-9
Köpjohan Stiftung, 36
KPM porcelain, 30, 48, 53, 68, 72, 90, 118
Kranzler, Johann, 48
Kreuzberg, 7, **32**, **66-7**
  architecture, 25
  hotels, 101
  walks, **37-9**, *38*
Kronprinzen Ufer, 35
Krüger, Andreas, 121
Krüger, Franz, 128
Krumme Lanke, 39
Kultur-Forum, 45, 46, 58, **67**, 68, 69, 79
Kunckel, Johann, 85
Kunstgewerbemuseum, 66, **67-8**, 72
Kunstgewerbemuseum Schloss Köpenick, 66, 67, **68-9**
Künstlerhaus Bethanien, **67**
Kupferstichkabinett, **46**, 54, 67, **69**
Kurfürstendamm, 42, 48, 54, **69-70**, 115

Landwehrkanal, 42
Lang, Fritz, 28, 126
Langes Luch nature reserve, 39
Langevelt, Rutger van, 68
Langhans, Carl Gotthard, 23, 51, 71, 88, 90, 97, 127
Language, words and phrases, 17, **135-7**
Lannoy, Baudouin de, 59
Lapidarium, 37, 66, **70**, 100
Laurana, Francesco, 93
Lavatories, 14
Laws and regulations, 14
Lee, Pieter van der, 30
Leibnitz, 18
Leipzig, 132
Leistikow, Walter, 40

141

Index

Lenbach, Franz von, 80
Lenné, Peter, 63, 85, 89, 91, 95-6, 100, 122, 124, 129, 130
Leo, Ludwig, 41
Leo, Wolf, 28
Lessing, Gotthold Ephraim, 35 95
Lessingbrücke 35
Libraries, 16
Lichtenau, Countess, 85
Lichterfelde, 41
Liebermann, Max, 26, 80, 98
Liebknecht, Karl, 74, 97, 98
Lindenufer, 43
Lindwerder, 43
Lost property, 17
Lübars, **70**
Lübbenau, 132
Lubitsch, Ernst, 28, 113
Lüdicke, Karl Friedrich, 30
Luise, Queen, 85, 90, 95
Lustgarten, 42, 46, *78*
Luther, Martin, 18
Luther Brücke, 35, 41
Luxemburg, Rosa, 29
Lynar, Graf Rochus von, 100

M-Bahn, 11
Manet, Edouard, 81
Mann, Heinrich, 28, 55
Männlich, Daniel, **60**
Maps and plans, 47
Märchenbrunnen, 98
Maria Regina Martyrum, 58, **71**
Marienkirche, 22, 42, 48, **71**, 80
Markets, **117**
Märkisches Museum, 36, 41, 43, 47, 56, **71-2**, 82
Marmorpalais, 120, 124, **127**
Marschallbrücke, 36
Marstall, 121
Martin-Gropius-Bau, 37, 67, 68, **72-3**, 81, 96
Martyrs' Memorial *see* Maria Regina Martyrum
Marx, Karl, 7, 74, 98
Marx-Engels-Brücke, 37
Marx-Engels-Platz, 41, 97
Maxim Gorki Theater, 97
Medical emergencies, 17
Medical insurance, 8
Mehringplatz, 38
Mendelsohn, Erich 42, 113, 120
Menzel, Adolph, 72, 81, 128
Metsys, Quinten, 60
Mexicoplatz, 41
Middlebrook, Martin, 31, 100
Mies van der Rohe, 142

Ludwig, 25, *25*, 81
Miller, Wolfgang, 53
Miró, Joan, 27
Mitlijanskij, Daniel, 62
Mitte, **32**, **73**, 101
Moabiter Brücke, 35
Moholy-Nagy, Laszlo, 47
Moltke, Count Helmuth von, 19, 95
Moltke Brücke, 35
Monbijou Brücke, 36
Monet, Claude, 81
Money, **8-9**
Moorlake, 43
Morris, William, 24
Movie industry, **28-9**, **111**
Movie theaters, **28-9**, **111**
Mueller, Otto, 53
Mühlendamm-Schleuse, 36
Munch, Edvard, 26, 53, 72
Museums:
 for children, **132**
 listed, 44
 opening hours, 14
Museum of Arts and Crafts *see* Kunstgewerbemuseum
Museum Berliner Arbeiterleben um 1900, **87**
Museum für Deutsche Geschichte, 47, **74**, 97
Museum für Deutsche Volkskunde, 54, **74**
Museum für Indische Kunst, **74-5**
Museum für Islamische Kunst, **75**
Museum für Naturkunde, **75**, 132
Museum für Ostasiatische Kunst, **75**
Museum für Ur- und Frühgeschichte, 129
Museum für Verkehr und Technik, 61, 62, 72, **75-7**, 132
Museum für Völkerkunde, 54, **77**
Museum für Volkskunde, **84**
Museum für Vor- und Frühgeschichte, **77-8**, 88-9, 132
Museumsdorf Düppel, *78*
Museumsinsel, 34, 36, 41, 42, 45, 50, 54, 73, **78-9**, *78*, 81, 92, 93
Music:
 classical and popular concerts, **112**
 discos, **114-15**
 jazz, **112-13**
 opera and ballet, **113**
Musikinstrumenten-Museum, 67, **79**

Nagel, Otto, 80, 83

Napoleon I, 19, 23, 52
National identity cards, 8
Nationalgalerie, 36, 43, 56, 57, *78*, **79-80**, 81, 83
Natural Science, Museum of *see* Museum für Naturkunde
Nauener Tor, 122
Nauener Vorstadt, 122
Nazis, 6, 7, **20-1**, 26-7, 28, 58, 71, 74, 82, 83, 85, 96, 97, 99, 120
Nefertiti, **45**, 118
Neoclassical architecture, **23-4**
Neptunsbrunnen (Neptune Fountain), **80-1**, 89
Nering, Johann Arnold, 22, 23, 68, 74, 88, 121
Neue Kammern, **126**
Neue Nationalgalerie, *25*, 43, 67, 80, **81**
Neue Orangerie, 120, 123, **126**
Neue Sachlichkeit, 26
Neue Secession, 26
Neue Synagoge, 65, 73, **81**
Neue Wache, 24, 42, **97**
Die Neue Wilden, 27
Neuer Garten, 120, 124, **127**
Neues Museum, 36, 46, 50, *78*, 79, **81-2**
Neues Palais, 123, **127-8**
Nicholas I, Czar, 65, 82, 105, 126, 129
Nightlife, **110-15**
Nikolaikirche, 22, 48, **82**
Nikolaikirche (Potsdam), 24, 121, 124
Nikolaiviertel, 36, 41, 55, 65, 73, **82**
Nikolskoe, 43, **82-3**, 91, 129
Nolde, Emil, 26
Novembergruppe, 26
Nudist sunbathing, 14

Oestelt, Carl, 48
Olympia-Stadion, **83**
Opening hours, 13, 14
Opera, **113**
Otto-Nagel-Haus, 36, 80, **83**
Owens, Jesse, 83, 133

Palaces, listed, 44
Palais des Prinzen Heinrich, 23, 97-8
Palais Unter den Linden, 97
Palast der Republik, 36, 97
Panorama, **83**, 132
Park Babelsberg, 43
Park Sanssouci, **122-3**
Parks, 44, **132-3**

Index

Passports, 8, 17
Patenir, Joachim, 60
Pechstein, Max, 26
Performing arts, **110-13**
Pergamon-Museum, 36, 41, 43, 46, 74, 75, 77, 78, 79, **84**
Persius, Ludwig, 91, 121, 122, 125, 131
Petit, Chris, 29
Pfaueninsel, 43, 62, 63, **85-6**, 90, 91, 98, 124
Pfingstberg, 122
Pharmacies, 24-hour, 17
Philharmonie, 67, 79, 110, **112**
Picasso, Pablo, 27, 46
Piscator, Erwin, 113
Platz der Akademie, 64, 73, **86**
Police, 17
Pomonatempel, 122
Porcelain, **30-1**, **118**
Post offices, 13
Poste restante, 10
Postmuseum, **86**
Potsdam, 62, 63, 98, 101, **119-33**
Potsdam Agreement, **21**, **120**, 124, 130
Potsdam lakes, **124-5**
Potsdam Museum, **128**
Potsdamer Platz, 7, **86**
Praunheim, Rosa von, 29
Prehistory and Early History, Museum of see Museum für Vor-und Frühgeschichte
Prenzlauer Berg, **32**, **87**
Prinzessinnenpalais, 97
Public holidays, 12
Public transportation, 10-11
Publications, 15
Pückler-Muskau, Hermann Fürst, 129

Quellien, Artus the Elder, 71

Raab, Ingrid, 28
Radio Tower see Funkturm
Rahnsdorf, 66
Railroads, 9
 S-Bahn, 10-11, **40-1**
Raphael, 58
Rathaus (Potsdam), 121
Rathausbrücke, 36
Rathenau, Walter, 20
Rauch, Christian, 80, 90
Reed, Carol, 29
Reading list, 31
Reichstag, 34, 36, 41, 42, **87-8**
Reinhardt, Max, 113
Rembrandt, 60, 69
Renting:
 bicycles, 12

 cars, 12
Rest rooms, 14
Restaurants, 14, **103-8**, **131**, 133
Riding, **134**
Riefenstahl, Leni, 28, 83
Riehmer, Wilhelm, 39
Riehmers Hofgarten, 39
Riemeisterfenn, 39
Riemenschneider, Tilman, 50, 92
Rieselfelder, 93
Rivers, 44
Rizzo, Antonio, 51
Rodin, Auguste, 79
Roller-skating, **134**
Römische Bäder, 120, 123, **128-9**
Rossellini, Roberto, 29
Rossi, Aldo, 88
Rubens, Peter Paul, 50, 60, 69
Ruinenberg, 123, 125, **129**
Ruisdael, Jacob van, 60
Running, **134**
Russian Orthodox Church, 122, 129
Russische Kolonie Alexandrowka, 122, **129**
Russischer Friedhof, **94**

S-Bahn, 10-11, **40-1**, 120
St Hedwigs-Kathedrale, 23, **97**
St Matthäi-Kirche, 67
St Nikolai-Kirche, 93
Sammlung Ludwig, **46**
Sanssouci see Schloss Sanssouci
Savignyplatz, 41
Schadow, Johann Gottfried, 30, 52, 55, 56, 80, 71
Schadow, Rudolf, 56
Scharoun, Hans, 67, 112
Scheib, Hans, 72
Scheunenviertel, 73
Schinkel, Karl Friedrich, **23-4**, 24, 25, 33, 37, 43, 46, 49, 55, 56-7, 64, 73, 78-9, 85, 86, 88, 89-90, 97, 98, 119-20, 121, 122, 124, 128, 129, 130
Schinkel-Pavillon, 24, 57, **89-90**
Schinkelmuseum, **56-7**
Schlachtensee, 40, 41
Schlemmer, Oskar, 47
Schleusenbrücke, 37
Schliemann, Heinrich, 51, 77-8
Schloss Babelsberg, 24, 120, 124, **129-30**
Schloss Bellevue, 23, 35, 42, **94-5**
Schloss Britz, **52**

Schloss Cecilienhof, 120, 122, 124, 127, **130**
Schloss Charlottenburg, 22, 23, 24, 42, 45, 54, 57, 79, 85, **88-90**, 93, 112, 134
Schloss Charlottenhof, 24, 119, 123, **130**
Schloss Friedrichsfelde, **90**, 96
Schloss Hechingen, 120
Schloss Klein-Glienicke, 63, 83, **90-1**, 98, 124
Schloss Köpenick, **68-9**
Schloss Lindstedt, 120, 126
Schloss Sanssouci, 23, 89, 112, 119, **122-3**, 125, 127, 129, **130-1**
Schloss Tegel, 24, **91-2**
Schlüter, Andreas, 18, 22-3, 36, 50, 74, 82, 89, 97
Schmettau, Joachim, 52
Schmidt-Rottluff, Karl, 53, 54
Schmuz-Baudiss, Theodor Hermann, 30
Schönefeld airport, 9, 10
Schwanenwerder, **99**
Schwechten, Franz, 49
Seyfried, Gerhard, 27
Shoe stores, **118**
Shopping, 13, **115-18**, **131**
Siegessäule, 41, 42, **92**, 92, 95, 133
Skarbina, Franz, 80
Skiing, **134**
Skulpturengalerie, 50, 54, **92-3**
Soccer, **135**
Solly, Edward, 58
Sophie Charlotte, Queen, 18, 22, 54, **88**, 89
Sophienkirche, 73
Sowjetisches Ehrenmal, 95, 96
Spandau, **32**, 42, 43, 62, 63, 73, **93**, 98, 99-100
Spandauer Forst, 135
Spar, Otto von, 71
Speer, Albert, 21, 25, 35, 70
Sports, **133-5**
Spree, river, **34-7**, 34-5, 42-3, 49-50, 66, **93**, 99
Spree island, 78
Spreewald, 132
Squash, **134-5**
Staatliche Museen Preussischer Kulturbesitz, 44
Staatliche Porzellan-Manufaktur, 30
Staatsbibliothek, 67
Staatsoper, 42, **97**, **113**
Staatsrat, 97
Stadtschloss, 23

143

Index

Stauffenberg, Graf von, 20, 58
Stegitz, 41
Stemmle, Robert, 29
Sternberg, Josef von, 28
Strade, Heinrich, 92
Strandbad Babelsberg, 124
Strandbad Tegel, 94
Strandbad Wannsee, **99**
Streets, major sights listed, 44
Stubbins, Hugh, 65
Stüler, Friedrich August, 45, 67, 79, 81, 83, 88
Subway, 10
Swimming, **132**, **134**

Taut, Bruno, 39
Taxis, 12, 14
Tegel, **32**, 42, 63, **94**, 101, 132-3
Tegel airport, 9, 10
Tegeler Forst, 135
Tegeler See, 43
Telegrams, 14, 15
Telephones, 13, 15
Television Tower *see* Fernsehturm
Tennis, **134-5**
Teufelsberg, **61**
Theater, **113**
Theater des Westens, 41
Theiss, Caspar, 63
Tickets:
 performing arts, 111
 public transportation, 11
Tieck, Christian, 56
Tiede, August, 75
Tiergarten, **32**, 42, **94-5**, 133, 134
Tierpark Friedrichsfelde, 43, 90, **95-6**, 133
Time zones, 12-13
Tipping, 14
Tobogganing, **134**
Topographie des Terrors, 37, **96**
Tourist information, 9, 15
Toy shops, **118**
Trains, 9, 10-11, **40-1**
Trams, 11, 120
Transportation and Technology, Museum of *see* Museum für Verkehr und Technik
Travel:
 air, 9, 16
 from airports to city, 10
 bicycles, 12
 boat trips, **42-3**
 buses, 10, 11, 16, **42**, 120, 132
 cars, 12
 ferries, 9-10, 11
 public transport, 10-11
 railroad, 9
 S-Bahn, 10-11, **40-1**, 120
 taxis, 12
 tickets, 11
 trams, 11, 120
 U-Bahn (subway), 10
Travel insurance, 8
Travelers checks, 8, 17
Treptow harbor, 42
Treptower Park, **96**
Tretbootverleih, 74
Trotta, Margarethe von, 29
Tschirnhausen, Graf von, 30

U-Bahn (subway), 10
UFA studios, 28, 124
Ulbricht, Walter, 21, 97
Underground (trains), 10
Unger, Christian, 23
Unter den Linden, 22, 23, 42, **96-8**
Ury, Lesser, 26, 40, 48, 72, 80

Value Added Tax (VAT), 9
Van Gogh, Vincent, 26, 53, 73
Vassiltchikov, Marie, 31
Vehicle registration certificates, 8
Velde, Esaias van de, 60
Velde, Henry van der, 24, 53
Vermeer, Jan, 60
Views, 44, **133**
Viktoriapark, 39, 66, **98**, 133
Volkspark Friedrichshain, **98**
Volkspark Klein-Glienicke, 24, 43
Vorderasiatisches Museum, **84**
Vostell, Wolf, 72-3, 103

Wagener, Joachim, 79
Waldbühne, **83**
Walks, 12, 16, **34-40**, 96-98, **135**
 Potsdam, **121-124**
Wallot, Paul, 87
Wannsee, 41, 42, 43, 63, **98-9**, 132, 133
Watteau, Jean-Antoine, 89, 130
Weather, 10
Wedding, **32**
Wegeley, Wilhelm Caspar, 30
Weidendammer Brücke, 36
Weigel, Helene, 52, 55
Weimar Republic, 6, **20**
Wellington, Duke of, 30
Weltkugelbrunnen, **52**
Die Wende (the change), 6, 7, 21
Wenders, Wim, 29
Werkbund-Archiv, **73**
Wilder, Billy, 28
Wilhelm I, Kaiser, 19, 61, 63, 64, 70, 97, 120, 129
Wilhelm II, Kaiser, 7, 19-20, 55, 63, 70, 120
Wilhelmine architecture, **24**
Wisniewski, Edgar, 79
Words and phrases, **135-7**
 emergency, 17
World War II, 7, 8, 22

Zehlendorf, 41
Zeughaus, 22-3, 42, 74
Zille, Heinrich, 99, 117
Zille-Museum, 49, **99**
Zitadelle Spandau, 73, 93, **99-100**, 132
Zoo *see* Tierpark Friedrichsfelde
Zoologischer Garten, 41, 42, 45, 47, 86, 94, **100**, 133
Zuckmayer, Carl, 66
Zürn, Martin, 92-3

The American Express Travel Guides

Amsterdam, Rotterdam & The Hague *
Athens and the Classical Sites
Cities of Australia *
Barcelona & Madrid
Berlin
Florence and Tuscany
Hong Kong & Taiwan *
London
Los Angeles & San Diego *
Mexico
Moscow & Leningrad/ St Petersburg *
New York
Paris
Rome
San Francisco and the Wine Regions *
Singapore & Bangkok
The South of France
Tokyo
Toronto, Montréal & Québec City
Venice
Washington, DC

* in preparation

BERLIN

1-4 BERLIN CITY
5-7 BERLIN ENVIRONS

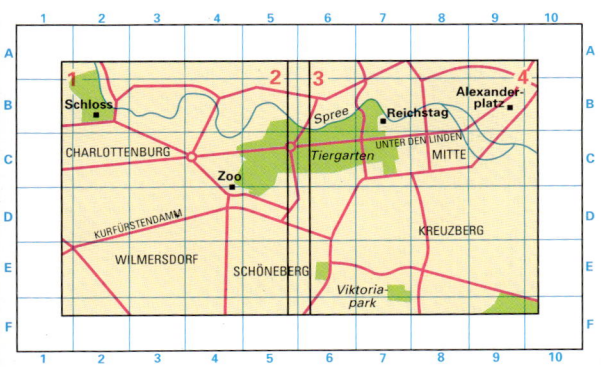

LEGEND

City Maps

- Major Place of Interest
- Other Important Building
- Built-up Area
- Park
- Cemetery
- † Named Church, Church
- ✡ Synagogue
- Hospital
- *i* Information Office
- Post Office
- Police Station
- Parking Lot
- U-Bahn Station
- S-Bahn Station
- Adjoining Page Number

Environs Maps

- Place of Interest
- Built-up Area
- Wood or Park
- Cemetery
- Autobahn (with access point)
- Main Road - Four-lane Highway
- Other Main Road
- Secondary Road
- Other Road
- Railroad
- Long-distance Station
- International Airport
- Other Airport
- River Boat Route
- Landing Stage
- *F* Ferry

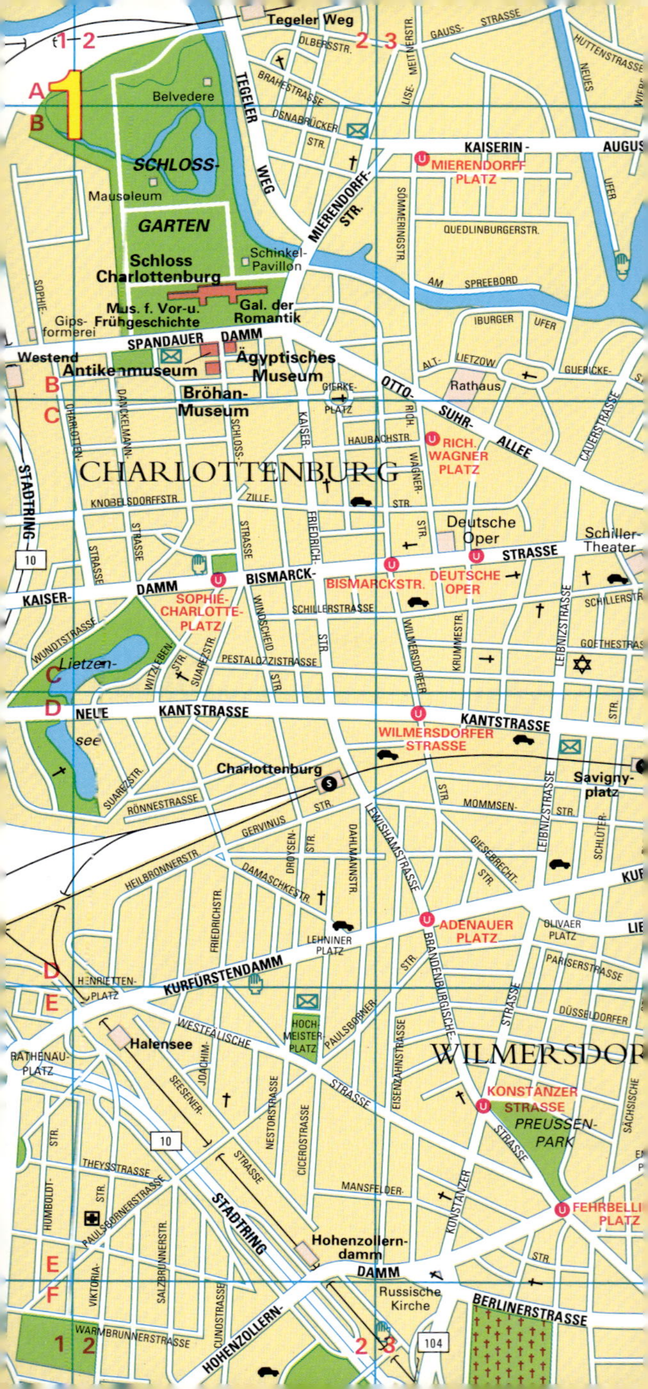
1
A
B
C
D
E
F
1 2
2 3
Tegeler Weg
Belvedere
SCHLOSS-
GARTEN
Mausoleum
Schloss Charlottenburg
Schinkel-Pavillon
Mus. f. Vor-u. Frühgeschichte
Gal. der Romantik
Gipsformerei
SPANDAUER DAMM
Westend
Antikenmuseum
Ägyptisches Museum
Bröhan-Museum
GIERKE-PLATZ
Rathaus
OTTO-SUHR-ALLEE
MIERENDORFF PLATZ
MIERENDORFF-STR.
KAISERIN-AUGUSTA
QUEDLINBURGERSTR.
AM SPREEBORD
IBURGER UFER
ALT-LIETZOW
GUERICKE-
CAUERSTRASSE
CHARLOTTENBURG
RICH. WAGNER PLATZ
HAUBACHSTR.
Deutsche Oper
Schiller-Theater
BISMARCK-STRASSE
BISMARCKSTR.
DEUTSCHE OPER
SOPHIE-CHARLOTTE-PLATZ
KAISER-DAMM
STADTRING
10
KNOBELSDORFFSTR.
SCHILLERSTRASSE
PESTALOZZISTRASSE
GOETHESTRASSE
Lietzensee
NEUE KANTSTRASSE
KANTSTRASSE
WILMERSDORFER STRASSE
Charlottenburg
Savignyplatz
MOMMSEN-STR.
LEIBNIZSTRASSE
LEWISHAMSTRASSE
RÖNNESTRASSE
GERVINUS STR.
HEILBRONNERSTR.
DAMASCHKESTR.
FRIEDRICHSTR.
ADENAUER PLATZ
LEHNINER PLATZ
OLIVAER PLATZ
KURFÜRSTENDAMM
HENRIETTEN-PLATZ
PARISERSTRASSE
DÜSSELDORFER
Halensee
RATHENAU-PLATZ
WESTFÄLISCHE STRASSE
HOCHMEISTER-PLATZ
PAULSBORNER
BRANDENBURGISCHE
WILMERSDORF
KONSTANZER STRASSE
PREUSSEN-PARK
FEHRBELLINER PLATZ
MANSFELDER-
SEESENER-
NESTORSTRASSE
CICEROSTRASSE
THEYSSTRASSE
PAULSBORNERSTRASSE
HUMBOLDT-
SALZBRUNNERSTR.
Hohenzollerndamm
DAMM
Russische Kirche
BERLINERSTRASSE
104
WARMBRUNNERSTRASSE
CUNOSTRASSE
HOHENZOLLERN-

2
A
B
C
D
E
F
4 5
5 6
3
TURMSTRASSE
KLEINER
ALT-TIERGARTEN
MOABIT
ALT-
BEUSSELSTRASSE
WALDSTRASSE
STROMSTRASSE
LÜBECKER STR.
BANDELSTRASSE
OLDENBURGER STR.
GOTZKOWSKY-STR.
ALLEE
Spree
HELMHOLTZSTR.
FRANKLINSTRASSE
LEVETZOWSTRASSE
ELBERFELDERSTR.
BUNDESRAT-UFER
LESSINGSTRASSE
HOLSTEINER UFER
KIRCHSTR.
CALVINSTR.
WIKINGER UFER
Bellevue
HANSAPLATZ
BELLEVUE
Schloss Bellevue
PARK
SALZ-UFER
BACHSTRASSE
ALTONAERSTRASSE
Hansaviertel
SPREEWEG
GROSSER STERN
Siegessäule
MARCHSTRASSE
Königliche Porzellan-manufaktur
Tiergarten
Berlin-Pavillon
Technische Universität
STRASSE DES 17 JUNI
ERNST-REUTER-PLATZ
HARDENBERGSTRASSE
FASANENSTRASSE
HOFJÄGERALLEE
Neuer See
ZOOLOGISCHER GARTEN
ZOO
Inter-Continental Hotel
CORNELIUS-
STÜLERSTR.
KLINGELHOFERSTR.
STEIN-PLATZ
British Consulate
Theater des Westens
ZOOLOGISCHER GARTEN
Aquarium
BUDAPESTER STR.
KEITHSTR.
LÜTZOW-UFER
LÜTZOWPLATZ
SAVIGNY-PLATZ
KANTSTRASSE
BREITSCHEID-PLATZ
Kaiser-Wilhelm-Ged.-Kirche
Europa-Center
TAUENTZIENSTR.
KURFÜRSTENSTRASSE
KNESEBECK-
UHLAND-STRASSE
KURFÜRSTENDAMM
WITTENBURG-PLATZ
AN DER URANIA
Post-museum
Berliner Flohmarkt
EINEMSTR.
Käthe-Kollwitz-Museum
MEINEKE-STR.
JOACHIMSTALERSTR.
RANKESTR.
AUGSBURGER STR.
NÜRNBERGER STR.
PASSAUER STR.
KLEIST-STR.
AUGSBURGERSTR.
LIETZENBURGER STR.
Ludwig-kirche
FASANEN-PLATZ
BUNDESALLEE
SPICHERN-STR.
MARTIN-LUTHER-STR.
MOTZSTRASSE
NOLLENDORF-PLATZ
WINTERFELDT-STR.
GEISBERGSTRASSE
WELSERSTR.
FASANENSTRASSE
UHLANDSTRASSE
SPICHERN-STRASSE
ANSBACHER STR.
VIKTORIA-LUISEPLATZ
EISENACHER
NACHODSTR.
DAMM
HOHENSTAUFEN-STRASSE
HOHENZOLLERN-
HOHENZOLLERN PLATZ
PRAGER PLATZ
MOTZSTR.
SCHÖNEBERG
BARBAROSSA-STR.
BAMBERGERSTRASSE
TRAUTENAUSTR.
GÜNTZEL-STRASSE
GÜNTZEL-STRASSE
GOLTZ-
EISENACHER STRASSE
GRUNEWALD STRASSE
BAYERISCHER PLATZ
PRINZREGENTEN-STRASSE
BUNDES-
BERLINER STRASSE
BLISSE-STRASSE
BERLINER-STRASSE
KUFSTEINER STR.
BADENSCHE STRASSE
MARTIN-LUTHER-
Rathaus
BELZIGER
AKAZIEN
HAUPT

3

KLEINER TIERGARTEN

Museum für Naturkunde
Brecht-Weigel-Haus
FRITZ-SCHLOSS-PARK
Hamburger Bahnhof
Lehrter Stadtbahnhof
INVALIDENSTRASSE
DOROTHE FRIEDHO
ORANIE
Charité
ALT-MOABIT
PAULSTRASSE
ALT MOABIT
FRIEDRICH LIST UFER
MOLTKE STR.
LÖBESTR.
BAUERDAM
Schloss Bellevue
Spree
Kongresshalle
Reichstag
SCHIFF-
CLARA ZETKIN
SPREEWEG
JOHN FOSTER DULLES ALLEE
Sowjet Ehrenmal
PARISER PLATZ
UNTE
BEHRN
Siegessäule
GROSSER STERN
STRASSE DES 17 JUNI
Brandenburger Tor
EBERTSTRASSE
HOFJÄGERALLEE
TIERGARTEN
ENTLASTUNGSTR.
BELLEVUE STR.
VOSS-STRASSE
GROTE
TIERGARTENSTRASSE
Kunstgewerbemuseum
Philharmonie
POTSDAMER PLATZ
POTSDAMER PLATZ
Gedenkstätte Deutscher Widerstand
Kulturforum
Musik-Museum
NIEDER-KIRCHNERSTR.
Bauhaus-Archiv
Neue Nationalgalerie
Staats Bibliothek
BERNBURGERSTR.
STRESEMANN
Martin Gropius Bau
LÜTZOWPLATZ
VON DER HEYDT STR.
SCHÖNEBERGER STRASSE
REICHPIETSCH UFER
LINK-
Anhalter Bahnhof
LÜTZOW UFER
GENTHINER
KLUCKSTR.
FLOTTWELLSTR.
SCHÖNEBERGER STR.
Lapidarium
HAL S
Berliner Flohmarkt
EINEMSTR.
KURFÜRSTENSTRASSE
POHLSTRASSE
TEMPELHOFER UFER
HALLESCHES
NOLLENDORFPLATZ
KURFÜRSTENSTRASSE
BÜLOW-
GLEISDREIECK
Museum für Verkehr und Technik
MÖCKERBRÜCKE
WINTERFELDT-
STRASSE
POTSDAMER STRASSE
OBEN-
MÖCKERN STR.
HORN-
PALLASSTRASSE
GOEBENSTRASSE
KÜL MER-STR.
KLEISTPARK
YORCK-
YORCKSTRASSE
YORCK STRASSE
Riehmers Hofgarten
GOLTZ-
KLEISTPARK
Grossgörschenstrasse
BAUTZENERSTR.
KREUZBERSTR.
GRUNEWALDSTRASSE
STRASSE
JÜGENSTR.
CRELLE
MONUMENTEN
VIKTORIAPARK
BELZIGER
ARCKENSTR.
HAUPT-
KOLONNEN
STRASSE
KATZBACH
DUDEN STRASSE
METHESSELSTR.

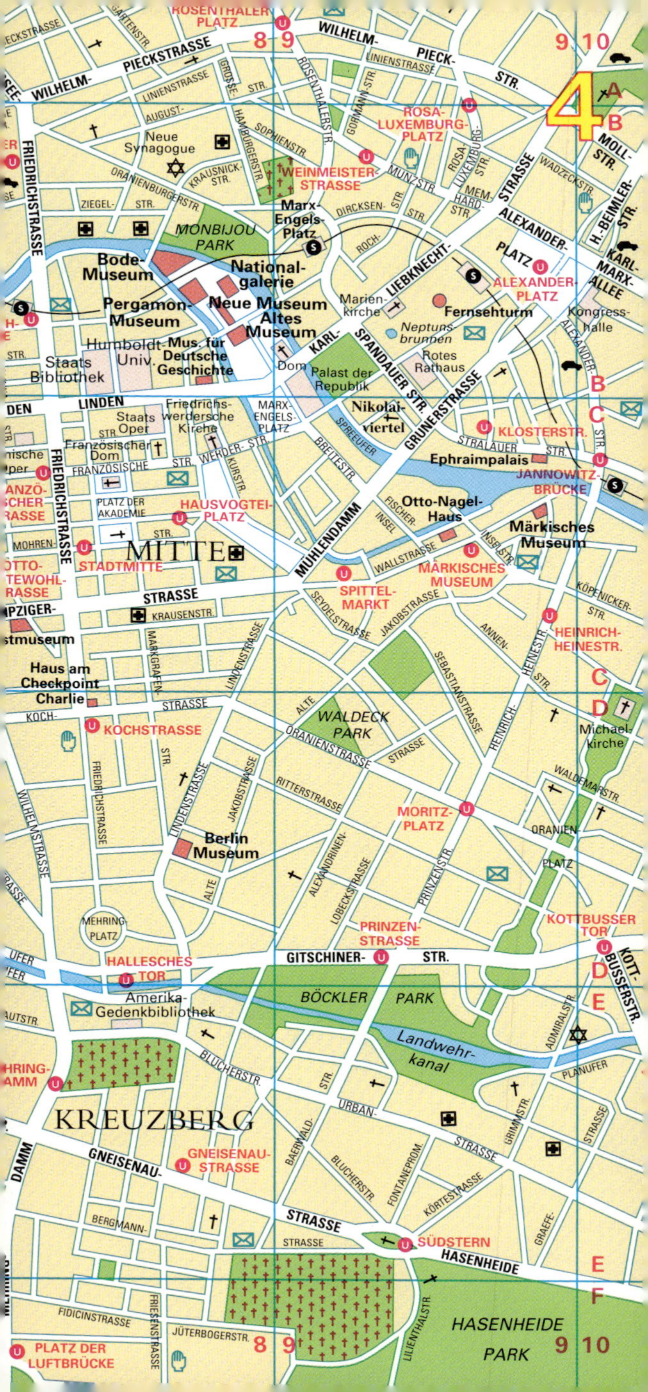
4
A
B
C
D
E
F
8 9
9 10
ROSENTHALER PLATZ
WILHELM-PIECKSTRASSE
WILHELM-PIECK-STR.
LINIENSTRASSE
AUGUST-
Neue Synagogue
ORANIENBURGERSTR.
KRAUSNICK-STR.
HAMBURGERSTR.
SOPHIENSTR.
ROSENTHALERSTR.
GORMANN-STR.
ROSA-LUXEMBURG-PLATZ
WEINMEISTER-STRASSE
MUNZSTR.
ROSA-LUXEMBURG-STR.
MOLL-STR.
WADZECKSTR.
H.-BEIMLER-STR.
FRIEDRICHSTRASSE
ZIEGEL-
MONBIJOU PARK
Marx-Engels-Platz
DIRCKSEN-STR.
MEMHARD-STR.
ALEXANDER-STRASSE
ALEXANDER-PLATZ
KARL-MARX-ALLEE
Bode-Museum
National-galerie
Pergamon-Museum
Neue Museum
Altes Museum
Marienkirche
LIEBKNECHT-
ROCH-
Fernsehturm
Kongress-halle
Humboldt-Univ.
Staats Bibliothek
Mus. für Deutsche Geschichte
Dom
KARL-
Palast der Republik
SPANDAUER STR.
Neptuns-brunnen
Rotes Rathaus
GRUNERSTRASSE
ALEXANDER-
LINDEN
Staats Oper
Friedrichs-werdersche Kirche
MARX-ENGELS-PLATZ
Nikolai-viertel
KLOSTERSTR.
STRALAUER STR.
Französischer Dom
FRANZÖSISCHE STR.
WERDER-STR.
KURSTR.
BREITESTR.
SPREEUFER
Ephraimpalais
JANNOWITZ-BRÜCKE
PLATZ DER AKADEMIE
HAUSVOGTEI-PLATZ
FISCHER-INSEL
Otto-Nagel-Haus
Märkisches Museum
MOHREN-
STADTMITTE
MITTE
MÜHLENDAMM
WALLSTRASSE
INSELSTR.
MÄRKISCHES MUSEUM
STRASSE
SPITTEL-MARKT
SEYDELSTRASSE
JAKOBSTRASSE
KÖPENICKER-STR.
KRAUSENSTR.
MARKGRAFEN-
LINDENSTRASSE
ANNEN-
HEINESTR.
HEINRICH-HEINESTR.
Haus am Checkpoint Charlie
KOCH-
KOCHSTRASSE
ALTE
WALDECK PARK
ORANIENSTRASSE
SEBASTIANSTRASSE
HEINRICH-
Michael-kirche
STR.
FRIEDRICHSTRASSE
WILHELMSTRASSE
LINDENSTRASSE
JAKOBSTRASSE
RITTERSTRASSE
MORITZ-PLATZ
WALDEMARSTR.
ORANIEN-PLATZ
Berlin Museum
ALEXANDRINEN-
LOBECKSTRASSE
PRINZENSTR.
MEHRING-PLATZ
PRINZEN-STRASSE
KOTTBUSSER TOR
KOTT-BUSSERSTR.
UFER
HALLESCHES TOR
GITSCHINER-STR.
Amerika-Gedenkbibliothek
BÖCKLER PARK
Landwehr-kanal
ADMIRALSTR.
PLANUFER
BLÜCHERSTR.
URBAN-STRASSE
GRIMMSTR.
KREUZBERG
DAMM
GNEISENAU-STRASSE
GNEISENAU-STRASSE
BAERWALD-
BLÜCHERSTR.
FONTANEPROM.
KÖRTESTRASSE
GRAEFE-
BERGMANN-STRASSE
SÜDSTERN
HASENHEIDE
FIDICINSTRASSE
FRIESENSTRASSE
JÜTERBOGERSTR.
LILIENTHALSTR.
HASENHEIDE PARK
PLATZ DER LUFTBRÜCKE

BERLIN ENVIRONS

0 1 2 3 4 km
0 1 2 miles

5

- Heiligensee
- AS Schulzendorfer
- Berliner
- Heiligenseestr.
- **SCHLOSS TEGEL**
- Schönwalde
- Sandhauser Str.
- Staakener Str.
- Havel
- Konradshöher Str.
- Konrads Höhe
- **STRANDBAD**
- Tegeler See
- Berliner Forst Spandau
- Falkenhagener See
- Niederneuendorfer Allee
- Schönwalder Allee
- TEGELORT
- Scharfenberg
- Jungfernhe
- Bernauer Str.
- Hakenfelde
- Spandauer Str.
- Gartenfeld
- Hohenzollernka
- Saatwir
- Falkenseer Chaussee
- Albrechtshof
- Siegefelder Weg
- **SPANDAU**
- **ZITADELLE**
- Haselhorst
- Siemensstadt
- Nonnendammallee
- Staaken
- Brunsbütteler Damm
- Spandau
- Spree
- Nauen 5
- Heerstrasse
- Pichelsdorfer Str.
- Ruhlebener Str.
- Charlottenburger Ch.
- Spandauer
- Seeburg
- **OLYMPIA-STADION**
- Reichsstr.
- CHAR
- Seeburger Ch.
- Heerstrasse
- **GEORG-KOLBE MUSEUM**
- **MESSE**
- Ab.-Dr. Funkturm
- Gatower Chaussee
- Gatower Str.
- Am Postfenn
- SCHILDHORN
- Berliner Forst Grunewald
- Avus
- allee
- Gatow
- Potsdamer
- Gatower Heide
- BADEWIESE
- Kladower Damm
- **GRUNEWALD-TURM**
- Hüttenweg
- 15
- Koenigs-
- **JAGDSCHLO GRUNEWA**
- LINDWERDER
- Grunewaldsee
- BREITEHORN
- Rittefelddamm
- Kladow
- Sakrower Landstr.
- Line 2
- Havel
- Krumme Lanke
- E51
- Onkel-Tom-Allee
- Hüttenweg
- Clay-
- D MU
- Schwanenwerder
- Line 1&2
- Havelchaussee
- Argentinische
- Berliner
- ZEHLENDORF
- 1
- Pfaueninsel
- **STRANDBAD WANNSEE**
- Schlachtensee
- Avus
- Str.
- **SCHLOSS**
- HECKESHORN
- Nikolassee
- Nikolassee
- Clauert Str.
- Dahlem
- Weg
- **NIKOLSKOE**
- Berliner Forst Düppel
- Grosser Wannsee
- **MUSEUMSDORF DÜPPEL**
- Teltower
- Wannsee
- Königstrasse
- 1
- Wannsee
- KLEISTGRAB
- Zehlendorfer
- Kleinmachnow
- Berliner Forst Düppel
- Potsdam
- **TELTOW**
- Teltow

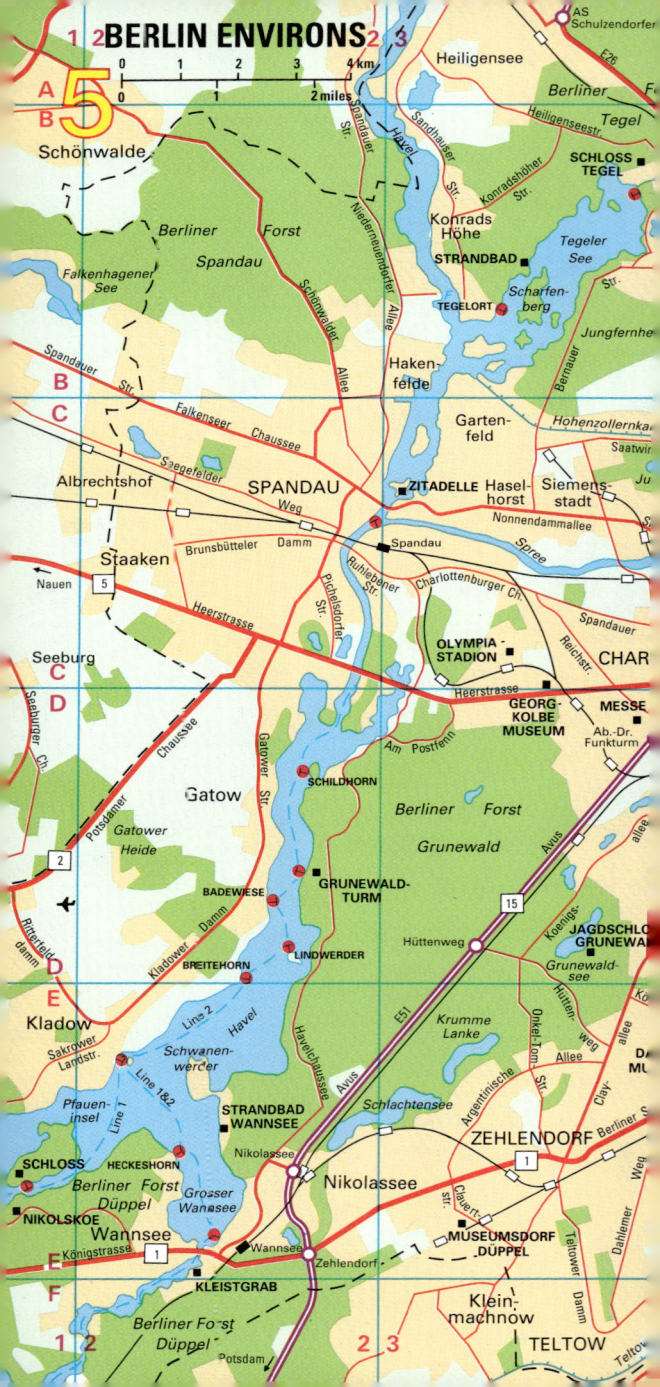

6
4 5
5 6
A
B
C
D
E
F
Hermsdorf
Hermsdorfer Damm
Zabel-Krüger-Damm
Lübars
Stralsund
Blankenfelde
Waidmanns-Lust
Waidmannsluster Damm
Märkisches Viertel
Mönchmühler Str.
Blankenfelder Ch.
Rosenthal
Buchholz
Wilhelmsruher Damm
Haupt-str.
Dietzgenstr.
Wittenau
Roedernallee
Nieder-schön-hausen
Pasewalker Str.
Holzhauser Str.
Eichborn-damm
Wilhelmsruh
REINICKEN-DORF
Course of Former Wall
Seidelstr.
Ollenhauer-strasse
Residenzstr.
Grabbe-allee
Schlosspark
PANKOW
Mühlenstr.
Prenzlauer Prom.
Berlin- Tegel
Müllerstrasse
Osloerstr.
Wisbyer Str.
Volkspark Rehberge
Damm
Markstr.
Seestrasse
WEDDING
Charlottenburg
SCHLOSS CHARLOTTENBURG
MITTE
Karl-Marx-Allee
Friedrichstr.
TIERGARTEN
Spree
Kantstrasse
Zoo
BERLIN
Kurfürstendamm
Skalitzer Str.
WILMERSDORF
Hasen-heide
AREA COVERED BY MAPS 1-4
SCHÖNEBERG
Berlin-Tempelhof
Tempelhofer Damm
Hermannstr.
Friedenau
Oberlandstr.
Britzer Damm
TEMPELHOF
Botanischer Garten
Steglitzer Damm
Attilastr.
STEGLITZ
Rixdorfer Str.
Britz
Drakestr.
Hindenburgdamm
Mariendorf
Buckower Damm
Kaiser-Wilhelm Str.
Grossbeerenstr.
Mariendorfer Damm
Britzer Garten
Goerz-allee
Ostpreussen-damm
Lankwitz
Lorenz-str.
Hildburghauser Str.
Marienfelde
Marienfelder Ch.
Rangsdorf
7
96
11
10
104
103
1
101
179

Map: Berlin (Northeast/Southeast Districts)

Grid references: A, B, C, D, E, F (rows); 5, 6, 7 (columns)

Roads and Routes
- E55 → Bernau
- E28
- Berliner Ring
- E55
- Route 2
- Route 158
- Route 15
- Route 96
- Route 179

Districts and Places

- Karow
- Lindenburg
- Blankenburg
- Malchow
- Wartenberg
- Ahrensfelde
- Falkenberg
- Werneuche
- Ahrensfelde
- Eiche
- Heinersdorf
- Falkenberger Ch.
- WEISSENSEE
- Klement-/ I. Gandhistr.
- Hansastrasse
- HOHEN-SCHÖNHAUSEN
- Obersee park
- Heinrich-Rau-Str.
- Lenin-allee
- PRENZLAUER-BERG
- Dimitroff-/ Bersarin-str.
- Greifswalder Str.
- Karl-Marx-Allee
- Frankfurter Allee
- Rhinstrasse
- LICHTENBERG
- MARZAHN
- Buchwitz-str.
- Otto-
- Heinrich-Rau-Str.
- Kaulsdorf
- Friedrichs Hain
- Hauptbahnhof
- Strasse der Befreiung
- SCHLOSS FRIEDRICHSFELDE
- Biesdorf
- Alt-Kaulsdorf
- Müncheberger Str.
- Stralauer Allee
- Rummelsberg
- Tierpark
- Am Tierpark
- KREUZBERG
- Elsenstr.
- Hauptstr.
- Köpenicker Ch.
- Waldow-allee
- Dunckerstr.
- Karlshorst
- Köpenicker Strasse
- Chemnitzer Str.
- Ulmenstr.
- Dammheide
- Kaulsdorfer Str.
- Trepto-ver Parc
- TREPTOW
- Rummels-burgerstr.
- Hermann-
- Karlshorst
- NEUKÖLLN
- Karl-Marx-Str.
- Sonnen-allee
- Baumschulenweg
- Grenzallee
- Buschkrug-allee
- Britzer Damm
- Wuhlheide
- An der Wuhlheide
- Mahlsdorfer Str.
- Britz
- Buckower Damm
- Spätstr.
- Königsheide
- Schöneweide
- Königsheide-weg
- Oberspree-str.
- Köllnische Heide
- KÖPENICK
- Course of Former Wall
- Rudower Str.
- Teltowkanal
- Johannisthal
- Adlergestell
- Adlershof
- MUSEUM
- Wendenschloss-str.
- Johannisthaler Ch.
- Neuköllner Str.
- Dahme
- Buckow
- Rudow
- Waltersdorfer Ch.
- Schönefelder Ch.
- Altglienicke
- Schönefeld
- Grünau
- Riviera